Masculinities in Transition

Genders and Sexualities in the Social Sciences
Series Standing Order ISBN 978–0–230–27254–5 hardback
978–0–230–27255–2 paperback
(outside North America only)

You can receive future titles in this series as they are published by placing a standing order. Please contact your bookseller or, in case of difficulty, write to us at the address below with your name and address, the title of the series and the ISBN quoted above.

Customer Services Department, Macmillan Distribution Ltd, Houndmills, Basingstoke, Hampshire RG21 6XS, England

---

Masculinities in Transition

Victoria Robinson
University of Sheffield, UK

Jenny Hockey
University of Sheffield, UK

First published 2011 by
PALGRAVE MACMILLAN

Palgrave Macmillan in the UK is an imprint of Macmillan Publishers Limited, registered in England, company number 785998, of Houndmills, Basingstoke, Hampshire RG21 6XS.

Palgrave Macmillan in the US is a division of St Martin's Press LLC, 175 Fifth Avenue, New York, NY 10010.

Palgrave Macmillan is the global academic imprint of the above companies and has companies and representatives throughout the world.

Palgrave® and Macmillan® are registered trademarks in the United States, the United Kingdom, Europe and other countries.

ISBN 978–0–230–20159–0   hardback

This book is printed on paper suitable for recycling and made from fully managed and sustained forest sources. Logging, pulping and manufacturing processes are expected to conform to the environmental regulations of the country of origin.

A catalogue record for this book is available from the British Library.

A catalog record for this book is available from the Library of Congress.

10   9   8   7   6   5   4   3   2   1
20   19   18   17   16   15   14   13   12   11

Printed and bound in Great Britain by
CPI Antony Rowe, Chippenham and Eastbourne

For Katie Picalli (1930–2009), a self-made woman.

For Peace Millicent Hockey (Pat) (1918–2005), in gratitude.

Contents

Preface and Acknowledgements

This book has been designed to meet the needs and interests of a variety of readers, something made possible by the different, though complementary expertise of its authors, Victoria Robinson and Jenny Hockey. For those wishing to explore theories of masculinity, particularly around men's work, embodiment, emotion and intimacy, Victoria draws on her established expertise in feminist theory (see, for example, Richardson and Robinson, 2008) and masculinity theory (see, for example, Robinson, 2008) in three extended chapters which front the book's three parts, framing the data chapters to follow. Her accounts provide critical analysis of contemporary research and theorising, setting it within the context of key debates within these areas. Jenny Hockey trained as an anthropologist and has extensive experience as a qualitative researcher. For those seeking case study examples which give insight into men's and women's embodied experience of everyday and life course transitions, each part provides four lively, case study chapters, each with a distinctive focus.

As Chapter 1 explains in more depth, the book's structure reflects a commitment to transition and it is the mundane materialities of dividing one's time *between* the place one works in and the place one calls home which provides its theoretical heartland. This is not to say that the data utilised in the book were gathered on the buses, trams, and private cars which connect these domains. Chapter 11 does take the reader into pubs, bars and cafes, as well as the bottom of the domestic garden and outside the city for scuba-diving and rock climbing. However, it is the way in which the separation of home and work meshes with the gendering of paid and unpaid work, and how this is reflected in the gendering of work *places*, that concerns us and which we understand to be a key route into the *mobility* as well as the diversity of masculinities. Thus, it is masculinity's fluidity within, as well as between, men that has concerned us (Spector-Mersel, 2006).

The writing of this book has, however, involved more than simply the distinctive expertise of its two authors, the grant holders for ESRC-funded project it draws upon. Alex Hall, Research Associate for the project between 2005 and 2007, devised its structure and provided helpful comments on its first draft. Victoria Robinson also undertook interviewing among hairdressers and estate agents, along with participant observation in two salons. Her knowledge of the area within which we had chosen to work, and her contacts, were invaluable, as was her launch of the qualitative study and the methods she developed in the process. This aspect of the project was taken on by Alex Hall in 2005. She undertook extended participant observation and interviewing among both estate agents and firefighters. Despite scepticism from audiences to whom we presented our initial research, as to whether a female researcher would be able to access and create trust and rapport among firefighters, Alex achieved this brilliantly, not only spending long days in the fire station where men drilled, cleaned their equipment and, always, waited for a fire call, but also accompanying them on nights out to the pub and community work within the city. The physical and emotional high of responding to a fire call was not something she was able to participate in – for reasons of both insurance and the scarcity of such calls (see Chapter 9). The quality of the data generated by both Victoria and Alex has been key to the theoretical insights and vitality of what it has been possible to include in this book. The richness of their data merited further work, long after the funding had expired and we are extremely grateful to Angela Meah who utilised the coding frame set up by the research team to help develop the content of this book's data chapters. As Chapter 1 explains, the inspiration for the project came from a previous ESRC-funded project on heterosexuality for which Angela was the full-time Research Associate. Angela's contribution to the development of the ideas for work on masculinity, and the proposal through which funding was secured, has been invaluable.

Throughout the life of the project we were fortunate to have an active and supportive Advisory Group who brought a wealth of expertise to our research and helped us with the methodological and theoretical challenges we encountered on the way: Richard Collier, David Jackson, David Morgan, Steve Robertson, Kath Woodward. Their publications have continued to be a source of inspiration and insight, as this book demonstrates. Those to whom we are most grateful are the firefighters, estate agents and hairdressers, and the women they nominated, all of whom found hard-pressed time (see Chapter 4), and were prepared to trust us, as we asked our questions and made our observations. Without their preparedness to reflect, openly, about their everyday lives – and indeed, to include us in them – this book would not have been possible.

1
Meeting Men on the Move

> The forgotten language of breadwinner
> gags in their pursed mouths.
> No work names to prop up lost men.
> (David Jackson, *Men without Work*, 2009)

David Jackson's poem about older working-class men made redundant within a post-industrial landscape of rusted cranes and silted harbours poignantly calls to mind a particular disposition of gendered time and space. Within this public world of paid work, men's 'work names' identify them. Once dispossessed, for them the gender order collapses and they 'get under their wives' feet. / They push shopping trolleys, grudgingly.' Home and the environments which resource it – the supermarket and the launderette – become problematic settings within which these men are now 'matter out of place' (Douglas, 1966).

Jackson's poem provides an initial example of men on the move, from youth and employment into later life and 'the end of doing', as he puts it. We witness not only the transition from one global economy to another, but also find out about these men's individual experiences of a historically situated life course transition. However, Jackson also refers to the 'the forgotten language of breadwinner', signalling that it is not just the materialities of industrial decline and ageing bodies that are in transition: a particular form of masculinity is troubled, its transitory – or mobile – nature revealed. We are therefore dealing with a language, a system of values and beliefs, a culture and an identity.

The 20 lines of this short poem effectively introduce the key themes pursued in this book. As we go on to explain, it is concerned with men's identities and their capacity to shift, as individuals move between differently gendered social environments. So, rather than treating

1

masculinity as stable and enduring, our work explores its mobility across different domains; in particular those of paid work, where men have for long secured their identities (Whitehead, 2002; Morgan, 1992), and home, where men are thought to find feminised refuge and solace (Davidoff and Hall, 2002). Our focus is therefore on the mutable 'doing of masculinity'. Grounding our perspective in men's embodied experiences of identifying *as* men has also required us to recognise that other, longer trajectory of change and transition as they grow up into expectations around employment, and grow old, potentially encountering 'the vacuum that the end of doing leaves', as Jackson explains. In the chapters to follow, then, we present the voices and embodied presence of men of different ages, exploring their status as representations of desired masculinity in the eyes of one another – or embodied reminders of how *not* to 'do' masculinity.

To close this section with a final line from Jackson's poem where he describes how older men 'envy the busy purposes/of younger men who've got to get on', the data we discuss show precisely the interplay of envy, desire, avoidance and ridicule, as our participants of *all* ages endeavour to 'do' masculinity in relation to those other men, who they emulate, pity, choose as 'top mates', compete with or have sex with. Women's voices are also in evidence, providing another level of interpretation, as they describe the domestic lives they share with our male participants, or witness as family members or friends. Importantly, though, they also provide an insight into heterosexuality's role as an organising principle which informs the doing of 'gender' as a lived, relational, intersubjective dimension of not only men's but also women's identities.

History

This book has theoretical roots in work from a previous ESRC-funded study of the making of heterosexual relationships within 22 extended families in East Yorkshire that was carried out by Jenny Hockey, Victoria Robinson and Angela Meah (see Hockey *et al.*, 2007). Two aspects of that body of research helped shape the empirical work that informs it. First, the heterosexuality study required Angela, the full-time Research Associate, to recruit participants for qualitative life history interviews within extended families, a method that revealed differences between women's and men's willingness to discuss the making and experience of heterosexual relationships. Although women, often in mid-life, would approach us with an expression of interest, their attempts to recruit their sons and male partners were often unsuccessful. However, once we were able to recruit men, towards the end of the study, we found that men themselves were much more successful at recruiting both other men in their own families, and men who would then recruit members of their own families, both male and female. The implications of this preponderance of women within our sample, we suggested at the time, were that women appeared to be 'self-defined guardians of their families' emotional lives' (see Hockey *et al.*, 2007: 18). This somewhat speculative interpretation is explored fully in Part III of the current work, where we present data from both women and men, comparing their constructions of potentially shared emotional lives.

The second way in which these experiences shaped the current book concerns the occupational identities of several of the men we finally recruited to the heterosexuality study. They were firefighters and they told us that divorce notices in the local paper often featured male firefighters and that their marriages were well known to be at risk. The reasons they gave for this were threefold: men in the fire service bonded more closely with work colleagues than their families; unsocial working hours meant that their leisure activities were likely to involve even more contact with men working similar shifts; and being a fireman was a passport to sexual conquest.

These two aspects of our previous study raised some fascinating theoretical and empirical questions about the relationship between men's working and home lives. We wanted to explore this link – and to talk to more men than had hitherto been possible. Given that our previous research had asked how the concept of heterosexuality was being lived out, the project we designed adopted a similar theoretical stance and asked how the related concept of masculinity is brought into being, or inhabited. In other words, a central component of this book is a set of theoretical questions about identity, something we understand as processual, always under negotiation, never 'finished', the outcome of ongoing performance (Woodward, 1997; Jenkins, 2004; Lawler, 2008). This led to a consideration of *different* performances of a masculine identity. While the notion that masculinity might be performed (Butler, 1990), or inhabited, in different ways is well established (Haywood and Mac an Ghaill, 2003; Connell, 2005; Whitehead and Barrett, 2001), what interested us specifically was the notion that the practice or 'doing' of masculinity (Morgan, 1992) might vary not just *between* men, but *within* the same man as his social context changed (Spector-Mersel, 2006).

The emic, or 'folk' theory, that aspects of being a firefighter make men less able or willing to integrate themselves into marriage or domestic life, led us to consider the experiences of men in other occupations. Might they too experience some sense of dislocation between their workplace and domestic identities? Or, as the emic theory implies, did the fire service bring specific demands and opportunities? Drawing on the notion that occupational cultures were potentially gendered, with firefighting being a particularly masculinised environment, we therefore selected three contrasting work cultures; from male-dominated, to gender neutral, to female-dominated.

Alongside the gendering of men's occupational identities, we also wanted to understand more about men's relationships with domestic space. The social changes of the nineteenth century – industrialisation and urbanisation particularly – have been understood to produce a gendering of social space, the public world of work being a male domain, the private world of the home being understood as both separate and highly feminised, a haven in a heartless world (see Chapter 3 and also Davidoff and Hall (2002) for a critical discussion of this view). To what extent, then, *do* men today move continuously between a public world of employment, which to varying degrees is masculinised, into a feminised home environment? Can we any longer sustain the notion of public and private as 'separate spheres', and can we think of these in terms of gender divisions?

To provide nuanced answers to some of these questions, we chose to address the domestic world through men's age-specific agendas such as leaving the parental home, setting up home independently, establishing partnerships and familial relationships, managing divorce and undertaking retirement. In other words, while we were interested in transitions between home and workplace, we did not treat either of these as static environments which somehow framed 'mobile' masculinities. Instead, we remained aware of major shifts within the occupational environments we selected, even within the life times of our older participants, along with the dynamic nature of the life course itself and its implications for context-specific identification. How men of different ages might engage with masculinity in the workplace therefore provided a link to a potentially different site of performance.

Our aim has thus been to understand the process of identification via empirical work. This has meant engaging critically with the notion of identity as contingent and unstable, realised through performance or practice. In this way, then, we address a lack of knowledge as to how a plurality of gendered identities actually comes into being, asking how social context – the workplace and the home – operates to give particular form to the identity category 'masculinity' – and how individuals moving between contexts both inhabit and manage their identities. By exploring, with men, their histories of movement across the social, spatial and temporal margins of domestic life and employment, we have sought to discover if and how masculinity might become subject to instability, reinvention or reinforcement. Throughout our study, we have also been concerned to make sense of the diversity of men and their experiences in ways that give theoretical emphasis to individual agency. By asking how men make accommodations in their performances of masculinity, as they shift between settings, what we highlight are both their conscious strategies and implicit negotiations, both their felt experiences of frustration and their unknowing conformity. The concept of transition has been crucial throughout this theoretical endeavour, and in Chapter 2 we introduce this concept as the framing for Part I of the book. In essence, then, our core problematic is to find out how men themselves understand the transition(s) they are experiencing, the extent to which their strategies for managing this change represent reformulations of their masculinity and the degree to which men discover themselves shifting between potentially contradictory forms of masculinity as they move out of and into a heterosexual domestic environment.

Identity and the process of identification

As noted, this book grounds itself theoretically in the notion of identity as 'never a final or settled matter' (Jenkins, 2004: 5). In other words, identity is treated as always in process, an outcome of what Jenkins refers to as an internal-external dialectic whereby the way one sees oneself and the way one is seen are profoundly intermeshed. By implication, then, identification is not only something the individual achieves or 'does' independently; it is also *contingent*, different social environments contributing to an internal-external dialectic in different ways.

This raises the importance of relations of similarity and difference. Thus, with respect to masculinity, it can, on the one hand, be located within heterosexual identification, the requirement for clearly differentiated genders: masculine and feminine. Weston, for example, explains the problem of same-sex desire in terms of 'the territory of difference and opposition' which has been 'ceded ... to heterosexual couples' (2002: 243). With regard to heterosexuality, therefore, masculinity is constituted through difference (Gutterman, 2001: 62). On the other hand, in the workplace, identification's other aspect, the seeking of relationships of similarity (Jenkins, 2004), is evident. Collinson and Hearn, for example, describe the 'unities, commonalities and mutual identifications between men' in the workplace (2001: 163). The relationship between these twin aspects of identity formation – identification and differentiation – are therefore key elements within this book's theoretical project. Jenkins describes them as 'dynamic principles ... the heart of social life' (2004: 5), the privileging of one, rather than the other, being simply a question of emphasis. In comparing men's performances of masculinity as they move across and between public and domestic spaces, then, it is precisely these shifts of emphasis which we aim to capture, so providing a nuanced, situated account of the processes of masculine identification.

Meeting men on the move

The empirical work which underpins this book was undertaken between March 2004 and February 2007. In following men's movement between home and work, we addressed what Woodward refers to as

> fundamental questions about how individuals fit into the community and the social world and how identity can be seen as the interface between subjective positions and social and cultural situations.
>
> (1997: 1)

Echoing Jenkins' (2004) internal-external dialectic of identification, Woodward's framing of identity led us to choose methods that would allow us to get at different dimensions of identity. Our research design combined three kinds of data: interviews with 54 men from the three occupational cultures which asked them to reflect on how home and working life might differ or be linked; interviews with 54 women, chosen by the men (partners, friends or children) which asked how the men do masculinity at home; and participant observation at each workplace that explored how embodied identity emerged within social practice. The three occupations chosen reflected a continuum from stereotypically masculinised work (firefighting) to a feminised work setting (hairdressing) (see Irving, 2008: 166–7). For example, although equal numbers of boys and girls overall were recruited to the Modern Apprenticeship scheme between 2002 and 2003, boys made up only 7 per cent of those undertaking apprenticeships in hairdressing (EOC, 2004). Less obviously 'macho' and becoming increasingly feminised, estate agency represented our mid-choice and a more ambiguous, if not gender neutral, work place.

Our sample also encompassed three age cohorts: young men begin-ning their careers, men in mid-life and older men around retirement age. Not only age but also class separated these men. Our study was located in a city in the north of England, where, like similar northern cities, previous scope for employment in heavy industry that had been available to working-class men was no longer available. Such industries were associated with the forms of traditional, 'macho' masculinity that Donaldson (1991) describes, and for some of the men we interviewed, this had been the social environment they had grown up in, their fathers and uncles recalled as men who worked with their hands, who had been apprenticed into occupations for life. Some of them were therefore the 'younger men who've got to get on', who were envied by older working-class men made redundant in a post-industrial city, those in whose mouths the 'forgotten language of breadwinner/gags' (Jackson, 2009). For younger men in occupations such as estate agency, however, wealth and status sufficient to transcend social-class distinctions was represented in the careers of their successful peers (see Chapter 5).

What men described to us about their working lives during inter-views fell into categories such as how they came to enter a particular occupation and what settling into that occupation involved; how they understood their identity within that occupation, for example, in terms of success and how they might measure this; how their job might have changed over time; and whether they felt they 'fitted in' to the social environment of the workplace and what media resourced or undermined the experience of 'fitting in' (for example, dress, attitudes and values, styles of interaction, degrees of closeness and disclosure, shared leisure). When they and a female partner, family member or friend, spoke about their home lives, they described, for example, life course transitions which involved moving out of or into particular accommodation; the nature of their life as a partner and parent, including leisure, domestic labour, conflict; how they experienced the relationship between their domestic and working lives. These data also gave us a sense of men's worldviews, their values, hopes, ambitions, worries and regrets.

We found that men responded well to opportunities to reflect upon different aspects of their lives and how they understood themselves and those with whom they shared their working and domestic lives. However, in treating identification as a process we have concerned ourselves not only with the play of social interaction as the site of an internal-external dialectic of identity formation, but also with the body as the location at which the experience of oneself at particular points in time is *felt*. Thus, it is through and within embodied engagement that identification occurs; not only with colleagues, friends, clients, and family members such as parents, partners and children, but also with the materialities of the workplace, its setting, the tools and equipment one utilises and those of the home, whether experienced as some kind of refuge from the demands of work, or a set of recurrent demands which are, perhaps, never satisfactorily met.

Moreover, the body is not simply the receptor of externally generated demands and definitions; it is also the vehicle through which men exercise agency, whether by manifesting their sense of themselves in the way they dress, walk or speak, or by more directly acting upon the social and material world through which they are moving. Jenkins sums up this perspective when he says: '[t]he self participates in an environment of others .... like mind, selfhood does not stop at the skin. But it always begins – literally and figuratively – from the body. There is nowhere else to begin' (2004: 46). Moreover, in our desire to understand men's experiences of themselves within and in relation to varying social contexts, the concept of embodiment, as understood phenomenologically, is key. Woodward argues that such an approach 'seeks the meaning of experience as it is embodied and lived in context rather than looking for essences so that the subjective and objective merge, thus emphasising both the primacy of people's own experience and the routine practices in which the embodied self engages' (2007: 75). The body, she explains, 'is not only composed of perceptible qualities; it perceives, that is it is seen and it sees' (2007: 75).

It was the methodological implications of this theoretical approach that led us to look beyond men's testimonies, however self-aware they might be, and to consider ways of getting at their embodied enactment of 'being a man' in different settings. This, we argue, cannot simply be extracted from what men put into words since it constitutes a tangible, materially grounded practice of engaging with both the body one *has*, the object body, but also the body one *is*, the subject body, and indeed the bodies of those who share particular spaces and activities (Turner, 1992). As such, 'being a man' encompasses body-based knowledge and emotion which may be difficult to articulate, even partly. For this reason, then, we undertook participant observation in all three workplaces, so making ourselves part of the environments within which men 'did' masculinity. Adopting this strategy within the private sphere is, however, challenging and, within the more confined social context of a couple or family's home, disruptive. What we decided, therefore, was to utilise the proxy access that women, who in some way shared men's lives, were able to share with us; we therefore interviewed one such woman for every man who participated in interviews, each man choosing the woman he felt could speak best about his domestic life.

The data set we were able to generate thus encompassed both field notes and interview data. Those deriving from among hairdressers were gathered by Victoria Robinson; Alex Hall carried out parallel work with firefighters; and data from among estate agents was collected by both Victoria and Alex. Access to a typically masculinised workplace, such as a fire station, might appear problematic for both these female researchers, yet barriers turned on issues of trust rather than gender, and the firefighters in particular were concerned that we might betray information to management. Indeed, access to men's emotional concerns was, overall, enabled by the gender of the researcher. Thus men would indicate that it was easier for them to talk to a woman, rather than a man. Among firefighters, for example, men would confide personal or domestic worries to Alex in fleeting moments away from the main group of men, when they would adopt a more reflective style of expression. That said, our analysis of data involved reflexively taking account of how gender differences, as well as age and social class, might inflect our material (see Chapter 16).

Participant observation was conducted at workplaces in the city, though some interviewees came from surrounding areas. Work among hairdressers took place in two salons that were selected to reflect very different social and geographical locations: one was in a working-class area, owned and run by a man in his fifties, and catered primarily for an older population; one was set among fashionable city-centre wine bars and shops and employed nine staff, including its female owner and two male stylists. Its clients were mainly 30-something professionals and young people looking for the latest hairstyles. Two estate agents were also chosen to reflect contrasting field sites: one a small, local business run from a cosy office in an affluent area of the city (Timpkins); the other a large city-centre office that was part of a chain and dealt in properties from the entire area, with a lucrative interest in fashionable city-centre lifestyle apartments (Saddleworths)[1]. Fieldwork among the firefighters was conducted in a busy fire station with one particular 'watch'[2] – a group of roughly ten firefighters who work and sleep together through a 'tour' of two day shifts and two night shifts. These were mostly local men, some with previous employment in the steel industry, the armed forces or trades such as plumbing or plastering, though a proportion had a university education.

Frozen moments?

This book is titled *Masculinities in Transition*. Mobility, whether of identity, time, place, the body or the emotions, is therefore what it sets out to address. Yet to provide a text-based account of the process of identification, the subtle shifts in one's sense and experience of oneself, both within everyday life and across the life course, means fixing words upon pages which are kept in place by hard or soft covers. Moreover, as boundaries to the content of the book, the covers are not its only points of punctuation. Regardless of how much one may seek to achieve continuity and 'flow' within academic writing, the conventions of chapters, subheadings and paragraphs divide the narrative, giving structure to what otherwise risks becoming an impenetrable ramble. Thus, in producing a text with transition as its primary focus, we found ourselves potentially defeated by the requirement to structure – and therefore break – the flow of what we were setting out to understand.

To divide the book in a way that reflected the three different occupations would imply insularity, the possibility of highly distinctive, bounded masculinities. While we do, indeed, question the notion of a single, hegemonic masculinity (Hearn, 2004), instead recognising the diversity of masculinities, to isolate them from one another would be to exclude the more pervasive repertoire of characteristics which inform the doing of masculinity more generally – and which have been addressed at length in the masculinity literature. For example, the notion of a sense of entitlement to women's care, support and sexuality (Whitehead, 2002); of complicit masculinity whereby men who do not conform to the criteria of hegemonic masculinity nonetheless benefit from the pervasive privileging of men throughout society (Connell, 2005: 79); and of an association between masculinity, rationality and emotional independence (Seidler, 2006). As Brittan argues, 'While it is apparent that styles of masculinity alter in relatively short time spans, the substance of male power does not' (1989, cited in Haywood and Mac an Ghaill, 2003: 10). Thus, as Haywood and Mac an Ghaill (2003) explain, the notion of 'masculinism' (Brittan, 1989) constitutes an ideology which all men are free to draw upon in order to rationalise and legitimise a privileging of their needs and achievements.

Somehow, then, what pervades different masculinities, the 'patriarchal dividend' (Connell, 2005) which pays out in different ways to all men, needs to be recognised. If a structure which worked against these kinds of connections was rejected, another framework might have been to divide the work on the basis of age, a strategy which would have foregrounded the distinctiveness of particular age cohorts' experiences of being men and indeed helped identify any reworking or transformation of masculinity. Yet to do so would, of course, have militated against understanding the incremental nature of the ageing process, the long trajectory of embodied continuities and changes that constitute the life course. In that we used different methods to get at men's processes of identification in the workplace and the home; another choice might have been to consider developing the work in two halves which, depending upon the occupational culture, might have helped focus on contrasts between 'doing' masculinity in one setting or the other. It is, however, nonetheless the case that each and every one of these ways of punctuating our narrative would insert a kind of stasis, freezing moments in men's dynamic and embodied processes of identification.

Sociologists and anthropologists, who have sought to explain how change is brought into being and managed within society, have drawn upon Van Gennep's ([1908] 1960) schema of the rite of passage to understand how identification operates, how, for example, individuals move between the categories of adolescence and adulthood, between being single and married or alive and dead. This schema also informs work on 'status passages' (Glaser and Strauss ([1971] 2010) which has been important in understanding socialisation into occupations and organisations. Van Gennep's ([1908] 1960) is, however, a stage model of change – even if it admits a liminal period 'betwixt and between' fixed identities. Used to address the structure and content of rituals of all kinds, such a framework has been criticised, for example, by Seremetakis (1991) who argues that, rather than the boundedness of ritual time and space, we need to think in terms of ritualisation. Thus, ritualisation describes a process rather than an event. As such, it is spatially, temporally and socially more inclusive, shedding light on ritualising processes which often unfold over time within the domestic sphere, at the hands of women. Chapter 11, 'Embodying Mundane and Life Course Transitions', develops this idea, referring back to the 'ragged boundary' between work and home explored in Chapter 4. What our data demonstrate are the ways in which transition or change is lived and indeed *created* through the establishment of buffer zones, such as 'time out' on the journey home, or changes of dress on re-entering domestic space. Change and transition thus emerge as anything but the outcome of tightly bounded status passages which enable individuals to move tidily between identities. Instead men, and women, who experienced ambiguous boundaries between home and work, were frustrated by their tendency to seep into one another, and found opportunities to create and benefit from the continuities and separations which constituted their everyday working and domestic lives.

We therefore found that to create a narrative which might enable the negotiated, sometimes fragile nature of 'mobile masculinities' to be addressed, meant working within a framework which in some ways resembled the processes outlined above. What we offer, therefore, is a book that foregrounds the key elements of identification, those features which pervade identity formation at any and all of its stages, constituting its holistic nature: transition, embodiment and intimacy/emotion. These themes are addressed at length in three chapters (2, 7 and 12) which offer extended discussions grounded in a broad range of feminist and related literature. Each of these provides the theoretical framework for four shorter chapters which explore data that give insight into embodied experiences of work and home-based masculinity, the ways in which being a man is 'done'. They show the pleasures, satisfactions and achievements that men access in these different settings, as well as their fears, disappointments and frustrations. Importantly, the data give insight into the unpredictable, often messy quality of everyday life, showing men and women reflecting on the gendered nature of their lives, the ways in which their beliefs and values, the materialities of work and family and the body, enable particular choices to be made and actions undertaken. Equally, the relationship between home and work can constitute a source of frustration, with individuals finding themselves unable to live out their lives as imagined and desired, and wearying of intractable features of their physical environment and being.

Conclusion

In investigating identification across the boundaries of gendered spaces, the project is thus well situated to demonstrate whether the notion of masculinities might best be understood as a diversity of stable identities, or an unstable and contingent potentiality for masculinity, realisable through practices and performance. Thus the chapters to follow ask whether particular identities pre-exist the encounters which go to make up everyday life. Or are they highly localised and emergent only in interaction? With a focus on men in life course and occupational transitions, this book captures some of the processes through which traditional, socially and emotionally distanced masculinities may be either reproduced or reappraised. As such, it contributes to the emergent, if limited, literature on emotions, intimacy and masculinity (Williams, 2001; Whitehead 2002) which are explored in Part III.

Note

1. These are pseudonyms, used to protect participants' anonymity.
2. A 'watch' is a group of men and women on duty at the same time at a given fire station. There are four watches at any station – blue, red, green and white. In any brigade, the same colour watch is on in all the stations. A 'watch' refers back to the military and naval origins of the fire brigade. The watch system is a way of organising cover for an area, and the watches are on duty in rotation. That means that all the men in the same colour watch get to know one another as they are on duty at the same time and will attend incidents together. In the course of a tour of duty (two days, two nights), a watch would meet members of other watches as they finished work in the evening or started work in the afternoon and new watches would come on duty. An individual can move between fire stations as a member of the same watch, if there is a vacancy.

Part I
Transitions

2
Masculinity and Transition

Introduction

This chapter introduces the book's first part where our theoretical and substantive approach to transition is laid out in relation to the three occupational contexts we outlined in our Introduction; that of hairdressing, fire fighting and estate agents. Transition is also conceptualised in relation to how the nature of masculinity can be conceived, for example, as processual and fluid and in terms of the practices and the 'doing' of masculinity across spheres and across the life course, that is, men in motion. What it argues is that transition can be as much about connection and continuity, as separation and difference. Thus, the nature of the boundary between public and private spheres can be seen as constituted differently for men and women of different ages and social class backgrounds (Whitehead, 2002). Furthermore, within individual men's lives, 'key' transitional moments can encompass first entering employment, career progression and retirement, through to becoming or being single, divorced or separated, becoming a couple or having a family. How men situate themselves in time, therefore – the role of memory and imagination, of subjective notions of the past and future – are all under-theorised aspects of the masculine experience.

This chapter places transitions centrally, with the aim of answering Seidler's (2006) call for a reflection upon the tensions men feel between family life and work. Its role is to introduce a set of chapters which will explore the extent to which the identity category 'masculinity' is fractured, but also sustained across the boundary between the working and domestic lives of men employed in different occupational cultures. In making sense of this diversity, what we emphasise is the theoretical centrality of a proper concern with individual agency. In investigating the way in which men make accommodations in their performances of masculinity as they shift between settings, what we highlight are their conscious strategies and implicit negotiations, as well as their unknowing conformity and experiences of frustration. To this complex picture, we add the question of how the private sphere of the home should be brought into the theoretical picture, and indeed the degree to which it is useful to conceptualise the home as separate from the public world of work in the consideration of masculinities. In later chapters, we also frame these discussions in the context of embodiment, emotion and intimacy, as well as our fundamental grounding of masculinity in relation to identity, the latter aspect which runs throughout the book.

This chapter will explore masculinity in relation to identity, briefly place the study of men and work in a historical context before more specifically using a case study of theories of men at work in female occupations to raise some general issues our study is centrally concerned with. This reveals how we both utilise, but also add to, and extend such work, before going on to look at our concept of 'masculinities in transition' in relation to historical notions of 'separate spheres', to enable us to reflect on how the concept of transition is used empirically and theoretically in the book. Finally, the (fluid) boundaries of home, transitions in a work context, as well in as a chronological and life course context are initially explored to enable the forthcoming data-based Chapters, 3, 4 and 5 to take their specific form and shape.

Masculinity: Challenge or Crisis?

The concept of a 'crisis of masculinity' has resulted in men's behaviour increasingly being called into question; in relation to crime, parenting, working with children, sexuality and marriage (Scourfield and Drakeford 2002: 621). It is not, however, clear what we might make of the masculinities that have (apparently) emerged over the 1990s, masculine forms which lead us to believe that we are now dealing with a 'new man'. Gill argues that labels such as 'new man' and 'new lad' may be signal the 'emergence of a more fluid, bricolage masculinity' (2003: 34). Such labels, in Gill's view, reflect competing cultural constructions of contemporary (largely white British) masculinity and suggest that men as social agents can arguably '"do" "new man" or "new lad"' according to context (2003: 39). The possibility of contextually located masculinities provided the impulse for the project drawn upon here, a more theoretically adequate position from which to appraise labels such as 'new man', or 'new lad'. Our data on the whole demonstrate a proliferation of challenges to traditional forms of masculine identity rather than a 'crisis of masculinity'.

While we have critical accounts of these and other 'masculinities' in both private and public spheres, we argue that a focus on men's transitions between the domestic sphere and the workplace provides a way of generating a more nuanced understanding of the nature of contemporary masculinities and has been neglected. As such, our discussion of men in transition is placed within the context of debates regarding a possible 'crisis in masculinity'. Nonetheless, masculinity remains an experience about which we know little, from the perspectives of either men or indeed women who are connected with men's lives in both private and public spheres. Within the masculinities literature, for example, these spheres tend to be addressed separately. Such theorising starts from assumptions about fluid and multiple masculinities, but tends to assume a static framework within which to explore men's experiences. Men are treated as if they inhabit and perform masculinities in one space alone, for example, either the workplace or domestic sphere. Little consideration has been given to how men exist in different spaces, sometimes simultaneously and at various stages of the life course, and how they manage transitions between work and home life, between being a colleague, friend, father and partner.

It is therefore precisely the gap between them which this empirical project has attended to – in order to both enhance understanding of masculinities, and contribute to the theorising of social identity. In addition, by investigating the experience of men of different ages, the project asked whether masculinities and femininities are now less centrally defined by difference than they were for men now entering retirement. Thus, its data explored whether and how the lives of younger men and women might be converging – and what scope older men might have for reframing traditional or hegemonic masculinity. Therefore, our focus is also on age-based and life course transitions, as discussed in Chapter 5, for example.

We now move on to consider the literature on men, masculinity and paid work. While much of this restricts its focus *to* the workplace, as argued above, we nonetheless highlight its contribution to understanding the work/home boundary and the scope of particular occupations to require, or enable, particular gender identities, of which, some are traditional and hegemonic, others more innovative or transgressive.

Men at work

Marchbank and Letherby (2007) state that paid work is considered to be part of the 'public' world and separate from the 'private' world of family and household, yet feminists and others have challenged this notion of two separate spheres pointing out that gender relations in the labour market are related to gender relations in the 'private' sphere. For example, it has been argued that women's greater contribution to domestic tasks is a crucial element in permitting men to freely compete in the labour market (Garmarnikov et al., 1983). According to them, both feminists and writers of critical studies of masculinity, have pointed out that this division has played a major role in defining femininities and masculinities in that women have been either excluded from, or disadvantaged in, paid employment; and that men have been restricted by definitions of masculinity related only to the world of work.

Morgan (1992) argues that paid work is a key issue for understanding men as it has been a source of status, while Collinson and Hearn (2001) state that paid work has been a chief source for masculine identity and power. For Whitehead (2002), work connects men to the public sphere and provides men with a (gendered) identity in that paid work, historically, has been managed, organised and engaged in by men. Crucially, work has been seen as a major influence on definitions and performances of masculinity. Men's sense of who they are is constantly re-affirmed at work, but also open to scrutiny and question. Whitehead (2002) also argues that men respond to changes at work, for example, technological change in diverse ways and individual men (and women) are under pressure at work, for example, the pressures induced through performance indicators. Increasingly, work pressure and insecurity is linked to globalisation and the global recession (Seidler, 2009)

Feminist studies, in particular, have revealed the way that most organisations are permeated through and through with masculine values (Burton, 1991; Gregory, 2009). As Collinson and Hearn (2001) point out, various, well established studies have revealed how, for example, shopfloor life is a very masculinist culture (Cockburn, 1983), or how labour market strategies of male dominated trade unions have served to segregate or exclude women (Walby, 1986). The development of masculinity studies has since gone on to demonstrate, as Whitehead (2002) observes, that men can never 'perform' masculinity seamlessly. If they do, damage to themselves occurs, and therefore, work can provide both assurances for men and also contradictions around their sense of being a man. Thus, work embodies 'masculine' values (but also increasingly, 'feminine' ones) (Simpson, 2009).

Not all men, however, are comfortable with a masculinist culture or a living up to hegemonic masculinity. Others seek to manage inherent tensions at work by focussing on work at the expense of the private sphere, family relations. Men are often seen to compartmentalise public and private spheres: work and relationships/ family lives. (Whitehead, 2002), and it is these assumptions the volume investigates and problematises, both conceptually and empirically. We begin with an examination of the literature which is concerned with men working in a woman's world and the 'feminisation' of the workplace for men. This highlights some of the more general concerns we have just raised about masculinities and work and, through the particular case of men employed in a feminised occupational culture, introduces some of the key issues we are concerned with in our study of the relationship of work to the private sphere. The broad issues raised within this case study area are then addressed in subsequent discussion of the occupational cultures of firefighting and estate agency.

Men in a woman's world

Interest in men who work in female-dominated occupations has grown since the mid-1980s. Feminist analyses note that men may be advantaged in these circumstances by accessing a glass accelerator to promotion (Bradley 1993; Williams, 1995; Lupton 2000). Williams' (1995) data on men working in female sector occupations, such as nursing or elementary school teaching, reveal an interaction between gendered expectations which are deeply embedded in organisations and the socially determined ideas that men bring to work. She argues that until more men 'embrace' more sensitive 'feminine' traits, and thus develop 'alternative' masculinities, such expectations will work to men's advantage.

Simpson's (2004) work on four occupational groups where men worked-; cabin crew, librarians, primary school teachers and nurses, utilised a typology of different male workers to explore men's contradictory experiences of working in female dominated professions. Thus, these men in her study were characterised as those who had actively sought such a career, those who entered the profession in the general course of thinking about which career to enter and those who entered such professions after working in more male dominated occupations. Men across these professions were seen to capitalise on being in a minority occupational position in a variety of ways, for instance, because their 'token status' allowed them special consideration through being allowed to have an 'easier ride' (2004: 357) or through an assumption that they would be allowed more authority than women as well as the 'comfort zone' effect (2004: 258) which meant they felt particularly relaxed when working with women, as opposed to when they had previously worked with men.

However, all these effects could be seen as contradictory for the men in question with over expectations of expertise or assumptions of strength or technical skill which meant they sometimes undertook extra or unsuitable tasks. Simpson concludes: 'it suggests that men undertake considerable "gender work" to re-establish a masculinity that has been undermined by their female occupation. At the same time, it demonstrates how men can feel comfortable with "female" discourses of service and care while drawing on resources from other, more privileged discourses to overcome any disadvantage associated with their minority status' (Simpson, 2004: 366).

And yet, men who choose 'non-traditional' careers may find their masculinity and sexuality coming under scrutiny (Lupton, 2000; Sargent, 2000). Williams (1995) has argued that men who work in occupations which are assumed to be female both upset a traditional gendered division of labour as well as risk being seen as effeminate or homosexual. While Lupton (2000) argues that working in a female-dominated occupation often does not allow men to easily confirm hegemonic masculinity, either within the workplace, or their lives more broadly, and men risk being both feminised and stigmatised as a result, Bradley (1993) suggests that men move across gendered work boundaries 'only in very special circumstances' (cited in Bagilhole and Cross, 2006: 39). By contrast, however, there is evidence that feminised occupations can positively attract men; as Bagilhole and Cross's (2006) interviews with male care workers showed, the nurturing dimensions of these jobs can appeal to them directly.

Sargent (2000), in his discussion of U.S. male elementary teachers cites Allan (1994) to further outline the contradictory position in which men find themselves in feminised professions, trying to fit in with the 'the proscriptions and prescriptions regarding masculinity' circulating among men's relevant others (Sargent, 2000, 413). He argues that men and boys who violate dominant definitions of gender-appropriate behaviour (by working in feminised professions, for example, or showing loving and nurturing behaviour) are viewed suspiciously. According to Allan, this acts to undermine any association between masculinity and responsibility, caring and nurturing. Sargent's research shows that men in elementary teaching must fight to be seen as 'real men' in environments which set up a 'dizzying array of options through which the men must negotiate regularly, yet inconsistently, depending on the immediate situation' (Sargent, 2000: 426).

Sargent's case study has interesting parallels with the male hairdressers in our study. Hairdressing is an overwhelmingly feminised profession in Britain. Our research, as later chapters detail, aimed to investigate what this ongoing feminisation of hairdressing means for men in the profession: for example, the extent to which men felt that they had had to negotiate a distinctive 'hairdressing culture'; how this might have manifested itself in personal styles of dress and hair, their conversation and their leisure activities, and how becoming a hairdresser might have altered men's relationship with their natal family and new partners. As we detail in Chapters 8 and 11, we have investigated changing perceptions (and management of) their bodies as they grow older. We have also explored how men navigate change, conflict, and relationships at work and at home as well as how they 'frame' and understand their emotional responses, and how these emotions in turn, shape their interactions in Part III.

Furthermore, we draw more broadly on studies such as Boyle's (2002) which have found that multiple masculinities, for example, both hegemonic and other 'compensatory' more caring masculinities are in tension in organisations. In particular, the concept of 'gender identity strain' is helpful, as evidenced by the work of Alvesson (1998) whose research among men in a Swedish advertising agency recognises that the feminisation of work puts strain on men's gender identity. The concept of gender strain has therefore informed our analysis of all three occupational settings, including the estate agents and firefighters. Moreover, Simpson's (2004) argument, detailed above, that men employ various strategies to re-establish masculinity which has been undermined by the 'feminine' nature of their work, is extended in our analysis of different gender associated professions when we consider how the private sphere of family and relationships can inform such strategies.

In this way, by working across and within spheres, we have asked how and whether men in different professions challenge traditional/dominant notions of gender roles, identity and power or merely *appear* to reinvent them, while in reality simply reconstructing old ones. Or indeed, is it possible, as Winlow (2001) suggests, that within the limits of any given culture, an individual can define new patterns of behaviour which are suggested by (and, we would add, fashioned from) the variations among old ways of being? Further, in parallel with Faizan Ahmed's (2009) work on the life histories of men employed in 'beauty work' in South Asia, our study revealed that just as different work situations produce different masculinities, the *same* work context can also encompass different masculinities. As she argues, within the beauty parlour 'other divides – provincial town, urban metropolis, caste-class, and so on – are critical in framing the gendered divisions of work' (2009: 168).

In addition, given our theoretical interest in the idea of 'masculinities in transition', we are in agreement with Martin (2001) that we need a conception of 'mobilising masculinities' in which men's individual and collective practices bring into play masculinities at work. Mobilising masculinities is defined here as any practices 'wherein two or more men concertedly bring to bear, or bring into play, masculinity/ies' (2001: 588). In other words, their gender practice is ongoing, expressed through, for example, dress, demeanour, routine, hairstyles. Through a focus on these dimensions of practice, Martin aims to make normally unacknowledged and routine masculinity practices both visible and subject to critique. Our work is also concerned with the routine, mundane practices of men in the public sphere of work, yet, as Martin says, we do not know the implications of such understandings of masculinities and gender relations at work, for either home/family or recreational/leisure contexts. However, it is precisely this which our focus on and problematising of their inter-relationship has addressed.

Moreover, as Martin also contends, the growing body of work on organisations as sites for men to construct diverse 'selves' has tended to focus on *men's* experiences and to ignore women 'except as objects of men's actions' (2001: 589). Martin asserts that studies of men from women's standpoints can show gendered dynamics which are both omitted from more mainstream organisational theories and 'illuminate how gender affects workplaces through interactions and interpretations between sexes' (2001: 589). For Martin, this means interviewing women who had their own stories of working with men to tell. For us, in addressing her plea to bring home/family, and leisure/recreation into the conceptual picture, this meant interrogating data from interviews with women who are partners, relatives or friends with the men and observe men's work in the private sphere, either when doing child care or carrying out domestic tasks or, for example, when they bring their 'public' work home, as the hairdressers and estate agents sometimes did. As well, through participant observation, we absorbed the stories of women in the hair salons having a 'cut and blow' or working alongside male hairdressers, or in the estate agency offices where female estate agents work with men to clinch a sale, or in the fire station where female firefighters are prepared to respond to emergencies, all with tales to tell of men's routine, but tellingly significant practices.

Thus far, we have introduced the implications of paid work for gender identities, focussing on the notion of occupational cultures, which, in themselves, enable and restrain feminised or masculinised identities and practices. But, as argued above, should work and home be seen in taken-for-granted opposition to one another and what might the gender implications of their relationship be?

Separate spheres?

The polarity or otherwise of 'separate spheres' has been much debated from within different disciplines and can be usefully placed in a historical perspective. Summed up by Segal (2007) with reference to Dennis et al.'s (1956) study of Yorkshire mining communities in the 1950s, and where this divide is portrayed, she states 'husbands and wives are seen here as living separate – almost secret lives, neither being able to properly enter into the other's world: the wife will know little or nothing of her husband's job and social life, the husband will take no responsibility for the housework or childcare' (2007: 6). Central to this conception of the public and private have been historical notions of separate spheres in a Victorian context where men were associated with the public sphere of politics and business and women with the private world of all things domestic. However, Davidoff and Hall (2002) in a revision of their earlier, classic work *Family Fortunes*, state that 'Family Fortunes is a story of exclusion and contestation, of boundaries which could never fully be fixed, yet had to be dismantled' (2002: xv). Indeed, central to their argument was the idea of separate and gendered spheres, which, even then, were conceptualisations these authors had started to question and move beyond, exploring the way 'autonomous' male actors were embedded in families, how 'dependent' women provided the contacts and capital, not to mention the labour and personnel which made countless enterprises possible: 'Public was not really public and private not really private despite the potent imagery of "separate spheres"' (Davidoff and Hall, 2002: 33).

Furthermore, they see the crossings of these boundaries as both material and imagined, something which informs our study of any reconceptualisations of, and transitions between, the spheres. In addition, and interestingly for our purposes, Davidoff and Hall (2002) assert that though sociologists have recently turned their theoretical gaze to the

private sphere as opposed to the public, for example, in their consideration of intimate friendships and relationships, they play down aspects
such as reproduction and children, thus, still tending to obscure the
family and gender relations and home, 'those people and places where
daily life goes on behind closed doors' (2002). Linking these historical
concerns with the public and private spheres with a concern with masculinities, Tosh in *A Man's Place* (1999) argues that the middle class male
of Victorian society re-valued the home as a reaction to the disquieting
effects of urbanisation and as a response to the teachings of Evangelical
Christianity. Domesticity still proved problematic in practice, however,
because men were usually working outside in the public sphere, and so,
Tosh argues, the role of the father began to shift and form the modern
day equivalent of a father's 'role'.

However, conversely, from the 1870s, men were becoming less
enchanted with the pleasures of home, mirroring the increasing rights
of women. Masculinity though, however contradictorily, had now
been linked irretrievably for the modern era, to domestic life. While
Olsen (2007), though arguing that Tosh recognises that this 'flight from
domesticity' was not universally accepted by all men, still finds (post
1880s), that 'historians generally agree, there was a refashioning of what
it meant to be a man. This has been a remarkably consistent idea, marking a shift from domesticated, spiritual and intellectual manliness, to
imperial, secular, bodily "muscularity"' (1999). Therefore, in her study
of the Religious Tract Society, the "flight from domesticity" is seen to be
combated by an insistence on men's central importance still within the
private sphere of the home. Citing Francis's work which has revealed
that men 'could simultaneously embrace and reject domestic manliness
(2007: 643)', she further argues that 'Men could have all the trappings
of a traditional family life, while maintaining an escape in the homosocial environment of the club or even in an adventurous imperial
fantasy life through reading.' (Olsen, 2007: 643).

In addition, as Edwards (2006) argues, historically, successful masculinity has been equated with success at work, either through middle-
class career building, or working-class physical labour. The centrality
of occupation to men's identity and its place as a privileged standpoint
cannot, however, be assumed. The changes identified by Beynon (cited
in Edwards, 2006: 8), such as the decline of Western manufacturing
industries, led Edwards to suggest an 'undermining of any direct relationship of masculinity with work *per se*' (2006: 9). Male unemployment
and women's increasing workforce participation have also destabilized
this relationship. Though the male breadwinner has not been entirely

eroded, Irving (2008) argues that this model may have been 'stirred', but it is only just beginning to be 'shaken'.

These sources, give insight into the gendering of paid work and domestic division of labour. But where is home located in men's lives? The assumption that the workplace is a masculinised setting where men feel 'at home' and the home is a feminised world, bankrolled and ultimately controlled by men, requires critical scrutiny. As Jackson (2008) reminds us, 'traditional' family life was a practice specific to nineteenth century middle-class westerners and emerged out of the removal of most forms of production from the home. As detailed in Chapter 2, home became the preserve of middle-class women who, along with their children, were supported by a male breadwinner. However, as Jackson also says, this model was 'an historically short-lived product of particular social circumstances' (2008: 129). Changes in the location of paid work were one part of the picture, therefore, but other aspects of this period also influenced conceptions of masculinity.

In the following example of a contemporary theorist working with a notion of transition, in an illuminating parallel to ours, we find discussion of the separation of spheres within everyday life; in this case between work settings and leisure venues. Thus Rapport has examined the lives of hospital porters in terms of 'how the boundaries between the Hospital and the outside world, as between the work environment and the time and space of recreation and "leisure" beyond it, are routinely permeated by Bob's [a porter's] actions and intentions' (2009: 93). Though in this particular instance he is concerned with the bodybuilding practices of an individual man, Rapport concludes that some of the porters he was investigating turn work into leisure through banter, jokes and 'good crack'. Also relevant for our work is his finding that for 'Bob' there was a 'slippage' between the status of the hospital as either work or leisure, so that while he escaped the hospital as a site of work to go to the leisure space of the gym, his workplace also served as a respite from the 'rigours of the gym'.

This example has resonances with the ways our participants transitioned between fire station and home, estate agency office and the golf club, and hairdressing salon and going clubbing. Therefore, this could be seen, for instance, in terms of the fluidity and interchangeability of these sites. Further, Rapport's idea that '"work" and "leisure" among the porters at Constance pertained not to certain fixed times or locations nor to certain circumscribed practices; rather they were attitudes, frames of mind, by which times, locations and practices were approached and juggled' (2009: 105), helped us conceptualise men's experiences of such boundaries and men's agency within them in terms of reflexively creating their own (gendered) identities.

In addition to our focus on men's movement between experiences of work and domestic settings we are also concerned with masculinity itself in transition. Thus, by situating itself at the boundary between domestic life and paid work, our project investigates the role and status of this division in either reinforcing, or enabling transcendence of hegemonic masculinity. Historically, the home has been an environment within which women's work practices have contributed significantly to the shaping of gendered identities (Jackson, 1997). By incorporating men's experiences of occupying transitional, potentially precarious positions vis-a-vis the domestic environment, this book captures the ways in which traditional, socially and emotionally distanced masculinities are potentially both shored up and reframed as men move into or out of such a context. Alongside this perspective, however, the continuing centrality of the public sphere to masculine identification needs to be recognised; in Walby's view (1986) it is the primary site of patriarchy.

Therefore, echoing the research on men and paid work discussed above, Collinson and Hearn describe how 'particular workplace cultures appeal to highly masculine values of individualism, aggression, competition, sport and drinking' (2001: 146). Indeed paid work, politics and leisure are often seen as integral to the practice of masculinity. In reality, however, the separation of public and domestic spheres is blurred, emotions and work practices often producing slippage between them. Conceptualised as separate domains, the notion of 'leaving home' can be central to masculine identification (Whitehead, 2002: 117). This transition to a public world often materialises as immersion within a workplace culture which can indeed compartmentalise and undermine men's domestic participation. For example, a male firefighter interviewed during our previous ESRC funded project on heterosexuality, described how the close bonds of interdependency between his male colleagues made his work and its related leisure environment into 'one big family'. Coupled with shift work, such ties disrupted firemen's marriages. Whether public/private boundaries therefore operate conceptually or materially is a question which we address in this book. For example, evidence for a stable material boundary is not only undermined by the permeation of home life by aspects of the workplace, but also by a view of the family itself as less a bounded entity, than a set of practices (Morgan, 1996).

We therefore start to identify the ways in which home and workplace intersect in the lives of men, in many cases undermining the notion of a clear, gendered division between public and private. These perspectives inform our concerns with diverse transitions across these, and other, traditional divides: the body and embodiment; the negotiation of gender boundaries; the sometimes risky, contextually located ways in which men draw upon particular forms of masculinity; and the meshing of working and domestic lives in life course planning projects and age-based transitions at significant moments.

No other place like home?

As Chapter 3 argues, the relationship between paid work and home has not only undergone marked historical change; it is a relationship which reflects differences between social classes, occupations, ages, ethnicities and regional and national identities. Spatially, while home has been seen as a core site for displaying ourselves to advantage, Chapman (1999) contends that home is neglected within theories of identity which privilege the public world. As a private environment we can more confidently control, the rooms to which visitors are admitted, for example – 'reception' rooms – can provide 'stages' for favourable performances of self, as Goffman (1971) argues. An exception to Chapman's (1999) critique is Barley's (1990) anthropological account of the lives of the English which asks what 'being English' means as a national identity means and how it is pursued. While ancestral houses or indeed ancestral tombs can be central to notions of self within some non-Western societies, Barley (1990) notes that for the English the private home occupies this role, a centrality reflected in the high price of housing, yet curiously at odds with the amount of time individuals actually spend in their own homes. As our data indicate, for some men, the time spent earning the money needed to help pay for their home frequently restricted their access to it.

Hepworth (1999) describes the emergence of the private home as a middle class retreat from the public world of nineteenth century industrialised urban life – and the agency of home to benefit its occupants' lives, realised by women's labour. Situated within this environment, women married to male members of a new middle class, grown wealthy through factory production, materialised the class-based status they aspired to through this wealth. Similarly, McNair Wright's *The Complete Home: An Encyclopaedia of Domestic Life and Affairs* (1881) states that '[b]etween the Home set up Eden, and the Home before us in Eternity, stand the Homes of Earth ... Every home has its influence, for good or evil, upon humanity at large' (cited in Hepworth, 1999: 25).

Davidoff and Hall (2002) note strong links between masculinity and domesticity between 1830 and 1870, citing Tosh's (1999) argument above that a more interiorized sense of personal identity reflected the influence of romanticism and a privileging of the individual. This can be understood within the context a British landscape radically transformed by industrialisation and urbanisation, where romanticism and the privileging of home and affective family ties became a counterpoint to the harshness of a world of scientific rationality and clock-time factory labour (see Lupton, 1998). However, as noted, Tosh (cited in Davidoff and Hall, 2002: xxii) suggests that by 1860 the questioning of orthodox religious belief had disrupted domestic commitment and engendered a male flight from domesticity. This once again gave homosocial activities a central role in men's lives, one previously located in the clubs, coffee houses, gin shops and street gatherings of the eighteenth century.

The agency of home to bring positive dimensions to its occupants' lives, effected by the hands of women, might have been generated during the early nineteenth century, yet this notion persists in more contemporary imaginings, as our data indicate. While social class and occupational differences shaped men's experiences of home, most saw it as somewhere that admitted aspects of identity not accommodated within the workplace.

While in temporal terms, we have assumed a distinction between a public world of work and a private environment of home – aiming to find out how movement between the two might influence the 'doing' of masculinity, closer scrutiny showed something more complex. For example, a boundary between work and home can be an aspiration rather than a reality; and the distinction between work and home mirrors both work/leisure distinctions and those between kinds of work – which may themselves be gendered. Our data therefore describe the gendered dimensions of creating distinctions between home and work. This is a particular focus in Chapter 4 which examines how both male interviewees and their partners attempted to construct boundaries between work and home both in spatial and temporal terms, and highlights the gendered implications of the diverse and occupationally different methods used by our participants to create home/work distinctions. In this way, we reveal how a complex gendered meshing of work, home, childcare, domestic and emotional labour, and leisure pervade our data. For instance, men's hours could confine partners with children to the home and a traditional gendered division of labour. Equally, their absence could increase women's access to home's positive associations, a 'private retreat within which a personal life can be lived in peace and security' (Hepworth, 1999: 17). Further, in Chapter 4, we reveal clearly how the ambiguous status of home as a site of both leisure and work – and the gendering of this distinction – profoundly influences the identities men discover on leaving work. Enmeshed in these changes are a whole series of apparently more specific transitions, which, nonetheless, carry implications for the gendering of women's and men's lives across different domains.

Work transitions

Arguably in crisis, contemporary accounts of masculinity suggest that it is currently subject to endless, processual reinvention. Whether such reinventions reflect an unfolding crisis, and if so, how this might connect with, for instance, the changing nature of technology within post-twentieth century culture, are core questions which we address in later chapters. In order to contextualise this, however, we need to begin by asking what implications occupational transitions might involve for masculine identification.

Edwards (2006) argues that historically, successful masculinity has been directly equated with success at work, either in middle class terms of career building, or in working class terms of effective physical labour. He then asks whether the changes identified by Beynon (2002), such as the decline of manufacturing in Western societies, might lead to an 'undermining of any direct relationship of masculinity with work per se' (Edwards, 2006, 9). Such changes include an associated rise in male unemployment, resulting from downsizing and market-driven policies, and a broader sense of occupational insecurity and precariousness in service, financial or professional sectors, where the increasing workforce participation of women is clearly evident. Whitehead, meanwhile, argues that men's search for ontological security through work is far from straight forward, and, furthermore, this public world of men at work is characterised by 'a rich, complex combination of myth, mystery and materiality' (2002: 125). In a historical context, for example, a man's sense of self may be re-affirmed at the workplace, but also is subject to both scrutiny and question. Whitehead points out that new technology, which is often seen as male in design and in use, 'also creates organisational transformations that can undermine traditional displays of masculinity' (2002: 125). It is these arguments which the data to follow exemplify. Thus, for example, men, like women, are increasingly under pressure to perform, finding themselves measured against pre-set targets over which they have little control. As Karasek and Theorell (1990) demonstrate, it is the extent to which individuals are able to exercise control over their work, rather than the volume of work itself, which is key to the degree of stress experienced. An overweening emphasis on performance thus reflects men's desire to achieve control. Yet in practice it can be seen as a form of obligatory 'presenteeism' that is both a consequence and a cause of an unproductive, 'long hours' work culture in the industrialised world (Whitehead, 2002: 126)

In terms of gendered identities, then, such changes have unpredictable implications. Irving (2008), for example, describes industrially advanced countries undergoing a period of economic globalisation, and the shift to 'knowledge' and 'information' as commodities and sources of economic advantage rather than manufactured goods, or even services. She then argues that one of the most prominent features in the recent analysis of women's employment, the expansion of jobs in services, conceals a much more complex and contradictory collection of advances and declines in gender equity. These recent changes, she suggests, allow us to reconsider gendered notions of 'work' and 'care'. Such changes also add new dimensions to the industrial shift from 'male' manufacturing to 'female' services and the increased supply of jobs for so-called secondary earners, which disrupted the idealised post-war family model of male 'breadwinner' and female 'housewife'. However, she goes on to contend that though this model has been stirred, it is still only just beginning to be shaken. Gendered work relations are in transition as we shift from the traditional male breadwinner model of family life to, as yet, unestablished models in response to economic change. What she also suggests is that with transition comes choice and a window of (gender equal) opportunity through which further progress can be made.

What is key to our argument here is Whitehead's (2002) view that men respond in different ways to such transformations at work, so to generalise about how these historical changes in production processes, gender relations and technological shifts affect individual men denies the potential of men's agency for change regarding their subjectivity. From the accounts of the female partners of our male participants, it becomes clear that a man's income and his social, emotional and physical well-being cannot be addressed as purely work-related phenomena. Masculinity, femininity and the changing nature of paid work intertwine within the materialities of family life and – in the cases we present here – it becomes evident that the instabilities and disjunctions which emerged within these men's working lives, at times, bound women more securely than ever to traditional gendered stereotypes.

Edwards (2006) argues that if masculinity is now less defined through work, one needs to ask, what does define it, and so, by asking this, it is then possible to undermine the notion that 'masculinity equals work'. However, it is by no means inevitable that changes at work in technology or techniques or organisational practices, will bring about a corresponding shift in masculine subjectivities, and therefore men's behaviours. Men might renegotiate their masculinity within organisations, but there is also clear resistance to change from some men (Connell, 2005).

Therefore, an understanding of the contingency of masculinity involves taking account of the historical processes which have resulted in particular occupational cultures and seeking then to make sense of how these processes might be reflected in biographical material which gets at the experience of being a man within a workplace which is undergoing radical transformation. Hegemonic masculinity thus emerges as context specific and vulnerable to change. What our three case studies show, however, is that while some men exercise agency in seeking to conform to these changing conceptions of masculinity, for others their identify is constituted through differences between themselves and the men who now dominate their occupational culture. Identification's twin aspects – the seeking of relationships of similarity and of difference, are therefore evident within our data.

In focusing here on agency and distinctions between not only occupational cultures, but also individual men at work in these settings, age needs to be recognised as an important dimension of identity. We move on, therefore, to the chronologies of different men's life course trajectories and their implications for masculinity.

Divergent life course temporalities

Sociologists of ageing have offered competing interpretations of the contemporary life course. Featherstone and Hepworth (1991), for example, referred to a 'post-modern life course', an emergent trend with the potential to overturn 'scheduled development' (Featherstone and

Hepworth, 1989: 144). They called for 'a flexible, individualised, bio-graphical approach which takes into account human diversity' (1991: 386), suggesting that during 'mid-life', a plateau phase of the life course which has arguably replaced 'middle-age', individuals may seek to max-imise and sustain the cultural capital of youthfulness. Their arguments are extended in work on the 'yo-yo-ization' of the life course (Elchardus and Smits, 2006), a concept which sees it transformed from 'a sequence of transitions and stages' to 'a series of positions that are simultane-ously accessible and between which individuals can increasingly hop' (Elchardus and Smits, 2006: 304).

Counter arguments, however, suggest that freedom and creativity in life plans bring increased individual responsibility, fragmentation and anxiety (Bauman, 2007; Beck and Beck-Gernsheim, 2002; Furlong and Cartmel, 1997: 44). Other authors, such as Elchardus and Smits (2006), present quantitative data that suggest that a standardised life course retains a place within contemporary society. Brannen and Nilsen (2002) also critique arguments for a post-modern heterogeneity of individualised 'planning projects' (Beck-Gernsheim, cited in Brannen and Nilsen, 2002: 515). Their data reveal that reflexive strategies for negotiating the life course, 'continue(s) to be shaped by structural influ-ences' (Brannen and Nilsen, 2002: 520), which means that '[i]mposing a dichotomy upon young people's lives in terms of either the "choice biography" or the "standard biography" is too simplistic' (2002: 531). In addition to the effects of relative (dis)advantage, our data show vari-ation within particular individuals' orientations towards their futures. As we argue, 'multiple masculinities' can be discernible within as well as across particular men (Spector-Mersel, 2006). In the case of our younger participants therefore, we suggest they are likely to experience tensions between standardised and de-standardised, or post-modern, approaches to planning their futures.

As Chapter 3 demonstrates, changing orientations towards the life course are enabled and constrained by the broader cultural, social and emotional dimensions of a changing culture of work. In so doing it takes account of men's life transitions already noted: leaving home, divorce, and retirement, drawing its sample from among young men starting out in life; men in mid-life and older men around retirement age. Chapter 5 explores the implications of particular temporalities for the contingent nature of the categories 'youth' and 'adulthood', showing the poten-tial intersection of masculinity, femininity, occupational identity and social class at the site of contemporary life course transitions. Its focus is prospective time and the configurations of masculinity which young men in different occupations imagine and indeed plan for, the calendars and maps through which they 'make' and mark the passage of time. Rather than a purely work-focussed structuring of an individual man's aims and objectives, however, the chapter details a potential meshing of professional and personal age-based transitions: for example, home ownership; marriage; fatherhood; level of income; position within company. In addition, rather than a structured trajectory driven by male career goals, for young men in some occupations this prospective life course chronology may be planned and operationalised by their female partners, particularly when they too share a commitment to personal career development.

Rather than simply foregrounding familial considerations, then, men with female partners may find that these women are defining the broader range of chronologised achievements which both parties then orient themselves towards. That said, a couple's potentially divergent life-planning strategies can produce anxieties and tensions which may be difficult to reconcile. Moreover, the younger hairdressers we interviewed were not living as part of a heterosexual couple. Their data therefore offer a contrast which points up the contingent nature of the categories 'youth' and 'adulthood', not only in terms of distinctive occupational identities but also the diversity of men's domestic lives.

Conclusion

The theoretical agenda identified so far has highlighted key issues which we will consider throughout the book. These have included the relationship between identification and differentiation as men move within and between public and domestic space and whether men move between contingent performances of masculinity as they negotiate their relationship with domestic space. We are also interested in whether contrasts, or indeed, conflict between these performances stimulate reformulations of gendered identities, or reinforce complicity with hegemonic masculinity as well as how different masculinities might correspond to the relationship between public and domestic space. In addition, it is important to consider how the degree of contrast and separation between public and domestic space might relate to identity formation among men, as well as how age and masculine identity intersect, and, further, ask if gendered organisational cultures contribute to wider processes of identity formation.

As noted above, what anchors this project is a core theoretical question: if the identity category 'masculinity' is shaped through opposition to or difference from the category 'femininity', how, in practice, does this relate to identification with the identity category 'masculinity'? By making home and work its focus, the project addresses this theoretical question through a materially grounded approach to the embodied, discursive practices through which identities are lived out or renegotiated. Examples of transitional times and spaces within men's lives are therefore proposed as sites of empirical investigation and explored in the following chapters.

3
Home and Work in Historical Context

Important within the study of masculinity have been critiques of foundationalist explanations which locate the nature of men within their bodies (Connell, 2005: 45–66). Instead, social scientists drew on theories of discourse, language and performativity, arguing for the contingent nature of masculinity. Masculinity, nonetheless, is a matter of embodied practice, not simply a concept or representation, however powerful. Moreover, men's bodies are *mutable*, across days and life times, and *mobile*, dwelling in different spaces at different historical moments (Hall et al., 2007). These features of masculinity are our core agenda. This chapter discusses two key spaces of everyday life – the workplace and the home, taking account of their materiality, yet recognising their openness to historical change. Even for our project's eldest participants, the nature of home and workplace and the relationship between them had changed. These men had grown older within environments which themselves were in transition.

As Chapter 2 described, the relationship between paid work and home has not only undergone marked historical change; it is a relationship which reflects differences between social classes, occupations, ages, ethnicities and regional and national identities. Just as any notion of a traditional family proves elusive when compared with empirical evidence, so the division between a public world of work and a private environment of home cannot, in any broad sense, be fixed in time and space. This chapter develops these debates as they inform the context of men and women's everyday lives, focusing on the occupations chosen by our male participants. Occupational histories therefore provide one part of the context within which masculine identification can be located; but the homes from which men left for work and to which they later returned also have their part to play.

Historical transitions

We therefore ask what meaning home had for our male participants, what investment did they make in it? This raises issues of standpoint: did men regard home as the place they went back to, a waiting haven; or the place they set out from, the location of their primary attachment? As Chapter 2 explained, although success at work and masculinity have been elided, historically (Edwards, 2006), the decline of western manufacturing industries and shifts in the gendering of work *per se* have destabilised this connection. Thus, the intersection of notions of masculinity, home and work has undergone transitions of many kinds. Below, we trace the histories of hairdressing, estate agency and fire fighting, partly through historical records but also via embodied experiences recalled during interviews with men around retirement age. The names and other identifying details of these and all our participants have been changed to ensure anonymity. The data which follow in this chapter give us our first evidence that masculinity, as an identity, is 'done' differently in different work settings. In addition, however, they shed light on the relationship between changing occupational cultures and men's domestic lives.

Comparing these men's lives highlights the need for a gender analysis to incorporate the marked contribution of social class to men's responses to change. In that our life history perspective reveals men's scope for agency within larger-scale structural processes of change, social location is an important factor in enabling or constraining such potential. Thus, in two out of the three occupations selected, men's higher social class position – one achieved through 'working their way up' – allowed them to redefine both themselves and their work, thereby securing status, income and respect.

Woodward (2007) addresses the intersection of masculinity with social class (and also race) in her ethnographic work on masculinity, identity and boxing. She draws on Bourdieu's notion of cultural capital and its scope for transformation, demonstrating how human agency allows different kind of capital to be activated. Thus, for example, she examines the scope of working-class men to mobilise what she terms 'physical capital' in order to achieve wealth, status and a reputation as a hero, an insight with particular implications for physical capital for working-class men discussed here.

In contrast with the advantages for working-class men that Woodward (2007) identifies in boxing, some occupational cultures offer limited scope of this kind. In the following analysis, then, the forms of capital available to men encountering occupational change are an important focus. Certain occupations, we suggest, permit class-based social locations to be transcended, as particular skills and knowledge open up relatively more secure, middle-class locations.

Importantly, however, evaluating the 'success' of different ways of mobilising capital raises questions about their implications for men's domestic lives, their health and well-being, their relationships with families, and, not least, the costs and benefits to a female partner. In terms of hegemonic masculinity, then, we ask whether these are forms of 'accommodated settlement' (Woodward, 2007: 36); or, by contrast, evidence of the capacity of hegemonic masculinity to reinvent itself in tandem with shifts in the world of work. Does participation in hegemonic masculinity potentially override differences based on social class, as Woodward (2007: 41) asks? Or, as Whitehead says, acknowledging the patriarchal nature of wider systems of power, 'the question remains as to what extent masculinity is simply a by-product of social and cultural change' (2002: 17). Further, discussing state power, for example, Connell represents it as 'a resource for the struggle for hegemony in gender, and hegemonic masculinity is a resource in the struggle for state power' (2002: 105).

Locating occupational identities

As Chapter 1 described, the occupations we selected reflect contrasting and stereotypical associations with masculinity and femininity; they also make different contributions to men's class-based identities, occupation being a key indicator of social class position (Rose, 1995). Not only do gender and class intersect here, but their inter-relationship changes over time. For example, as an occupation becomes feminised it may lose status; if it acquires a higher status, its workforce may succeed in directing the nature of historical change. As data from hairdressers and estate agents show, their skills and knowledge represented forms of cultural capital that opened up relatively secure, middle-class locations, when compared with the physical capital available to firefighters (see Woodward, 2007). Scope for 'working their way up' potentially allowed some hairdressers and estate agents to redefine both themselves and their work, thereby securing status, income and respect. In exploring the broad historical changes which have occurred within particular occupations, we utilise biographical data from three men who have negotiated a life time of occupational transition, considering its implications for their gender and class-based identities.

The hairdresser

While hair 'styles' undergo enormous change over time, the quality of hair's presentation remains an enduring marker of identity, status and gender (Herzog, 1996). Hairdressing skills can therefore be linked with other important bodily interventions: dental work, blood-letting, cupping and leeching, extracting teeth and treating wounds. During the eighteenth century, hairdressers were valued by rich and powerful individuals for whom elaborate hairstyles and wigs announced social status. Here gender intersected with social class: not only were men were seen as the best hairdressers but a trained wigmaker, such as Legros de Rumigny, who started work as a baker, later became a court hairdresser in France.

Until the twentieth century, however, fashionable hairstyles were the prerogative of the upper classes and hairdressing was practiced in the home, by resident or travelling male hairdressers. With the gradual democratisation of beauty and fashion, however, came the growth of hair salons in the US in the 1900s (Banner, cited in Gimlin, 1996: 506). In the US today, 'half of every beauty dollar is spent' is spent in the hair salon (Freedman, 1986 cited in Gimlin, 1996: 507). In Britain, hairdressing has become increasingly feminised and salon-based over the twentieth century. In that hairdressers are strangers who break the norms of bodily space, this may explain the rise of women tending other women's hair (Herzog, 1996). Nonetheless, men have achieved status as celebrity stylists: for example, Nicky Clarke at Birmingham, Manchester and Leeds; Sergio Valente in Rome; and John Barrett and Garren in New York (see also Chapter 10).

While there are clear distinctions between men who defined themselves as 'gents'' hairdressers and those who worked in unisex salons, Russell Talbot, a men's hairdresser for 50 years, described changes in men's hair styles since the 1960s that made techniques previously reserved for women in demand among young male clients. He adopted these techniques and when a local college began vocational training, agreed to 'help', a challenging move into a more middle-class role which meant, in his words, that 'I've never sweated so much in my life'. The son of a newsagent, Russell and his wife still lived in a neat semi in a respectable working class part of the city. His father had advised him that a hairdressing apprenticeship would provide him with a skilled trade for life. Now Gloria, his wife describes them living, not 'luxuriously', but 'comfortably', with 'enough to go round'.

Russell thus moved into what Connell (2005) describes as a 'new middle class', men with expertise but not the social authority of older professions. Russell's lack of social authority was compounded by the absence of job security or pension. For him, therefore, home was partly the place to which he withdrew during periods of unemployment. When asked whether Russell's job had introduced stresses into home life, Gloria said it was periods without work that had been challenging, referring to his heart attack as a younger man.

Now semi-retired, home was a place where Russell had a finite list of *'things to do'*, rather than the ongoing task of keeping it 'ticking over' undertaken by Gloria. She described him assuming a traditional gendered role on semi-retirement, relieving her of 'gardening duties' and 'helping' with shopping when needed. Russell's occupational trajectory had thus enabled him to transcend the working class life he was born into; he had, however, responded to the requirements of his job by adhering to a traditional breadwinner model, suffering when this proved unviable. While Russell had subsequently become an active grandparent and sold booklets of his poetry to raise money for charity, hairdressing remained his core identity. Giving it up was difficult to envisage; he said: 'I'm not sure I'm yet ready to, to give in ... it does feel that I would be giving everything up'. In terms of retirement offering scope for reinventing masculinities (see Chapter 2), then, Russell was clearly ambivalent about making any radical shift into more feminised activities.

The estate agent

Prior to the 1980s, estate agency had been undertaken by small firms with defined geographical boundaries (Beaverstock et al., 1992: 168). Establishing a business was cheap; and there were no set qualifications or licensing (although many agents are qualified surveyors or auctioneers) (Bragg, 1992: 368). However, the UK state's shift to the logic of the market in the 1970s brought concentrated growth and change in estate agency (Beaverstock et al., 1992: 166). Moreover, the Thatcherite promotion of property owning meant that those previously excluded from home ownership entered the housing market, fuelling demand for property. Associated with Thatcherite economic values, estate agency became a lucrative opening for go-getting individuals who needed only a gift for selling, ambition and confidence (Beaverstock et al., 1992: 167).

Falling interest rates at the end of the 1980s, however, saw estate agency go into recession. Branches bought up by large corporations in the 1980s 'acquisitions war' were closed, although some former agents then bought back their businesses cheaply (Beaverstock et al., 1992: 176–8). Local knowledge of the sector, the mainstay of traditional practice, once again prevailed over the techniques of large financial institutions (Beaverstock et al., 1992: 180). That said, the 1980s image of the untrustworthy estate agent has persisted, testimony to a time of cut-throat dealing and 'sharp practices', an image not helped by estate agency's longstanding lack of regulation (Bragg, 1992: 368).

Like Russell Talbot, Brett Hardwick, a semi-retired estate agent, had entered a profession which afforded him the cultural capital needed to transcend his working-class origins: he said he had 'lived in a council house, I'd grown up in that environment ... had no experience of buying or selling property'. He recalled the thrill of driving the firm's car:

> bumping into my old school mates... saying 'Look at me! I'm in a posh Triumph Herald', because if I could get in the Triumph Herald rather than the Morris Minor I was in heaven.

Finding himself in a different social milieu, Brett adjusted his speech to fit in with the firm's 'awfully nice' public school-educated partners. Over time, he weathered the storms of an unstable profession and saw this as an outcome of marketing a trustworthy self: 'you don't sell houses, you sell you ... when I first started, you know you'd shake hands on a deal and a gentleman's word was his bond and that was it'. He now offered part-time, lucrative consultancy among other estate agency-related services. Across his life course, then, Brett had undergone a whole series of age and also class-based transitions.

For him, home had two aspects. On the one hand owning a home was a key indicator of his new social class location:

> Most of my colleagues, friends, had all, you know, it was sort of post War years and so on, but we became very much a, it was aspirational to own your own home, it's part of the British psyche really isn't it?.

That said, while home was central to his 'British psyche', Brett spent little time there. a reflection of particular gendered identities and their implications for masculinity. Married as teenagers, Brett and Chrissie, his wife, lived according to traditional gendered stereotypes. Referring to his youth, he said, 'your wife was pregnant, she had a baby she didn't go back to work... I'd got to be, I'd got to be the breadwinner, I'd got to support my wife and new child'. Providing for his family gave Brett a measure of his career success –a large commission cheque from early sales paid for his wife's first washing machine, a real luxury

Though still driven by a work ethic, Brett was described by Chrissie, his wife, as less stressed now he had relinquished some work pressures. Being an estate agent had made Brett 'uptight and frazzled', particularly during moral battles with colleagues, said Chrissie. Like Gloria, Chrissie's domestic life was dominated by a partner's long working hours. Although stoical, she had been lonely.

Chrissie and Brett, a working-class couple, grew up when home ownership became an achievable reality and class location was less of a barrier to 'making it' in professional sectors like estate agency. Negotiating shifts in a cut-throat industry, riding economic booms and busts and investing wisely to pursue security and raise a family while adhering to a moral path, had been the trajectory of Brett's life.

The firefighter

Though the provision of a fire service dates from the Great Fire of London in 1666 (Segars, cited in Baigent, 2001), it was in 1833 that insurance companies together formed the 'General Fire Engine Establishment' (Baigent, 2001: 3). Firefighters became feted as cult figures, epitomising a preoccupation with 'manliness', heroism and chivalry. Battling industrial blazes, firemen represented a 'spectacularly visible' masculinity (Cooper, 1995: 164).Though poorly paid, firefighting offered working-class men a sense of purpose and worth. Baigent argues that the 'fire service remains one of the few havens where men can celebrate their physical strength and embodied skills in *permanent* employment with a pension' (2001: 11; italics in original).

Firefighting has, however, undergone change. Major strikes in 1977 heralded the 'halcyon days' of conditions and morale (as a participant put it). However, the 2002/2003 strike undermined confidence in the Union, revealing only mixed public support. Working conditions are now perceived to have deteriorated along with the erosion of the brigade's military model. Baigent (2001: 5) now describes a 'them' and 'us' attitude dividing firefighters from management over the future of the service.

Key points of fracture include health and safety legislation that now prohibits officers from tackling fires first hand, reducing their respect among lower ranks (Baigent 2001: 7–8). Fighting fires itself is less a part of everyday, embodied work, fire prevention and public education growing in importance. Men's scope for demonstrating a particular kind of hegemonic masculinity is thus limited; and the entry of women into the service is seen to have undermined standards of health and fitness, while also putting traditional homosocial comradeship under pressure (Baigent, 2008).

For Clive Bell, a 53-year-old, retired fire fighter, these issues were core to the narrative of his life. Becoming a Junior Fireman at 16, firefighting had been Clive's life. Indeed he acknowledged that 'love of the job' played *some* part in ending his 19-year-long marriage. In terms of his relationship with home, his job has 'always, always come first', said Helen, his girlfriend. However, unlike Russell Talbot and Brett Hardwick, whose cultural capital had helped them ride out radical changes at work, the physical capital Clive developed through embodied strength and skill was insufficient as a resource when changes occurred (see Woodward's (2007) parallel discussion of the physical capital working-class boxers accrue through bodily strength and skill). When interviewed, then, Clive spoke of Chief Fire Officers who had:

> never been to a bloody fire ... they don't strike you as physical guys who've ever struggled in their lives to do anything ... they've never pulled anybody out ... they've never been cold and the Deputy Chief ... used to work in a bank ... it's a joke.

Lowering entry standards to accommodate women, in his view, meant allowing 'weak' men and 'weak' women into the service: 'let's have equal but let's have a good equal, you know and not a weak equal', he said, reiterating the importance of bodily resilience:

> when you're a fireman, basically ... you're a mule, you've got to get equipment from one place to another to operate ... You know it's a physically demanding job ... you get dirty, you get cold, you get wet ... how many women do you know that really want to do that?

For Clive, however, that resilience was time-limited. He feared being unable to live up to the job and had chosen retirement at 50:

> It was becoming hard work ... responding to fires ... in the middle of the night ... you're thinking 'Jesus Christ, it's hard work, it's a young man's game' ... 50's no time to be running up stairs with a BA [breathing apparatus] set on.

Home, for Clive, during his first marriage, was somewhere he spent little time, dividing his days (and nights) between work and a fire service archive he set up. Subsequently he came to live with Helen, the girlfriend he'd met as a teenage volunteer at the archive. In the flat below, his father tended his mother who had chronic arthritis. When interviewed Clive was wearing an American fire service T-shirt, the walls of the flat crowded with fire service memorabilia. Not only did he undertake cooking and ironing, skills developed as a firefighter, but he spent considerable time with Helen, socialising and travelling. Yet after retirement his nights were still disrupted: he remained alert for a fire call. And when a fire engine ('pump') passed in the street he recalled being in it.

That said, Clive became a car mechanic post retirement. 'You've got to think about more than putting fires out at the end of it, you think, I've got a life to lead'. Once in this new role, he rarely visited the fire station and did not park his car in the yard: 'I'm not part of that fraternity any more ... (free parking) is a privilege you get when you're in the job'.

Conclusion

Home and work thus stand in a changing relationship with one another. While Russell Talbot and Brett Hardwick fought to 'succeed', they often absented themselves from home and family life. For Russell, being at home was what happened when the precarious nature of his job lost him work; nearing retirement he still seemed committed to not 'giving away everything', and retaining his professional commitments. Home, for Brett, was an indicator of his success as working-class man who had succeeded in a professional job; but not a place to spend time or undertake domestic tasks. Clive too had prioritised work, his first love, spending little time at home. Rather than leaving his wife to a traditional gender role, it was his wife who left him, effectively severing connections between Clive and his son. Unlike Russell and Brett, Clive had subsequently distanced his identity as a firefighter, not wishing to compromise the status he had built up at the point when he left. Different social class locations carry different penalties for men responding to change at work, its cost in terms of relationships with their family, and their health, varying. Men such as Clive, were less free to innovate; having lost his family he then sought refuge in a new relationship, downplaying his earlier firefighting connections.

4
Continuities, Conflicts and Contradictions

The notion that a man's occupation is central to his identity has now been questioned, along with the elision of masculinity, a breadwinner's income and a public world of work (Edwards, 2006). Using biographical and historical data, Chapter 3 detailed the recent social and economic shifts which have put this particular framing of masculinity under pressure. This chapter makes the relationship between masculinity, identity and home its starting point in a discussion of how home and work might each shape, bound and give significance to the other. Moreover, data about the domestic and working lives of men in three different occupations show that any adequate answer to this question needs to take account of the particularities of different lives.

As Chapter 2 described, home can be seen as a core site within which identification takes place, despite the experience of many of the men interviewed, that home was somewhere their income resourced, yet their work tended to exclude them from. Hepworth's (1999) account of the nineteenth century separation of the paid workplace from the home provides an explanation for the initial gendering of the public and domestic spheres, home coming to constitute a retreat or haven from an industrialising society. The agency of home to bring positive dimensions to its occupants' lives, effected by the hands of women (Hepworth, 1999), also persists in more contemporary imaginings, as our data indicate.

As this account shows, therefore, not only the three occupations discussed in Chapter 3, but also the space, place and practices we call 'home' have been in transition. This chapter takes up this point and, via the beliefs and practices of firefighters, estate agents and hairdressers, shows not only how home was conceptualised and lived, but also how their working lives contributed to the practices through which home was brought into being – and indeed how home life contributed to men's occupational identities. While men's experiences of home varied, depending on their occupation, age and social class, it tended to be viewed positively as an environment that permitted behaviours and aspects of identity not accommodated within the workplace. That said, commitment to working lives often restricted men's access to home, quite significantly. This chapter does not, therefore, treat home simply as the bricks and mortar which men's incomes helped them own or rent; rather, we draw on Morgan's (1996) notion of practice as the mechanism through which institutions such as family come into being. How men carry out their working lives, then, in relation to home, can be seen as integral to the production of home as both an environment and a concept. In understanding home as a practice, we also take account of the ways in which key elements of identity are brought into being, particularly masculinity and femininity. As VanEvery (1995) argues in her discussion of housework, the outcomes of practices such as cooking, shopping and cleaning are not restricted to the materialities of eating and personal comfort. Gender itself, via individuals' accountability to particular conceptions of being a man or a woman, comes into being as floors are mopped and lawns mown.

As noted in Chapter 1, the project that produced the data we discuss below derives from our previous research on heterosexuality. In the course of that work, male interviewees who happened to be employed as firefighters argued that features of their work made their marriages unstable. This notion was reiterated by Carrie Morse, female partner of a young firefighter, interviewed for the current project. Enticed by the stereotype of the heroic, sexually hot firefighter, Carrie's women friends would seek introductions to her partner's workmates; she would jokingly rebuff them, saying surely they'd heard about the high divorce rate among firefighters. While dubious about this rate herself, she did discuss the implications of shift work. That, along with the strong bonds between firefighters who shared a watch, and the sexual opportunities afforded by their public image, supposedly undermined men's domestic lives. This might seem to suggest that, for firefighters, there are tensions between their working and domestic lives, though our data show a potential for harmony between these spheres as well. Certainly, as we discuss below, the temporality of shift work sets these men on a different course, giving them access to leisure when others are at work, and removing them, sporadically, from family meals and the marital bed. How this shapes the gendering of home is, however, more complex than stereotypes admit. Nonetheless, the notion that there may be different kinds of (in)compatibilities between workplace and home provided a key starting point for the project overall – and for this particular chapter. We begin now by considering the spatial and temporal location of working life and the extent to which this might be at odds with men's and women's life aspirations and their sense of who they are,

The boundaries of work

Many interviewees, both men and their female partners, described their attempts to contain men's working lives, both spatially and temporally. Its boundaries were experienced as ever vulnerable to collapse. For example, among hairdressers, references to 'the door' were used both literally and figuratively to describe work's potential intrusions upon private life. Pat and Gordon Bristow owned their own slightly run-down salon in a mixed middle- and working-class area of the city and were now comfortably off, despite a relatively impoverished start in their lives. Pat spoke of the salon door when relating conflict between Gordon, her husband, and their son, Terry. With Gordon nearing retirement, father and son worked together in the same salon. However, as Pat said,'(the conflict) finishes when they, when they close the door, it finishes'. Working alongside other family members, particularly partners, was not uncommon among the hairdressers we interviewed, but another challenge to sustaining a boundary to work was the embodied nature of their skills – plus the portable nature of much of their equipment. When they finished work, their skills came home with them and family and friends would expect to visit them for hair styling. Paula Flint, friend of Steve Richardson, a young hairdresser, said that Steve kept hairdressing 'a professional thing'. 'At least then that's it', she said, 'he closes the door. If he kept doing people at home then you never leave work'. Joyce French , partner of Derek , an older men's hairdresser with a shop in a working-class area of the city, made references to the fabric of the home and the salon when echoing this point: 'You never ... you might as well live over the shop', she said. What these references to closing the door indicate, therefore, is the need to create rather than simply cross a boundary between home and work.

The all-day proximities of the salon could also be problematic between friends, as well as family members, who worked together. Again, interviewees used the metaphor of the door to make this point. Sam Cartmell, a young hairdresser, described needing a boundary between himself and a work friend who lived in the same apartment block. Without it, he said 'he's there in the whole of my life, there's no separation, you can't shut the door in your home life and be able to breathe and think – ah, you know, this is my space, you know, I'm happy'. Notions of the public and the private which were implicated in the gendered division between paid work and family life during the nineteenth century here surface as an ongoing aspiration – but one not necessarily accessible in the everyday life. Brendan Amies, a 37-year-old gay hairdresser had cut people's hair as part of his hectic social life, but now wanted time in the flat he had recently bought after leaving his parents' home – he had hardly sat on his own sofa, he said.

Though the notion of home and work as the outcome of practice is important, the references made by hairdressers and their female friends, partners and relatives to a material item – 'the door' – do point towards the less mutable spatial dimensions of work's boundaries and its potential intrusion into home space. Not only did hairdressers seek to annex their working practices from home, but estate agents too were often faced with work-related matters such as phone calls while at home. These calls could even surface in holiday locations. Chrissie Hardwick described her husband Brett, a retired estate agent, sitting on the beach in Barbados perturbed to find there was no signal for his mobile. In retirement, Brett ran a small lettings business in an office set up at home. Though work and home were spatially elided, they remained separate in terms of the gendering of practice. Thus, while Brett would sit in his office, perhaps taking phone calls, Chrissie made the evening meal on her return from work. Of Brett, Chrissie said, 'People just think you're on call 24 hours a day', yet her own paid and domestic work similarly extended across many of her waking hours. Phil Cruikshank, a 41-year-old estate agent in a small independent company, said he did leave work behind at the end of the day; he was not paid enough to take it home. But, he went on, 'obviously the directors when they go home, they're, they've got an office at home, they go straight into that one them, and finish off jobs that they haven't done in the office'.

For men in full-time employment, these intrusions into home space reflect the ragged nature of work's temporal boundaries. When the nineteenth century migration of agricultural populations into cities brought an end to working days shaped by the weather, the seasons and religious festivals, it was the clock which replaced these influences as time spent at work was measured precisely in money, employees quite literally clocking on and off (Voth, 2000). Now the long but bounded nineteenth century hours of industrial production are echoed in the widespread commitment of the UK labour force to a longer working week than any other in Europe; but this commitment is one without clear boundaries. Paid employment now involves a flexibility which in practice means more – unpredictable – work time, whether in the work place itself, the commuter train or the home (Burke and Cooper, 2008). While men spoke regretfully of missing time with their children and – repeatedly – of their tiredness after long hours and sometimes long commutes, time at home was frequently colonised by the requirements of work.

Time spent at work, then, proved crucial in shaping men's relationships with home. Among hairdressers and estate agents, the *volume* of time was critical. As a relatively junior estate agent, Phil Cruikshank rightly assumed that older, wealthier estate agents indeed made virtually unbounded temporal commitments to their businesses, a process of attrition as days extended into evenings and weekday work colonised weekends. And as commitment to domestic life reduced in terms of time spent, it increased in terms of financial resources contributed, a shift mirrored in the social class transitions enabled by success within estate agency. However, the temporal demands of ownership were not restricted to the wealthy or middle class; limited hours of domestic life did not necessarily mean financial compensations. Older hairdresser, Derek French, owned a salon on a working-class estate in the city but had made more money working 'on the buses' (which he hated). His annual holiday allowance was two weeks, but he had not taken that time for the last five years. As Joyce, his wife, pointed out, 'the trouble is with working such long hours, the time you have off, you've got to do work on the house. Or he's got to go to the dentist and have a lot of work done at the dentist, now he's off for a week in August, so that week will be taken up going to the dentist, so really it's not a holiday'. While the home/work boundary is ragged and unpredictable among estate agents, for hairdressers, like firefighters, the actual hours worked reflect the particular demands of their occupation. Being open for customers on a Saturday was essential for Derek French, with time 'off' during the working week. But, said Joyce, 'I mean we have Thursdays, your day off Thursday, that's going to the wholesalers, going to the bank, so really there's only Sunday'. Refusing haircuts to friends and relations was thus insufficient as a way of sustaining work's boundaries.

For firefighters, in particular, work did not expand in *unpredictable* ways. Indeed, some female partners found the rigidity of shift patterns problematic, leaving no scope for requesting particular leave times, for example, when a wedding came up. For these men, the shift system (2 days and 2 nights tour at work, four days at home) quite literally 'shifted' them – onto different temporal tracks, removing them from home entirely during a tour, returning them to home while others were at work. This asynchrony had a variety of implications for men's lives at home and outside work and these are discussed in the section below on home. And even so, while firefighters' equipment remained within the fire station, unlike a hairdresser's portable tools, their embodied skills could blur the boundary between what for them were the more separate worlds of home and work. Retired firefighter Clive Bell (53) said 'even in civvy street you still step forward ... because of your training and your frame of mind, you're always there to assist the public'.

In sum, men's working lives intruded into their home lives in ways that neither they nor their female partners felt in control of, regardless of class and age differences, resulting in tiredness and a sense of exclusion from home. Home, as described by some estate agents, was a place they visited briefly at the very end of the working day or working week. Patrick Thompson, for example, at 57, said 'you want to recharge your batteries, you're in bed and you're up the following day and you're back into it ... it's limiting in that sense and ... when I go home on a weekend, my weekend doesn't last forty eight, it lasts for twenty four hours... but I do so much gardening on a Sunday, so much work at home, I come in on Monday and I'm knackered'. Similarly, Tim Dawson (29), another estate agent, said 'when I was working in Leeds, the biggest factor would be the travelling ... I wouldn't get back until late and also my girlfriend's working towards becoming a qualified accountant, so a lot of the time she'd be studying and I'd get in about half seven and then cooking tea, she's studying, so it really was a case of having to sit down for an hour, ten o'clock, go to bed'. Tim laughed at the end of his statement, yet went on to describe 'constantly feeling fatigued in, not really an even keel to judge, judge things sometimes'.

In contrast with these experiences, some men's workplace identities could be deliberately sustained when they got home – in ways that female partners welcomed. Derek and Joyce French, for example, had both been hairdressers when they met, but when perming solutions inflamed Joyce's potentially cancerous dermatitis, she had to retire. Now, she said, 'I mean he comes home and he tells me about the customers and I enjoy it, you know it's, always got plenty to talk about'. Similarly, younger hairdressers' work could extend into events outside the salon and they enjoyed the associated social life. Michael Dunbar 'used to know all the hairdressers in the city', and said 'I suppose a lot of the events that we do, hair colouring and take place in town, that's .'. Like Derek and Joyce French, estate agent, John Sargent and Susan his partner worked alongside one another. After their children left home, Susan had decided to undertake administrative work in the business John set up later in his professional life, having become disillusioned with the company he worked for. After suffering his earlier, very long working hours and his eventual depression, she said that after work it was 'good to go home and I want to potter in the kitchen and one part of the garden, and he'll be down the garden or he'll be somewhere else ... and occasionally it's handy, you think oh did I remember ... but we wouldn't sit and spend an evening, unless it was something like I'm doing a salary spreadsheet and I want to talk about it at home ... I think I was worse to start with, but as I'm sort of mellowing, and various things happen in life, I think you calm down and mellow a little bit more'.

Implications for home

So far we have prioritised the ways in which men's work can either encroach upon home, or require their lives to follow a temporal trajectory which is at odds with the patterning of other family members' lives. As these data indicate, home and work constitute one another's boundaries, boundaries which, by implication, represent the demands of working rather than home life. In ways that reflect differences of age and social class, tensions between the two are evident.

That said, interviews with female partners do not reveal overt gender-based conflict around this issue. Fifty-seven-year-old Chrissie Hardwick said of Brett, her estate agent husband, 'I do nag him sometimes, when he comes in at nine o'clock at night you know, or and he's just sat down to eat his tea and the phone rings', but then described her response as, 'just a wife thing isn't it really?', going on to assert that 'It's not his fault and he can't help people phoning but people just think you're on call'. Her 'wifely' worries about Brett's well-being are amplified in female partners' emotional responses to firefighters' lateness home, these carrying more urgent health implications. 40 year-old Cara Simpson said 'I think I worry more when he's on nights because there's more dangers for him on a night shift than what there is on a day shift, I worry if he's late home ... (but) my time span's expanded now, I actually allow him half an hour to be late now which only used to be five minutes, five minutes, clock watching'. Sharon Armstrong, at 27, described hearing of a major fire in the city on the radio during her husband's first week in the service: 'I thought shit, he's there, you know, I know he's there'. She went on, 'I text him and I went, look I know you're at this fire can you text me when you're alright and ... I didn't get no text message back, he were supposed to finish his shift at nine o' clock and I didn't get a text, ten o' clock I didn't get a text message and eleven o'clock I didn't get a text message and I were at work and my boss went, you alright? And I went no, just burst'.

Consistent throughout data where women were describing the problem of men's absences from the home, and the associated threats to their health, were assertions that their partners loved their job, and their earnings meant that the family were 'well looked after'. While these data may be less than transparent, and anger and resentment were perhaps being concealed, women sometimes actively welcomed men's absences from home. Asked about the implications of nightshift, firefighter's partner Cara Simpson said 'It's heavenly [laughs] ... because I have my time, it's just me, I can watch what I want on telly, I can get in bath and just relax and not have to think oh I've left him downstairs on his own and you know go to bed when I want and have all quilt to myself, it's just things that you just sort of take for granted when you're single'. A similar view was expressed by, Sharon Armstrong, describing her firefighter husband being away for 14 weeks' training, 'at beginning I were like, I didn't want him to stop there ... but at end it were ... nice to go out and for me to come home and still have everything in it's place [laughs] you know, like instead of coming in and there's like shoes on floor ... like t-shirts chucked somewhere else, cups of tea all over ... I found it more stressful when he come back than when he went'.

While data show that long working hours could confine female partners with children to the home and a traditional gendered division of labour (see Chapter 3 for the example of estate agent Brett Hardwick and Chrissie, his wife), men's absence also gave women access to home's positive associations, a 'private retreat within which a personal life can be lived in peace and security' (Hepworth, 1999: 17). To what extent, then, is this view of home shared by the men we interviewed? Estate agent, Phil Cruikshank, worked during weekends with time off during the week – then looking after his pre-school son. Regarding himself, at 41, as an older dad, he described the combined demands of home and work life as 'intense' and said that it was returning to work that could be 'a relief' after childcare, a contrast with the notion of home as a retreat. Also 41, Kevin Kirkpatrick, a firefighter, drew a more positive contrast between his extended contact with his children during off-duty days and the very limited time his successful brother spends with his children.

Clearly the ambiguous status of home as a site of both leisure and work – and the gendering of this distinction – profoundly influences the kinds of identities men discover, perform and inhabit on leaving the workplace. For firefighters in particular, the days between shifts allowed them to develop what they saw as a privileged parental identity from which men tied into a conventional working week were excluded. Sally Carling (29), partner of Nick, also 29, was asked 'Would Nick be quite hands-on in the future when it comes to it?' 'Oh God, yeah', she said, going on to recall that 'quite early on when he joined up one of the guys said to him that one of the best things about the job was being there to meet your kids at the end of the school day, you know where, for every other child it's the mums who are meeting them but he was really proud to be the only dad standing at the school gates and I thought, yeah, that's really cool, no he, that, that has always been a big plus, you know even if, I don't know say we never have children, it was always a sort of a potential plus if you like, that Mark would be able to take on a lot of the childcare stuff'.

When the gendered division of domestic labour (cleaning, cooking, washing, childcare) was discussed, it became apparent that older female partners of men in all three occupations undertook this work with little questioning, mainly regretting their male partners' lack of availability for companionship and leisure rather than domestic work. While this was also the case for younger women such as Sharon Armstrong, who saw men's absence as potentially 'helpful' in that it reduced 'mess', among many couples who combined parenthood with employment, time and energy for domestic work was limited and tasks were undertaken on an ad hoc, needs basis. Although this might, ostensibly, reflect little by way of a systematic gendering of these tasks, when Ceri Treadwell (34), criminal lawyer and partner of firefighter Dominic Treadwell (44) described him taking on a feminised gender role in principle, he failed to perform that role in the way she understood it: 'Dominic will stand and watch pasta boil for Lily [their toddler], you know, whereas I'd be like emptying the dishwasher, you know, loading up the washing machine, probably on the telephone as well if someone phones you know, listening to the radio and probably cooking something else for dinner for later you know and he'll just stand and watch it, I don't think they can do two things more than one sometimes'

Where gender does inform working practices at home is the performance of tasks which many women associated with their male partners: gardening and home maintenance. Where men fail to undertake these tasks, women may question their experience of heterosexual coupledom, finding it somehow inauthentic, as shown in our previous research (Hockey et al., 2007): for example, Sarah (43) felt that 'I'm very practical and I do nearly all the maintenance but it would be nice if he suddenly sort of came home and he said "Oh well, I'll clear the gutters out, they need doing"'. For men such as estate agents, these were opportunities for physical activity that work did not permit; for others they were jobs that never happened and as such were a source of friction between men and female partner who saw this as men's work.

5
Masculinities in Prospect: The Life Course and Chronology

Chapters 3 and 4 made the spatialities of home and work their focus. Time was nonetheless important, whether historical time and associated changes in the nature of work and home, biographical time and the shifts within men's occupational histories and home lives, or everyday time's unstable division into the porous categories of 'work' time and 'free' time. This chapter develops the implications of particular temporalities for the contingent nature of masculinity as men move between occupational and domestic environments. Chapter 3 made time recalled by older men its focus, but here we engage with prospective time and the configurations of masculinity which are imagined and indeed planned for. Through data from among younger men and female partners, we explore the implications of both occupationally specific notions of ageing and also heterosexual coupledom (see also, Hockey et al., 2009).

As Chapter 4 argued, for young estate agents and firefighters conceptions of ageing and the life course were likely to shape, and be shaped within, the tensions and negotiations that constitute heterosexual coupledom, revealing not only differences between forms of occupationally specific masculinity, but also the potentially divergent life-planning strategies of men and women. Thus, female partners may 'manage' the way men understand and undertake their unfolding life course trajectory. The young hairdressers interviewed were not, however, living with a female partner – and for them masculinity in prospect was more likely to concern tensions between future economic stability and the paradoxical requirement to retain not only the appearance but also the cultural capital of 'youth' and its associations with unconstrained sociality.

The life course destructured?

The data we present in this chapter do testify to the view that while shifting patterns of work, and the notion of a sequence of sometimes quite different occupational identities across the life course, may be welcomed by some as an opportunity for freedom and self discovery, strong evidence for the persistence of conventional life aspirations remains (Bradley and Hickman, 2004; Lewis et al., 1999). Shifting class and gender locations further complicate this picture, as the chapter explains. For example, where both men and their partners were career oriented, the time limits on women's fertility were a particular focus for concern among partners who might challenge men's willingness to remain within the less rigidly temporalised category of 'youth'. Chronological age therefore emerges as an important organising principle, one that reflects different, gendered priorities as it is drawn upon in decision-making and practice.

As discussed in Chapter 5, Elchardus and Smits (2006) concept of the 'yo-yo-isation' of the life course, one which sees it transformed from 'a sequence of transitions and stages' to 'a series of positions that are simultaneously accessible and between which individuals can increasingly hop' (2006: 304) is countered by the notion that freedom and creativity in life plans bring increased individual responsibility, fragmentation and anxiety (Bauman, 2007; Beck and Beck-Gernsheim, 2002; Furlong and Cartmel, 1997: 44). Moreover, strategies for negotiating the life course reflect gender and class differences, making simple distinctions between a 'choice biography' or the 'standard biography' conceptually inoperable (Brannen and Nilsen, 2002: 531). What the data presented below indicate quite strongly are tensions experienced *between* standardised and de-standardised, or post-modern, approaches to masculinity, and femininity, in prospect.

'Footloose and fancy-free' or 'standing on your own two feet'

Faced with uncertainty in a globalised labour market, young people lack the meta-narratives which framed the employment experiences of their parents (Bradley and Hickman, 2004: 120–2; Furlong and Cartmel, 1997; Mythen, 2005). This, in turn, can generate an extended period of youth dependence (Furlong and Cartmel, 1997: 1), with 'traditional' markers of adulthood – sexual activity, becoming an active consumer, leaving home and gaining full-time permanent work (Roche et al., 2004: xiv) becoming 'desequenced'.

When men spoke to us about the relationship between – and indeed conceptions of, 'youth' and 'adulthood', their data showed both continuities and differences. Thus 'youth' was likely to be characterised by: being single, spending money on age-specific socialising, renting accommodation, being in training, travelling or having a 'rubbish job'. Mickey Smith, a 26-year-old graduate firefighter said

> the whole living in the city with my mates ... I did it at university. I did three years and I did it well.

Similarly, Paul Lewis, a 28-year-old graduate estate agent said: 'It was fantastic ... yeah, mates round on a Friday and a Saturday and not having to worry about anything, making a total mess of the place and not getting told off [laughs]'. Fieldnotes record him as: 'on the cusp of settling down properly with his girlfriend ... a bit ambivalent about the changes in his life ... really enjoyed the youthful fun of his twenties ... lots of "lady" friends for football, pub-crawling and beer drinking ... he is fond of the bachelor life'. Sam, a 28-year-old hairdresser, had a similar 'youthful' life and described how 'at the time this city was my playground, it was a big city, you know I'd come from kind of country ... it had got a lot more happening'. He chose a salon in 'an area in town where I went out a lot at night, so it had got that kind of glamorous side to it'. Nonetheless Sam was keen to further his career and had moved salons, thinking 'I'm going to be propelled to, you know, new heights.' Unlike younger estate agents, discussed below, Sam believed that *retaining* a fluid, youthful approach to his identity through dress was integral to meeting his career goals: 'I'm the kind of person I'll get up in the morning and if I want to be rock Sam, I'll be rock Sam, if I want to be serious, smart Sam. Like today I got up and obviously wanted to be kind of like, Addams family/ funeral parlour worker and I think I've achieved that'.

Another estate agent, Joe White (24), however, compared his current circumstances with those of other men still living a 'footloose and fancy-free' life stage, an endless present with no future:

> a lot of the youth today just don't give two hoots about anything. They just take each day as it comes and they're not really bothered about their future and their career.

However, as we go on to discuss, our data also reveal identity transitions – from a junior to a more established member of staff; from 'boyfriend' to 'husband' and, potentially, 'father' – that are reflected in the distinction between being 'footloose and fancy-free' and 'standing on your own two feet'. Not only chronologised distance – that is numerically grounded conceptions of age (Hockey and James, 2003), but also observable differences resourced the distinctions men made. As Joe White said, 'I've got this conscious thought that I do need to grow up and it's good that I've got that'. Looking back, Steve Richardson (44), a hairdresser, said 'when you're young you're out at night, you're partying, you're clubbing etc. As you're getting older, I mean, you've got responsibilities, you can't be trolleyed every night, because your business'd go down the pan'.

However, while informants *perceive* a chronologised trajectory leading to the achievement of 'adulthood' by 30, *experientially* a gendered, contradictory and ambiguous distinction could blur 'youth' and 'adulthood'. Among firefighters and estate agents, these contradictions emerged *within* men's views and *between* their own and those of female partners. If firefighter John Smith's youth was comfortably located in his past, he remained concerned not to settle down too young: 'I'm just still scared', he said. Pondering promotion to Station Officer, he saw it as at least 35 years away. Indeed, the prioritising of money over personal relationships and a failure to properly relax and enjoy oneself were counted among the costs of growing up. Unconstrained by female partners, however, some younger hairdressers were less equivocal about forgoing pleasures associated with 'youth': Jamie (28), for example, had previously been in the army but now, as a hairdresser, he had 'got slipped back into my laid back ways'. In his profession, he said, 'it's which image you're trying to portray rather than clean and neat, clean cut, office type worker, but more of a laid back stylish approach I suppose … I've had office work stuff before where I had to wear shirt and ties and I hated it'.

By contrast, Adam Black (23), an estate agent stated: 'My worst fear is waking up and I'm thirty and I'm in the same job, you know, middle management'. His dream was of being *'comfortable'* in 10 or 15 years, something he jokingly represented as 'owning a Ferrari'. Like Adam, Joe White wanted to 'get in there early and work your way up', comparing himself with youngsters who 'come out of school [and] expect to walk into a good job'. The imperative to exercise both careful choice and individual agency comes through strongly. For example, at 24 Joe had already made a false start at college, then entered the armed forces, and then taken an arbitrary job away from home before becoming an estate agent. During this time he had experienced loneliness and depression and said 'the guys who are not happy in their job at 25, 26 (ought) to change career (but) I think it's very daunting … well, I've had to. It's frightening, absolutely frightening'. At 21, estate agent Kevin Johnson was already identifying what he calls the 'stepping stone' of becoming a valuer by 24. These are therefore issues that young men address within the context of quite specific time frames.

Doing masculinity differently: the intersection of class and occupational identities

The data above suggest a sometimes uncomfortable meshing of individualising trends and a standardised life course. Moreover, for young estate agents and firefighters, gender differences constituted through heterosexuality could influence these shifts between different conceptualisations of time and the life course. In addition, structural differences of class and occupation inflected all the men's orientations towards the future.

Unlike estate agency and hairdressing, firefighting remains a traditional, working-class 'job for life' (Baigent, 2001), a perspective reiterated by the firefighters we interviewed. While the service is undergoing change (see Chapter 3), firefighting still represented the social and economic stability that men's fathers had achieved through industrial labour. Combining a 'secure future' with good pay and pension prospects and boisterous male sociability, firefighting was perceived as a practical, honourable profession.

In contrast with this emphasis on becoming a team player, estate agency promotes strong imagery of 'self-made' individualism and power. Personal dynamism, flair and perseverance are key to 'making it', with success measured financially, both in company targets and personal bonuses. In a competitive market, men (and women) pursue a career that offers not a traditional 'job for life', but the potential for huge financial rewards – and thereby security. Young men relished the challenges of a competitive environment: 'you know you want to be top of the valuers and you want to make sure you've got the best fees and you're getting "Valuer of the Quarter", it's all about that, yeah definitely', said Paul Lewis. Joe White echoed this point, saying:

> The qualities you have to be very proactive and very, what's the word I'm looking for? You have to have a lot of drive and then to come to work every day to succeed to do it.

Admired colleagues were those who had 'made it' (through property development, for example) and retired early. In an insecure job market, some young men viewed getting a 'suit job' as a better strategy than pursuing their fathers' manual trades.

Hairdressing, however, offered men the glamorous sociability of youth culture. Young hairdressers enjoyed the aesthetic aspects of their work, identifying as creative individuals and skilled technicians. Renting a chair allows them career flexibility and a chance to live in the extended present Brannen and Nilsen (2002) refer to. 'Youthfulness' represented cultural capital as well as the pleasure of a highly sociable work and associated leisure environment. Men were nonetheless aware that 'youthfulness' was time-limited and that career flexibility could result in insecurity. At some stage, therefore, many envisaged pursuing the capital and contacts for opening their own salon – or perhaps leaving the profession. Some men expressed ambivalence about the responsibilities of this prospect, an unwelcome contrast with their current present-oriented life style. Steven Richardson, the 44-year-old hairdresser cited above, was asked how he saw himself in five or ten years' time. 'I can't, I don't wanna go there', he replied.

Within masculinity's diverse manifestations, then, contrasting possibilities are apparent – the 'hands-on', practical member of a secure hierarchy; the dynamic, 'self-made' individual; and the artistic party-animal. Very different 'planning projects' and strategies are associated with each one.

Gender, time and the life course

While estate agent Joe White found that 'it's hard to grow up', he also asserted that 'now I've got a lot more drive and determination. I was so immature at college ... just couldn't be arsed with anything, didn't take life seriously.' Being grown up, he said, means having 'nice things and ... nice people around you'. Such aspirations did however carry risks: for example, overwork and the prioritising of money over family and friends. Other perceived 'pitfalls' were seductive status symbols, such as inappropriately 'flash' cars and houses, as well as insufficient time for family, never letting your hair down and delayed retirement.

'Growing up' was a less ambiguous category of ageing for the female partners of estate agents and fire fighters; not only readily identifiable, it evoked none of the ambivalence expressed by their male counterparts. Setting up home was a taken-for-granted, chronologised transition for Sharon Armstrong (27), an art technician married to Daniel Armstrong, a firefighter. She said 'I'd paid bills. I know that you need to get your money sorted and you need this and you need this .' 'I'd always like said I'll be married and got a house before I'm thirty', she went on, and 'I very rarely change my mind'. Yasmin Ford (21), partner of estate agent Kevin

Johnson, also said 'When I want something I want it there and then. I can't wait'. Both Sharon and 40-year-old Sarah Ward, an estate agent and partner of Paul Lewis, had told their male partners that 'you need to stand on your own two feet. You're nearly thirty years old. You can't always go running back to your mum and dad'. Sarah, like Sharon, described how 'I have stood on my own two feet from being seventeen.'

Uncertainty about adulthood, for these women, concerned their limited years of high fertility, a worry which had implications for both their own and their partners' career trajectories and a perceived need for financial independence. Sharon, for example, wanted a child by the time she was thirty: 'I've got more friends that can't have ... children or are struggling to have children and my mam tried for six years to have me and if I'm trying for six years, I don't want to be 36 when I'm and if there is a problem '. Exercised by this goal Sharon was considering buying an expensive predictive fertility testing kit. Childbearing too soon, however, could curtail career development and home-building, in their view. As Irving (2008) demonstrates, compared with other European countries, the UK has the lowest rate of female unemployment, and is one of the few such countries where women's unemployment is lower than men's. In addition, compared with 1984, fewer British women now withdraw from paid work upon the birth of children and afterwards, as Smeaton, (2006) shows, are returning to work more quickly than in the past.

What these data underscore, then, are the different ways in which women and men experience tension between their occupational and age-based identities. For young estate agents and firefighters, to grow up into (successfully employed) adulthood incurred the risk of losing their *youthful* identity as a fun-loving individual who is open to new possibilities. For their female partners, the adult status resulting from occupational achievement put 'motherhood', an alternative form of female *adulthood*, in jeopardy.

The data we present are drawn from occupational cultures associated particular masculinities; these in turn reflect structural differences associated with social class. What they show, then, is the relationship between particular workplace-based masculinities and the tension different men might experience between standardised and more individualised life course trajectories. Among firefighters and estate agents, we find gender differences in the extent to which women and men draw upon standardised or destructured models of the life course. At the intersection between patterns of economic activity, of consumption, and of fertility, couples sought to plan shared lives which nonetheless cleave to sometimes competing priorities and values.

Importantly, the *relationship* between 'youth' and 'adulthood', and the transition between them, emerges as the area where differences grounded in occupationally-based masculinities and gendered identities are most apparent. Thus, estate agents, Paul and Joe, experienced contradictory desires for a more extended period of youthful independence alongside a concern with the adult goals of furthering their careers and maintaining a stable partnership. They offer a contrast with firefighters, many of whom emulated their father's life course patterns: taking on a respected job-for-life and settling down early. However, their work involved – indeed required – participation in boisterous male sociality and preparedness to tease and be teased, sometimes ferociously. Their ascent to adulthood was perhaps a shallower incline. Firefighters talked openly of the watch atmosphere letting them 'behave like children'. They can be compared with the young hairdressers who did not have well-established or traditional lives as part of a couple. They would cultivate their youth as a form of cultural capital which enhanced their professional life, both socially and economically. However, data from among older hairdressers showed that extending 'youth' well into mid-life was ultimately self-limiting, the body's capacity to support this identity eventually terminating. This meant either loss of earnings, or the demands of salon ownership or management.

In sum, the men we interviewed who in some way continued inhabiting the category 'youth' were likely to be either firefighters or hairdressers. In both cases, however, the future contained potential penalties: in the former case, being 'one of the lads' became problematic when juggled with the responsibility of taking on management roles and going for promotion; in the latter, body-based youthfulness was a time-limited resource, the loss of which could undermine a man's capacity to identify as a successful hairdresser, sought after by clients and esteemed by peers. Most starkly, however, for estate agents, 'adulthood' introduced a tension between the loss of an autonomy epitomised in 'laddish' socialising and the desire for power, status and 'nice things'. Feeling impelled to exercise personal agency within standardised chronologies, young estate agents' concerns evidence the persistence of modernity's regulated life course alongside late modernity's trend towards individualisation. Through data which represent the views of men and women who have chosen to share their lives with each other, we are also able to show how occupational demands and trajectories are compounded by reproductive imperatives, and the gendered consequences of this additional, body-based, chronologised agenda.

6
Belonging: Scrutiny, Irony and Performance

The temporalities and spatialities of 'work' and 'home' have been a focus in Chapters 3, 4 and 5. Together, these have introduced the gendered dimensions of the environments within which mobile masculinities are lived out. In this chapter we sharpen our focus on the nature of identification itself, exploring data which show how men both practise but also *imagine* masculinity. Chapter 3 placed the occupations selected for our study into a wider context of historical shifts, not only in their status and gendering, but also in the characteristics of masculinity valued in those settings: for example, the go-getting entrepreneur of the Thatcherite era who replaced the honourable gentleman estate agent who had preceded him. While the men who staff estate agents' reception areas, undertake valuations, and broker deals may themselves manifest these qualities in only a limited sense, if at all, masculinity, for them, is nonetheless lived out in relation to particular constellations of characteristics. It is this relationship which we now take up, seeking to understand identification as a process that unfolds in relation to distinctive models of what it means to be a (particular kind of) man. As Chapter 4 argued, aspects of masculinity are selectively required, rewarded or 'released' at home and at work, the extent to which those associated with home and the workplace differ from each other varying across the three occupations.

In this chapter, men's testimonies show how they negotiated their relationship with the nature of masculinity within the occupations that employed them. Did 'belonging' mean conforming, for example? Rapport's (1993) ethnography of a British village brings out the incongruities between individuals' observable behaviours – through which belonging may be achieved – and how they actually understand themselves and the world about them. Thus, while individuals may 'communicate' with one another and achieve some sense of belonging, they may simultaneously talk *past* each other, with little sense of one another's internal worlds. Social reality, Rapport (1993) argues, is constituted through individuals' active engagement with, and indeed self-interested mobilisation of the values and norms of their social context, an abstract repertoire of possibilities which come alive to the extent that the individual inhabits or deploys them. At the heart of this chapter, and indeed the research it represents, lies a focus on this capacity of individuals to reflect upon the environments within which their lives unfold, to measure the extent to which they conform, and to assess the 'authenticity' of their belonging. It is an aspect of sociality that is often ignored, greater value being placed upon observations of what people *do*, rather than what they say they do, a hierarchy that downplays the importance of everyday reflexivity. While the approach we adopt here does echo Jenkins' (2004) internal-external dialectic of identification, as well as Mead's (1934) distinction between the 'I' and the 'me', we give particular emphasis to the individual's capacity for awareness of differences between themselves and other people, and indeed their scope for motivated performances of particular ways of being. 'Passing' (Goffman, 1968) and lying are but extreme examples of this potentiality.

As noted, our project is rooted in interview data from our previous study of heterosexuality (Hockey et al., 2007). In those interviews, men cited an emic, or 'folk' theory that firefighters' unstable domestic lives and high divorce rate were outcomes of their bonds with other men, their shift system and the sexual opportunities afforded by their 'heroic' reputation. The extent to which these features were constitutive of firefighters' *lives* is therefore part of the question we are asking. The data gathered during the present project give few indications of men exploiting their occupational identities for sexual ends and while such practices may continue, open reference to them was not part of the everyday conversation we accessed during more than three months' participant observation at a fire station. Firefighters' shift system, if anything, allowed some men at least opportunities for domestic work and childcare during their regular four days off, particularly if their partners were out at work.

In the data to follow, then, we consider the role of men's conceptions of their occupational masculinities within their everyday practice and, moreover, the reflexive reach of their orientations towards these conceptions. For example, living up to popular conceptions of the heroic, sexualised firefighter was something that could attract men's scorn.

Alan Proctor, who had been in the fire service for 10 years without seriously pursuing promotion, derided men who 'strut about being a Fire Fighter'. He spoke ironically about the World Firefighter Games, a mini-Olympics where men compete individually and teams. The event had been held in the city and Alan said, sarcastically, that he could well have won the Toughest Firefighter Alive competition if he had had the 'firefighter' tattoo his more committed colleagues wore, along with the 'Thermal Warrior' T-shirts they'd had printed.

Alan's partner, Patsy, described how this ironic humour could be expressed not just in words but also practical jokes. Referring to a fire museum in another city where Alan had worked previously, Patsy described 'a Fireman all kitted up, like a model'. Together with a close colleague, she said, Alan 'put stockings on underneath his uniform, he's got red knickers on and red bras and stockings if you ever look beneath his uniform he's cross dressed'. In this way Alan simultaneously evoked and subverted the stereotypes of both the firefighter who takes himself too seriously and the firefighter who avails himself of the occupation's reputation for sexual desirability. By combining them in a single figure he effectively distanced himself from both. Hegemonic masculinity was thus evoked through comparison with the cross-dresser and so irreverently debunked.

In addition to maintaining an ironic distance from popular conceptions of firefighting, men also cited mismatches between the ways in which the fire service itself constructed their job during training - and the work they subsequently undertook. Young firefighters, Daniel Armstrong and Richard Shawcross, for example, both described their difficulty with book learning, yet once at work, other skills emerged as key to being seen to do the job well. They recalled the 'golden boy' recruit who had won the Silver Axe during training who was rumoured to have panicked when he 'got into real world'. Belonging turned out to result from a capacity to subsume oneself to a team, to take direction from 'gaffers' and accept critical comments about one's performance during an emergency. Repeatedly firefighters of all ages would say: 'you've got to learn the hard way, that's what the fire service is all about, that's what I've found'; after training, men would 'keep basics but get your own ways of doing things'; 'experience is everything' they said. Nigel Saltash, at 50, said with irony, 'tell me how anything works straight out of a book'; and Victor Todburn, at 44, asserted that gaffers who did things by the book would 'wind firemen up big style'. In terms of earning respect, then, it was the layering up of experience which differentiated one firefighter from another, rather than rank. Men who achieved promotion without experience were scorned. When Nick Carling, a graduate with two years' experience behind him, was asked whether he tried to look after men new to the service, he replied:

> I do and I don't, I kind of help in some ways but I try not to in others because I don't want any of the elder ones thinking 'what do you know?', 'you've only been here two years, I've been here twenty', you know. But then when nobody's about I'll say, you know, 'do that way, don't, just ignore what he's saying, not ignore what he's saying, take it on, listen to what they're saying but don't take it literally, don't take it seriously, it's them having a bad day, it's not you'.

Paradoxically, the requirement to subsume oneself to a team and to the directions of a 'gaffer', to enter into the 'flow' of responding to an emergency, went alongside a need to sustain distances, whether social, practical or emotional. Socially, young firefighters understood a requirement to stay fairly quiet, to wait until invited to become part of the team. If a new person was talkative, others, reportedly, would think: 'Whoa, that's not the way we do things'. Those who had been outspoken, or challenged other men's views, discovered that this 'put people's backs up'. In terms of *practice* during emergencies, men described the importance of staying calm: 'don't rush into things, just look at the situation and deal with it, keep it simple'. Once a situation had been responded to, emotional distance became important. Asked about the impact of fatalities, Alec Simpson, at 41, said 'if you're somebody who would dwell on seeing somebody dead in a car crash, then it's going to carry forward and going to affect you in your next job potentially. You've got to be able to look at it and analyse it and then put it behind you' (see also Chapters 12, 13 and 14). These forms of distancing were lived out via the juxtaposition of being at the station, on the one hand, and responding to a call, on the other. As Richard Shawcross (23) said:

> It all changes when you get a job, everyone has a good laugh and takes piss and that, on station, but when you get a, like once bells go down like everyone's sort of different. Do you know what I mean? You sort of get into like a little zone for want of a better word and you just know what you've got to do.

Ten years into the service, Kevin Kirkpatrick remained aware of this transition: 'you go into a different state of mind', he said.

The ideal type firefighter, then, was a relatively 'laid back' character, someone who was 'a right laugh', yet could curb their banter in line with what others could cope with. Going too far risked other men 'getting a face on'. Men could be summed up as 'spot on', yet without reference to anything specific. Unpacked, however, being a 'spot on' person meant a capacity to meet requirements that were actively policed, whether through gaffers' routine comments on performances during emergencies, or the palpable risk of 'making name for yourself' if you got 'bigger than your boots'. Being interested in the job and looking forward to coming into work were orientations towards this occupation that men aspired to. For them, paradoxically, promotion to a managerial role undermined scope for proving themselves calm and level headed during emergencies and 'a right laugh' at the station. Those who had achieved high rank might be seen to have 'an urge to be in charge' which left them betwixt and between the banter and team spirit of lower ranking men and the demands of higher management. Leadership, men felt, required a capacity to listen to the men who were in the front line and find out what they saw as best practice in any one situation – but not all gaffers seemed capable of this.

Alongside the image of the heroic, sexualised firefighter we can place the stereotype of the cutthroat, city slicker estate agent. While popular myths did not intrude on the working lives of firefighters to a great extent, with the difference between *'the book'* and everyday practice being their greatest source of dissonance, the estate agents we interviewed *were* working alongside difficult public stereotypes. As noted, Rapport (1993) argues for the need to explore individuals' reflexivity vis-à-vis the persona they choose to present; Goffman's (1968) concept of 'passing' exemplifies this human capacity for self-consciousness. Repeatedly, estate agents engaged in a curiously circular discussion of the importance of personal integrity, honesty and openness. If a devious or untrustworthy agent 'oversells' a property, if they 'hassle' would-be buyers by ringing them up repeatedly, if they overvalue a vendor's property, then they will get 'found out', it will 'rebound on them'. So honesty and straightforwardness are essential to good business. Moreover, as Simon Pulling (52) put it, 'I shouldn't have to make an effort, it should be natural, you know it should be ... I shouldn't have to put on an act, for them to trust me, it should, they should ... look at me and listen to me and trust me because I'm being honest because I'm always honest whatever I do'. Implicit here is the notion that 'genuine' honesty will shine through as a 'natural' feature of the individual and his practice. Yet as other men sought to explain, honesty also has to be *performed*; that is to say, however genuine it might be, the client has to be made aware of it. When we asked Derek Chisholm (43), 'do you actually need to be genuine or do you just need to be able to inspire the appearance of genuine?' he picked up on the notion of performance and said, 'I think that's quite correct and I think that's a sales skill that some people don't have because they're, they don't actually project'. He went on to acknowledge the paradox that 'you know they are, you could say they're more genuine' (see also Chapter 16).

Rather than 'belonging' or 'fitting in', terms which convey firefighters' more collective orientation towards their relationships with other men in their watch, estate agents are keen to be seen as successful individuals, both by colleagues and by people in their lives outside work. And as already indicated, that success required a curious *performance* of 'natural' or 'genuine' integrity (Goffman, 1971), an integrity which may indeed correspond to an individual's commitment to hard work and ethical practice. Simon Pulling (52) expressed this in his choice of language when describing the need to get on with people of all kinds and with varying levels of knowledge about house buying. He aimed, he said, to 'hopefully create an impression whereby they trust you and want to do business with you, you know'.

Where we begin to find similarities between estate agents and firefighters is in terms of another paradox, that between the value attached to being 'laid back', 'relaxed' and 'confident', while at the same time aspiring to being 'proactive' and having 'drive'. Again, it is this 'easy' confidence that nonetheless has to be performed and Kevin Johnson, at 21, was able to explicate this process as he experienced it. Having asserted that estate agency means working on your own initiative without anyone looking over your shoulder to guide you, he was then asked whether he found this difficult. He replied, 'No, I, to be honest I don't think about it, I think if you think about it, that's when you start becoming nervous, it just comes second nature to me now ... sometimes you've not got time to think because this ... you're giving somebody advice, if you're thinking about it you don't sound confident, you've got to be sure'. In this kind of balancing act, then, it is the notion of *'second nature'* which enables him to pull off a successful performance. Without this, he says, 'they're not going to hundred percent believe what you're saying'.

For firefighters, manifesting 'confidence' was important as a way of both retaining one's place within a team and shoring up the collective confidence of that team as they manage the challenge of an emergency. Individually, however, firefighters were more diffident about claiming distinctively positive personal qualities. For example, Brian

Underwood (41), who had worked in management before entering the fire service in his mid-thirties, was 'acting up' as a Leading Firefighter at the time of his interview. He discussed the importance of communicating well with those he was managing, citing the loyalty of people within his department in his previous job – yet indicating concern about sounding boastful with the words 'sound as if I'm blowing my own trumpet, but ...'. By comparison, estate agent Joe White (24) stressed how much he had learned in a year, despite minimal training, asserting that 'I just kept telling myself that I would pick it up you know, it wasn't, I've never really struggled to do anything in life, that I've applied myself and gone to do so I picked it up really quickly so I didn't, I didn't have a struggle at all'. Thus, while there was some respect for an individual's capacity to hold his ground among firefighters, those individuals who set themselves above others and perhaps went for promotion were seen to pay the price of losing their place within the team. For Fergus Dart (24), sales consultant within an estate agency, however, the prospect of his boss's distinctive and luxurious lifestyle was, without question, desirable: 'Who wouldn't want to do what Brad's doing?'.

While firefighters were consistently *given* feedback on their performance in emergencies by the gaffers, estate agents gained insight into the requirements of their job by studying particular individuals. Indeed, they attributed an almost magical quality to the success of men who had 'made it', often citing their youthfulness to underline the rapidity of their progress (see also Chapter 5). Joe White (24) said of a senior colleague, it's 'just phenomenal of what he's achieved and he's only like 33, 34, he's just phenomenal, absolutely phenomenal ... what he's got and what he's done for himself is just baffling, absolutely baffling how he's done it ... It's just amazing the things that he's done and building his own empire basically ... a lot of admiration there and he does intimidate me quite a lot'. Fergus Dart (24) described moving beyond bafflement to analysis when he spoke of his boss, Brad Charrier, saying,

> He's someone that I do look up to and sort of see that brilliant, how has he done it? Can you ... I mean all the time I try and look at people ... see how, what their skills are and see if I can take any on board, whether it be how they talk to somebody, how they conduct themselves, what are they doing in business to allow them to retire at the age that they are doing.

These data therefore give crucial insights into the process of identification, showing how even '*second nature*' is something men deliberately sought to cultivate, monitoring one another's behaviours to identify secrets of success which were not inculcated through formal training. In this sense, then, identification's internal-external dialectic (Jenkins, 2004), as expressed through the relationship between the 'I' and the 'me' (Mead, 1934), is made quite explicit in men's self reflexive accounts. Success, on one level, was characterised by not having to 'put on an act' (Goffman, 1971), the successful individual instead coming to embody the characteristics which help secure membership of the company.

Among men working as hairdressers the notion of performance was also important. If we scrutinise the ways in which they talked about it, however, it becomes apparent that the concept carries a different meaning within an occupation where the relationship between client and practitioner is not potentially limited to a single encounter but instead may last a lifetime (see also Chapters 13 and 15). Like firefighters, the hairdressers we interviewed had an awareness of stereotypes, one of which was the association between hairdressing and being gay, a theme we explore more fully in Chapter 10. Sam Cartmell (28), for example explained that while he was gay, the assumptions made about him did not in any sense capture 'the full Sam'. He said, 'as soon as you mention hairdresser and gay, it just opens a box of all this stereotypical thing, which you know it just isn't me at all'. More broadly, he went on, 'I don't, try, I don't fit into that stereotypical hairdresser in that I change me hair every week, or do anything like that'. Sam explained his distance from this stereotype in terms of his age: 'but, er but that's 'cause I'm older'.

The notion that hairdressing was 'a young person's business', as Andy Hathaway (50) put it, was debated by many interviewees. To some extent, men's own ages were reflected in what they had to say; for example, Steve Richardson (44) said that 'when we went into this years ago, there was a shelf life attached to the profession ... you know you'd got 20 years and that was it'. Certainly many older hairdressers described the wear and tear on their bodies of bending over the chair where a female client was seated, something not required of barbers where hydraulic chairs allowed the client to be positioned exactly as they wished (see also Chapters 2 and 11, and Part II).

To fully understand the relationship between age and identity, however, the particular notion of performance that is understood among hairdressers does need to be scrutinised. Most men agreed that, in a service industry, it was important to be cheerfully sociable with clients, regardless of how the hairdresser was actually feeling. Yet Ed Niven (35), who had a reputation as a particularly good hairdresser, said that

'It can be an act sometimes, although I, I hope I don't put on an act but when I'm cutting someone's hair for the first time I'm always quite quiet, ask a few questions then the next time they come back, they come back because they actually like the haircut but not because I've performed'. This *qualified* notion of a 'performance', or 'act', was reiterated by Patrick Valentine (28) who said 'if you're in a bad mood, something bad's happened that day, it's hard for me I can't, I'm not that fake where I can put on a face and it is a really big smiley face, I mean I can do it to an extent but usually shows with me, people always say what's the matter? I just can't hide it really'. Patrick's reference to his clients' solicitude is an important clue to the centrality of communication in the fostering of long-term relationships with clients. As Gordon Bristow (64), said, 'You've got to become part of their lives, if ... this is the thing, that if you become part of their lives, they never even think about going anywhere else'.

Repeatedly, interviews with hairdressers contain words such as: 'you've got to talk, you've got to talk'. Andy Hathaway (50) expressed this in financial terms when he said: 'You can be the most creative hairdresser in the world and still not make money ... you know usually it's having good communication skills and be able to do what clients want rather than being the best hairdresser in the world because quite often the best hairdressers never take any money because they can't relate it to the client'. Steve Richardson (44), similarly made a direct equation between clients and income when he said: 'so I'm really pleased that I've still got the work coming through the door for me to do erm now, at my age'. Another hairdresser, Gordon Bristow (64), even went so far as to say that 'You can make an absolute mess of somebody's hair, but if you can make her feel comfortable and good in the shop, she'll come to you for life and I've proved it'.

This kind of skill was, however, understood to be something developed over time. Steve Richardson (44), for example, agreed that younger men might have trouble 'reading' a client: 'that's why at 16, erm 16-18 you, you're learning', he said, noting that 'they hopefully will pick things up from the rest of the people in the salon'. Gordon Bristow was unequivocal on this point, saying, 'in hairdressing, you've got to be a people's person, you've got to love people. I have worked with people who do not like people, they don't like having a laugh and a joke and making people feel comfortable ... and they shouldn't be hairdressers'.

In interviews, then, men were clear that they were selling their personalities, that they had to present themselves – and their hair – well, in order to attract new clients. Yet it was also the case that in an occupation where many men earn relatively little, the twin pleasures of creative work and sociability, in themselves, were rated more highly than income, particularly among younger men (Bagilhole and Cross, 2006). In other words, the centrality of a secure client base to an older man's continued income did not simply mean a cynical cultivation of dependency among those clients. Jamie Tindall (28), for example, said, 'The money's not too good but I get a lot of job satisfaction so that's more, that's more important to me than money. My friend he gets very little job satisfaction but then he started getting money ... as a sales rep, but he's always moaning about his job and like I'm just happy plodding along, as long as I get enough money to go out'. Gordon Bristow (64), again, repeatedly made the assertion that 'you've got to love people'.

Conclusion

While the careful management of relationships with other members of the watch was key to the experience of firefighters who sought to 'fit in', estate agents' perceived themselves striving for their niche within a markedly hierarchical business where acceptance followed *success*, whether in valuations, sales or property development. Among hairdressers, however, the key relationship discussed in interviews was between client and practitioner, one which for many men would outlive ties with the colleagues with whom they shared salon space for a period, before moving on to rent a chair elsewhere.

What these data allow us to engage with, more broadly, then, are the reflexive processes through which individuals develop an understanding of the roles they inhabit and the kinds of masculinity associated with them – while at the same time making choices about the extent to which they choose to live up to these roles, to creatively interpret them, and indeed to draw upon them in generating a sense of self worth and job satisfaction. Thus hegemonic masculinity (Connell, 2005) can be seen as a practice which men *recognise* and, moreover, are able to engage with agentically, at times, whether in pursuit, subversion, or adaptation of its characteristics.

Part II
Embodiment

7
Embodiment: Masculinity and the Body

Introduction

The previous chapters have focused particularly on life course transitions and men's everyday movement between work and home, exploring the 'elusiveness, fluidity and complex interconnectedness of masculinity in modern societies' (Haywood and Mac an Ghaill, 2003: 4). Through selecting occupations that are stereotyped as 'masculine' or 'feminine' (hairdressing, estate agency and firefighting) (*Labour Force Survey*, 2004), we asked how the juxtaposed cultures of workplace and home might evoke contradictory or congruent performances of masculinity. As Chapter 4 makes plain, we understand such performances as spatially located and, importantly, embodied. Here we move on to a critical discussion of theories of the body, especially in relation to masculinity, making the relationship between masculine embodiment and individual agency a key focus. Thus, in the following chapters we examine the male body in motion, situated within the materialities of particular times and spaces and in relation to a whole range of embodied others: female partners, friends and family members; male and female colleagues; clients; and members of the public. In so doing, the chapter develops the case for an investigation of embodied indicators of identity and of spatio-temporal boundaries; and of the ways in which sociability materialises, both in the workplace and the home. It therefore argues for the centrality of issues of embodied agency and the importance of a focus on complex performances around men's different identities. Thus, the contingent nature of embodied identification is explored contextually, the work-place and domestic environments of performance being viewed as 'scenes of constraint' (Butler, 2004:1) within which gendered identities can be both 'done' and 'undone'. Occupational cultures commonly stereotyped as 'masculine' or 'feminine' and domestic environments peopled by 'husbands', 'boyfriends', 'fathers' thus constitute the settings within which men conform to, draw upon and resist an array of hegemonic masculinities.

In making sense of the ways in which this is achieved, the chapter introduces a distinction between gendered conceptions of 'the body' and individual men's experiences of embodiment. What it argues is that processes of identification emerge via men's embodied experiences of particular kinds of gendered bodies. In the other chapters which make up this part, we explore the ways in which men negotiate the perception of these bodies in different workplace and domestic contexts; for example, through the use of clothing to become smart and professional, through training the body to become fit and skilled, and via the acquisition of embodied knowledge to 'fit in' within the workplace and the home.

Specifically, Chapters 8, 9, 10 and 11 take up and expand on the theoretical points made here, through their focus on data. Chapter 8 is concerned with revealing how the men we interviewed reflected upon the embodiments that were specific to their occupations, the diverse ways in which they understood and practiced the bodily styles associated with the office, the meeting, the client's small private home, the fire station, the site of the emergency, and the salon. As Simpson notes (2009: 88), spaces come into being through the embodied performances of women and men (see also Halford and Leonard, 2006). Chapter 9 focuses on men's bodies and sociability, drawing on data from among the fire fighters to explore their embodied movements between the different sites of the fire station and the outside world. Chapter 10 takes the performing body as its theme, specifically in relation to the notion of 'camp' and the masculinity and sexuality of hairdressers, while Chapter 11 is centrally concerned with men's strategies for identification as an embodied *process*, and in relation to both spatial home/work transitions and life course transitions such as illness.

This chapter presents theoretical debates and issues which allow subsequent chapters to make theoretical and 'embodied' sense. In that we understood embodiment as key to the processes of identification which informed the research questions our empirical study posed, we were faced with particular methodological challenges, explored more fully in Chapter 1. These concerned the ways in which embodiment might be investigated. As noted, however, Leder's (1990) argument that the human body is a vehicle for perceiving the surrounding environment, one directly experienced primarily during illness, means that investigating embodiment requires us to interrogate something which may lie beyond the individual's awareness for much of the time. We were, therefore, mindful of this issue when drawing on Connell's (2005) view of gender as a structure of practice. As she explains, 'gender is a social practice that constantly refers to bodies and what bodies do [...] it is not social practice reduced to the body' (2005: 71). The chapter, therefore, starts to explore the ways that men in our study engaged in the 'social practice' of masculinity as embodied individuals who inhabit the workplace identities of firefighter, hairdresser and estate agent (for detailed discussion of gender as a social practice in relation to organisations and work, see the special issues of *Gender, Work and Organisation*, 2006 and 2009).

Embodying identities

In exploring the relationship between workplace identities and the body, we draw on a distinction between 'the body', as it has figured within the social sciences, from feminist theory to medical sociology and 'embodiment'. Much of the work on the body is about the body we *have*, the object body that we might alter in some way, whether via diet and exercise or piercing and cosmetic surgery. It is the body through which identities may be claimed or imposed, through the materialities of clothing, or body modification. It is also the body which is open to the scrutiny of others – colleagues, employers or partners, as well as of the State, the media (B. S. Turner, 1992). From a Foucauldian perspective, the body we *have* can be seen as the site at which institutional control renders the body docile and disciplined (Foucault, 1977). The concept of embodiment, however, takes us towards the body that we *are* and, as such, provides a fruitful starting point from which to understand the dialectical processes of identification as they unfold within particular social contexts (see Nettleton and Watson, 1998; Williams and Bendelow, 1998).

Some theorists have therefore preferred the term 'male embodiment' to 'men's bodies' as this incorporates the corporeality and sociality of people's bodies over the gendered life course (Monaghan, 2005). For instance, Woodward (1997) draws on Connell's account of how 'muscle tensions, postures, the feel and texture of the body' enable the power of men to be naturalised, despite some men's lack of other resources (Connell, 1987, cited in Woodward, 1997: 85), as an antidote to the theoretical problems of both social constructionism and biological essentialism. She argues that it is a notion of embodiment which can expand on studies of the male body which have hitherto limited this analysis by not examining the corporeal, or by downplaying the possibility of positive male identifications with the body when seen over the life course; for instance, how men might gain body capital as they get older, as Robinson (2008) explores in relation to the 'extreme' sport of rock climbing.

While Monaghan argues that Connell (1995) and Watson (2000) are among the few sociologists who have researched male bodies using an embodied perspective, echoing Woodward, he also asserts that Watson's work, though grounding men's experiences in relational and processual bodies, simultaneously, does not consider more positive attempts by men to construct plural masculinities and sexualities. This can be compared with work done on men's bodies in other areas such as sport, where, often, the body has not been seen in positive ways, but as illustrative of men's capacity to take pain, or sustain injuries, sometimes in order to gain acceptance in sporting circles (see Robinson, 2008). Chapter 12 develops our discussion of sport, particularly in relation to the emotions. Further, gendered practices and images of the body become embodied for people, and affect, consciously or not, people's participation in sport, or as we discuss here in work and domestic spheres, over the life course. In Chapter 8, therefore, we examine the way images influence people's diverse experience of their bodies.

Gendering the body/embodying gender

Feminist ideas have been central to debates on the body, and have focused particularly on the female body. Woodward (2008) observes that feminist critiques have argued that a Western, post-Enlightenment split between mind and body has meshed with a gender hierarchy which links culture and the intellect with masculinity, and nature and the body with femininity (see MacCormack and Strathern, 1980; Battersby, 1998). This has often resulted in reductionist associations between women and bodily functions such as menstruation, reproduction and breast-feeding (see Firestone, 1970). In response, authors such as Butler (1990) and Grosz (1994), whose work is influenced by Foucault, highlight the social 'production' of bodies through discursive practices such as medicine. However, the body, as the material site of human *experience* remains a concern for feminists such as Moi (1999), who have developed Merleau Ponty's (1962) theories of embodiment, focusing on the lived body as their analytic starting point. This approach is also adopted by cultural phenomenologist, Csordas, who argues that, 'embodiment can be understood as an indeterminate methodological field defined by perceptual experience and the mode of presence and engagement in the world' (2002: 241). In other words, the body is the site from which we perceive and engage with our environments, the means by which we come to understand and 'objectify' who and what surrounds us.

Csordas (2002) perspective is reflected in work on men's bodies undertaken by medical sociologist, Watson, cited above. Watson (2000) views embodiment as a location at which the personal and the social interweave, citing Giddens' argument that identity is sustained through 'practical immersion in the interactions of day-to-day life' (1991: 99, cited in Watson, 2000: 111). If identity is 'the interface between subjective positions and social and cultural situations' (Woodward, 1997: 1), then human embodiment is core to this interface.

Notions of the body as an object do, nonetheless, remain important in that its scrutiny, mediatisation and objectification are important aspects of embodied subjectivity. Particular representations or objectifications of male bodies can contribute powerfully to who men think they *are*. Nettleton and Watson have argued that it is surprising, given the centrality of the body in relation to everyday life, that there has been little empirical research into how humans *experience* their body, particularly research which prioritises '... engaging ordinary men and women in talk about their personal bodily experiences' (1998: 2). Though empirically grounded work on the bodily experience has been undertaken since their pronouncement, at the same time, we still need more evidence of how men, in particular, actually experience their bodies in different ways according to their gender. In particular, the subsequent chapters reflect Morgan et al.'s (2005) observation, that an individual is the site of numerous bodies, for instance, here, the occupational and the domesticated male body. In this sense, men's bodies, when engaged in both public and private bodily practices are constantly under scrutiny from others, and from themselves. In this way, performances of masculinity through these 'bodies' are investigated empirically as complex and interactive in these later chapters.

Men's bodies

The feminist debates about the relationship between femininity and the body outlined above may have prioritised women and their bodies, yet men's bodies have by no means been excluded from this work. Indeed, as Jackson and Scott suggest, 'as well as criticising the all-pervasive pathologisation of women's bodies, feminists have called for the problematisation of men's bodies' (2002: 370). Morgan stresses the importance of this task, arguing that, 'at least superficially, women tend to be more embodied and men less embodied in social scientific, popular and feminist writings and representations' (2002: 407). In critically reviewing feminist debate on men's embodiment, then, we explore work which engages with both 'the body' we *have* and the embodied experiences through which we *'are'*.

With respect to the body we *have*, for example, Grogan's (1999) discussion of body dissatisfaction among both women *and* men highlights the increasing requirement that men be both slender and muscular, arguing that both sexes are now willing to submit themselves to dietary and surgical body modification practices. Differences between groups of men are also apparent as McArdle and Hill's (2010) research on gay and heterosexual men and their body image shows, for example, with gay men having greater body dissatisfaction than heterosexual men, among other differences. Thus, though studies reveal some men to be worried about not being tall enough, or having a slight physique (de Visser, 2009), McArdle and Hill's research found that more men in their study wanted to lose weight than to gain it. However, does this mean that women and men are equally concerned with body issues, and do they both face body dissatisfaction and stereotypical ideologies of the body too?

Monaghan (2005) discusses this 'dubious equality' through reference to Davis's (2002) work on cosmetic surgery. Although he concedes that male bodies are not generally 'objects-for-others' in the same way that female bodies often are, he does argue that men and boys are increasingly being subjected to normalising body discourses and practice. Nonetheless, Morgan remains critical of existing sociological accounts of male bodies, arguing that they tend to be represented as hard and aggressive, an 'over-phallusized picture of man' (Morgan, 2002: 407). Whitehead (2002: 189) argues similarly – that force, hardness, toughness, physical competence and applying physicality to the world are misleadingly associated with dominant masculinities. This view is explored in later chapters in this part.

While we develop critiques of such representations, we also, importantly, pay attention to their role within men's *embodied* subjectivities, their notions of who they should or might be. Whitehead suggests that while 'many men fail to achieve a seamless, constant, symbiotic relationship between their bodies and dominant discourses of masculinity', they may still attempt to do so and their masculine subjectivity is bound up in these attempts (2002: 191). Moreover, while feminists such as Delphy (1984) have argued that bodily differences are made to ground 'gender' via what Connell (2005) later described as 'gender projects', these projects have *local* contexts. This means that different masculinities emerge from what Connell refers to as 'configurations of practice generated in particular situations in a changing structure of relationships' (2005: 81). Thus, for example, historical location and class-based position provide contexts for these specific practices.

Csordas (2002) and Young (2005), who adopt a body-based phenomenological starting point, similarly argue that this must include wider cultural and structural dimensions of subjective experience. As our data indicate, it is through particular social configurations – class, age, historical location – as well as individual agency that 'restrictively normative conceptions of sexual and gendered life' (Butler, 2004: 1) are both done and undone. Via engagement with these data, as already noted therefore, it becomes clear that gender emerges as the outcome of particular forms of embodied practice, performance, interaction and play which can act to not only reinforce or 'do', but also destabilise or 'undo' masculinity in its hegemonic or stereotypical forms. In other words, the body as it is represented and also modified contributes to men's subjective experiences of themselves.

In this way, the volume, in part, speaks to recent calls for more work on how men's bodies and dominant social constructions of masculinity construct the experiences of men in female-dominated occupations where the masculine body does not correspond to traditional social and cultural expectations of it (Simpson, 2009; Evans, 2004), especially in respect of our data on male hairdressers (see Chapter 10).

While Morgan argues that hard, aggressive, 'over-phallusized' male bodies dominate representations of men's embodiment (2002: 407), Simpson (2009), makes the slightly different point that '[w]hilst in general terms, men may be considered to be largely 'disembodied' and divorced from considerations of the body, associated with the rational domain of the mind, this association is overturned when men undertake a non-traditional role' (2009: 108). In her study, male nurses' bodies were co-opted by institutions in an instrumental sense; yet Simpson also found that men's bodies in this context can be 'marked as dangerous, disruptive and problematic in ways that resonate with the ways women's bodies have been traditionally viewed' (2009: 109). For example, echoing Morgan (2002: 407), Simpson concludes: 'Nurses and cabin crew can be expected to deploy masculine bodily characteristics to subdue disruptive patients or passengers, while body attributes may be less relevant in gender assessment of male librarians' (2009: 165).

Yet, in Hall et al., we argued that '[f]or estate agents, then, doing gender involves bodily practices which generate a self identity as a man who "seeks to make his mark on and change the world through his drive, energy, self- discipline, initiative"(Whitehead, 2002: 122)' (Hall et al., 2007: 547). In this way, we problematise assumptions that, for example, the body attributes of some male professionals are less relevant than others. This allows us to appreciate both the obvious and the more nuanced differences and similarities between men's embodied practices and subjective experiences, and, importantly for our purposes, as they unfold *across* both public and private spheres.

Embodiment and body work

Having raised issues around the implications of feminised work environments for men's embodiment, and, indeed, the neglect of some men's embodied experience entirely, since notions of hardness and aggression have misleadingly been taken as the hallmark of the masculine body *per se,* we can consider, Seidler's (2009) argument that a dualistic Enlightenment vision of modernity is at work in a post modern culture. This is instructive, offering an explanation of why some dimensions of male embodiment have been misleadingly foregrounded, to the exclusion of others. Thus, it can be difficult to explore the intermeshing of men, their bodies and their emotional lives.

Yet bodies and emotions are, of course, intimately connected, as the work of Hochschild (1983) on the body and emotional labour in an occupational context revealed and Witz et al., (2003) further developed. As Irving (2008) points out, the ability to manage or control emotion is integral to newer service work such as cabin crew, to the more established welfare professions such as nursing, to contemporary work, in, for example, the beauty industry (see Sharma and Black, 2001) and the emotional labour of men across our three occupational groups is explored in detail in Chapter 13. For our argument here, however, it is Seidler's (2009) point that within this Enlightenment tradition, men relate to their bodies as machines that need to be controlled that is of specific interest. This instrumentalism, he argues, leads to men feeling estranged from their own bodies and the body subsequently becomes objectified as a performance or display. His work, and that of other authors to follow, now takes up the theme of men's difficult or troubled contemporary embodiment.

In relation to the sphere of paid work, for example, Seidler maintains that '[u]ndermined within a globalized economy with the decline of traditional industries that could sustain the identifications between masculinities and work, the body can become an exclusive site of threatened male identities' (2009: 16). As our chapters in this part on the body go on to reveal, the body as an unstable and threatened site can, indeed, become an opportunity for men to confirm and reconfirm masculine power in both public and private spheres. However, a focus on the body can also show men grappling with body uncertainties, due to age or health, for example, which both undermine a sense of bodily power and thus reveal men's changing and reflexive relationship to their body and through this, their relationships with others; at work or in terms of domestic relationships.

This kind of concern about the body, which authors such as Grogan (1999) have addressed, has been described as body work. However, as Wolkowitz (2002), argues we need to expand the concept of body work in its current deployment, since traditionally this has primarily been concerned with the work people do on their own bodies; for instance, in meeting the expectations and requirements of employers. What Wolkowitz (2002) argues, however, is that any investigation and theorising of the social relations of body work needs to acknowledge those whose paid labour entails a concern with 'the care, adornment, pleasure, discipline and cure of others' bodies' (2002: 497), for example. This perspective is instructive with regard to our concerns with the body work undertaken by hairdressers; this involves managing and grooming their own bodies, but also, importantly, the bodies of their clients.

There has, however, also been recent work published on male workers in beauty parlours which acknowledges the importance of work on the bodies of others. For instance, Faizan Ahmed (2009) is concerned with such workers in India, in relation to male beauty parlours and argues that '[c]aring for the body and the production of a new "beautiful" masculinity are a joint endeavor of client and worker who share a particular view of the male body and the presentation of the masculine self' (2009: 169). Given that most of our male hairdressers' clients are female, we add another dimension to the care of body work, in that it is largely the production of a 'beautiful femininity' which is the joint endeavour here. However, it is also the male hairdressers' subjective sense of their own embodied labour and masculine identity which informs the production of these femininities.

Wolkowitz (2002) further argues that the pre-occupation with the social relations of work in the service sector through the notion of emotional labour (Hochschild, 1983) can lead to a taken for granted 'mindlessness of the body'. However, this argument can be challenged on the basis of important work undertaken within corporeal feminism; for instance the 'leaky' bodies discussed by Grosz (1994, 1989) and Shildrick and Price (1998). Wolkowitz also stresses the need to extend a phenomenological concern with the lived body from the *inside*, to one which is concerned with how we experience the body from the *outside* 'in routinized workplace encounters, mediated by the cash nexus, and located within wider social inequalities' (2002: 505). Though a primary concern of ours is with men's gendered identification with their own (and others') bodies, and thus the lived body from 'the inside', we are also mindful of, as Wolkowitz puts it, 'the conditions under which patients', clients' or customers' bodies become merely counters in the bargaining between managers and workers' (2002: 505). This can be seen, for example, in general terms, in men's changed relationship to both the public and private, domestic spheres; changes in men's position as dominant or sole breadwinner, and thus, shifts in their traditional masculine status at home and at work (See Chapter 2 in this volume and Haywood and Mac an Ghaill, 2003).

These transitions have recently become more marked with the global economic recession; for instance, in the way estate agents manage their daily bodily routines in a changed financial climate as they go to see prospective clients in their homes, or how firefighters' bodies are routinely deployed by managers in different ways, when for instance, the ethos in the firefighting profession turns to a new managerialism, rather than a 'hands-on' approach to the job. Importantly, these two examples reveal that we are not merely concerned with the gendered body in relation to 'service' jobs such as hairdressing or with those occupations which are just *explicitly* concerned with the care of others' bodies, but also with those occupations which have a more implicit relationship to others' bodies, both in their practices and in relation to self identification. In this way, we also address Wolkowitz's (2002) plea to extend any analysis in this way to the relations between both givers and receivers of body work, across 'the social formation as a *whole*' (2002: 505, our emphasis).

Men at work: Embodied or non-embodied?

In exploring how the negotiation of occupational cultures contributes to ongoing gender projects, we take account of the 'heroic male project': that is, the imagery surrounding men's engagement with the 'public' world which often links male subjectivity with 'militarism, dreams of conquest and accompanying physical endurance' (Whitehead,

2002: 122). This 'heroic project' also includes the man who 'seeks to make his mark on and change the world through his drive, energy, self-discipline, initiative, but, most importantly, through his financial acumen' (Whitehead 2002: 122). Such performances link self-image – the body we *have* – with control of self and control of others, via alluring representations of 'powerful' men successfully manoeuvring in the public world (Whitehead, 2002: 123). Whether the working world enables embodied conformity with such images is another matter. Whether gender is 'done' or 'undone' in different occupational spheres (Butler, 2004) is the question we are therefore addressing, by asking how different occupations, with contrasting masculinised and feminised working cultures, support different expectations of what men should achieve, either in the body's appearance, its actions or its potential. As Woodward argues, '[e]very context or cultural field has its controls and expectations and its "imaginary"; that is, its promise of pleasure and achievement' (1997: 23). The implications of differing expectations – and imaginaries – for embodied masculinities are therefore constitutive of the gender projects occurring in the occupational environments we explored.

Morgan (2002), cited above, suggests that in modern society some men are seen as more embodied than others: 'Many images of men in sport, at war and in doing sex are highly embodied or, to be more exact, we are encouraged to read these representations in this way. Pictures of stockbrokers, bishops or dons might not seem as embodied as images of sportsmen or warriors' (2002: 407). He warns that 'if we fail to see their bodies in these cases this may be because of a prior framework of understanding that links men, bodies and action' (2002: 407).

This argument returns us to the notion of 'particular situations' and 'changing structure[s] of relationships' (Connell, 2002: 81). If some men's bodies 'disappear', this may reflect a privileging of those bodies which conform to notions of hardness, domination and physical competence. As our data reveal in the chapters to follow, embodied identity involves body-based perceptions, interactions and experiences within hierarchised landscapes of masculinity and gender relations more broadly. While certain occupational cultures cultivate the idea of body-based identity, as already referred to, we problematise assumptions that men who identify as 'stockbrokers, bishops or dons' (Morgan, 2002: 407), for example, are somehow less embodied.

Locating the men in our study within hierarchised landscapes of masculinity and gender relations also requires us to take account of differences of occupational status, age and also social class. Bourdieu

(1984), for example, describes the body as 'the most indisputable materialisation of class taste' (1984: 190). Yet if 'class' constitutes a marker of identity, it needs to be recognised as one among a plurality of centres generated by the dislocations of modern society (see Laclau, 1990). This perspective echoes Connell's (2005) view of gender as the outcome of social practices occurring within particular situations and social relationships.

Representation, image and bodily practices

The preceding discussion highlights potential mismatches between gendered or masculinised imagery and men's embodiment. This brings us to the question of representations of the body and their resonance within lived experience. Thus, the following chapters explore the potential gaps between *representations* of the 'heroic' fire fighter, the 'unscrupulous' estate agent and the 'camp' hairdresser, and the complex realities of men's embodied lives. Popular culture in the United States, for example, the TV drama 'Rescue Me' (Smith, 2005) which was concerned with the firefighting heroes of 9/11, reveals the gap between cultural representations and the reality of the profession for the firefighters involved. Smith (2005) argues that this programme was not so much concerned with fire fighting than with the 'celebration of the All-American Male in his sweat-stained, emotionally unavailable glory' (2005: 17).

In contrast, in a qualitative study of American firefighters and correctional officers who guard prisoners and inmates housed in local, state and federal correctional facilities, Tracy and Scott (2006) argue that '... firefighters labour to fulfill expectations as "America's heroes"' (2006: 6). They found that discourses of occupational prestige, as well as masculine heterosexuality, enable firefighters to present their work in privileged terms, while correctional officers 'struggle to combat taint discursively associated with low-level feminized care work or with brutish, deviant sexuality' (2006: 6). Further, they indicate that work can be tainted physically, socially or morally (Ashforth and Kreiner, 1999). In their study, for the firefighters, it was through their sexuality that the group identity was one which was seen to be associated with masculine conceptions of bravery and strength. They also found that, with the firefighters in their study, the external perception that society has of firefighters as being' sex symbols' (an image that they actively perform in their everyday embodied practices) had purchase. For instance, this could be seen in their actions which took place after a 'hoax call' where they made their presence visible in ways which drew attention to themselves, for example, ringing the fire truck bell to attract women's attention on the street, controlling others' bodily reactions as they made their own bodily presence explicitly felt. What is more, for the firefighters, in spite of the fact that they had to engage in dirty and mundane working practices, there were also internal audiences of their peers, as well as these external ones, on the street, which celebrated 'performances of gallantry and sexuality' (2006: 29).

In contrast with the correctional officers, firefighters' embodied working practices were enhanced by bells, big red trucks and hoses as well as these 'adoring' audiences. In addition, the firefighters managed the 'physical taint' of their occupation, for example, the fact that part of the job was dealing with dead and sometimes charred bodies, or more often, mundane dirty work, by being able to 'reframe their job's physically dangerous aspects into badges of honour', and so were able, through self deprecating humour, to deal with disgust in this way (see Chapters 9 and 13). Thus, for Tracy and Scott (2006) firefighters work with 'dirt' (i.e., embodied) forms of taint but through their special status, are able to manage this. Their conclusion is that dirty work and taint management need to be seen as occupational issues, but ones which take place in a context of discourses of power. It is these that 'constitute the meaning of a job and the identities of its workers' (2006: 35). Their study thus echoes Wolkowitz's (2002) stress on the necessity to look at the wider social relations of occupations.

However, such representation is not restricted to the more obvious example of the fire fighter, an image which, to some degree at least, rests on outward appearance and occupational 'props' such as uniforms. Mörck and Tullberg (2005), utilising Craik (2005), point out that there are three categories of uniform. These include those worn in a traditional manner by those in the armed services, for example; those which can be termed as 'quasi' uniforms, such as a style of dress that has no official code to regulate it, but informal rules of what is appropriate dress still operate and to deviate from this would not be acceptable; and 'informal' uniform, where styles of dress are very individual, but not very predictable. Mörck and Tullberg (2005) are concerned especially with the 'quasi' style of uniform, particularly in relation to male managers and employers of large corporations. For, as they say, 'Only women are properly described through their clothes in the dominant discourses of the Western world' (Mörck and Tullberg, 2005: 4). Arguing for the importance of performance theory in order to understand how a business masculinity is both a fashioned and so an embodied phenomenon, contextualisation is seen as important.

Thus, these authors note that any performance, when examined in a metaphorical theatrical sense, is constituted by a beginning and end time, which is structured in a particular manner, within a stage setting constituted of props and background. They conclude that men, through their working practices such as attending meetings, create hegemonic masculinity by consistently repeating acts wherein the image that 'managers' are both resolutely male and heterosexual is sustained. As they say: 'The tie or the pitch of the voice must be in good order' (2005: 4). Popp and French (2010) make a useful comparison here with their discussion of the dress codes of commercial travellers in the period from the start of the nineteenth century to the eve of World War Two. For their travellers '[s]elling is an inherently performative occupation, and identity creation is an always ongoing project in which process is "equally important"' (2010: 22). For Mörck and Tullberg (2005), this performance of masculinity is also relational, depending on men's interaction with female employees, who themselves take up particular roles through their dress and general appearance. The boardroom they found was one of the 'last bastions' for the performance of hegemonic masculinity in such a rigid way. The main impression yielded by these powerful managers was one of conformity through dress. Unity of presentation is key here, but differences in dress can 'create different statements and possibilities; here dress seems very important in defining the plot' (2005: 15). This aspect of the importance of dress, the 'quasi uniform', is also addressed in Chapter 8 which examines data on the estate agents; also, in the same chapter, hairdressers and their 'informal uniform' are considered. As Popp and French (2010) argue '[d]ress codes, whether implicit or explicit, reflect the workings of deep-seated organizational/occupational cultures and the spaces they create for the processes of creating roles and identities' (2010: 21).

In sum, therefore, a concern with this representation of self, but also of a collective group occupational identity illustrates Giddens' argument that people now fix themselves not through tradition and fixed roles, but by deliberate self identity choices over what to wear, or what group to belong to. Here, as Wellington and Bryson (2001) argue, we know rather little about how employees are either forced or encouraged to play particular roles or develop certain images or identity. Thus, they conclude: 'There can be no doubt that it is through aesthetically saturated acts, gestures and clothes that identities are constructed and programmed and self-positioned in the competitive market place. In the workplace image, appearance and dress are extremely important' (2001: 940). Citing examples of where employers issue guidelines for

how employees should be dressed appropriately at work, they therefore assert that pressures to conform to a particular image come from
employers and from the media. Furthermore, they argue that image and
performance have always been an integral part of workplace relations.
However, what is important to note is that now people can develop
very visible images in different kinds of media. That said, Wellington
and Bryson's (2001) argument, that such images are a mere facade, not
impacting onto the lives of most people, is one that our data, with its
focus on both the public and private lives of our participants, contests
(see Chapter 8).

This is especially true, where, for example, image is connected to
a concept of a very visible and regimented traditional form of dress.
Thus, an article in the UK newspaper *Guardian* (2009) reveals how fire
fighter's new uniforms will now include turban and hijab versions
and pregnancy uniforms for female fire fighters in a recruitment drive
to encourage as wide a range of applications as possible to meet new
diversity targets in respect of women and ethnic minority communities. (In 2009, 3 per cent of fire fighters were women and 5.5 per cent
are from an ethnic minority background in the UK.) This re-visioning
of a traditional uniform has implications beyond the way in which
individuals perceive their own, and others' embodied identities in an
occupational setting and extends to the image of a particular profession
in the popular imagination, and different gendered and ethnic groups'
sense of self.

Embodying representations

Who's who?

Jenkins (2004) stresses that this question can only ever be answered
contingently. For example, among his apparently 'less-embodied'
groups of men, Morgan (2002) has a category of 'mirroring' bodies.
This apparently feminised body – linked with bodily consumption and
commodification – suggests a passive experience of embodiment which
might encompass men in service industries such as hairdressing. Indeed,
hairdressers' bodies are gazed upon by clients and would-be clients, and
are a crucial resource for getting jobs in trendy city-centre salons, as well
as attracting business by 'looking the part'. Thus, clothes choice among
most of the young and middle-aged city-centre salon hairdressers in our
study contributes to their sense of embodied identity – in that men felt
themselves being surveyed at work. However, this was only one part of
the story and in Chapter 10 we go on to examine how successful male

hairdressers achieve a hybrid identity which is both macho and sensitive and where straight men may therefore present as more gay than gay men themelves. This appears to 'undo' the gender order through destabilising any simple straight/gay binary (see Kelan, 2010, for further discussion). In addition, the men in our study achieved the effective management of other people's bodies through the constant reinvention of their own youth-oriented, fashionable 'looks', particularly in up-market salons.

We also go on to explore in Chapter 10 how the camp stereotype can be appropriated as part of the expectations of manhood within the profession, but note how individuals are aware of their 'performances', and the ambivalences surrounding them. Men play with bodily, vocal and conversational styles enabling a special status in relationships with colleagues and clients, and overturn expectations of 'masculinity' while simultaneously asserting power, status and influence – even if such 'performances' were not always within their control.

As we have already noted in this chapter, estate agents might be seen as somehow less embodied than other men – relatively invisible when compared with the hairdresser mirrored around the salon and exposed to passers-by through picture windows. Yet body management is integral to appearing authoritative and securing clients' trust as they negotiate housing market uncertainties in a competitive field as we explore through the data in Chapter 8. By contrast, firefighting appears a primarily physical job, embodying ideals of the 'last working class hero' (Baigent, 2001) and 'immaculate manhood' (Cooper, 1995). Yet, as we have argued (Hall et al., 2007), despite occasional, intensely physical life-or-death interdependencies, firefighting is less grounded in the stereotypically hard masculine body than popular representations suggest: with age and seniority other forms of cultural capital become privileged.

Thus, the particularities of our participants' situations reveal not a transparent living out of stereotypes, but instead a complex environment of social negotiation. If the feminisation of hairdressing involves the clients' gaze on individuals' style and appearance, for example, there are also more masculinised dimensions to their embodied identities. What we arguing, therefore, is that individual men move between performances of gender which reproduce, but also act to transform, hegemonic masculinity; to not only 'do' but also 'undo' gender in ways which serve men's career aspirations. That which Butler describes as 'restrictively normative conceptions of sexual and gender life' (2004: 1) thus emerge as open to transformation. However, as she notes, such transformations, or 'undoings' are neither intrinsically negative nor positive. While potentiating critical distance and autonomy, they may simply allow socially mediated survival.

In addition, consumption features as another key arena for the construction of social identities (Miles, 1998: 2; Miller, 1987; Mort, 1996), a practice concerned with the marking and creating of similarities and differences. In consuming 'lifestyles', individuals locate themselves in relation to other people, so making statements about the self. Yet while goods, leisure and services enable the pursuit of status, any narration of identity is dependent upon an individual's *competent* use of cultural forms and goods, with attached symbolic, cultural and social value (Chaney, 1996: 5, 16, 93).

Barber (2008) notes the work of Bordo (1989) in *The Male Body*, where women's contemporary consumption of the male body and the sexualisation of men in the media can help to destabilise stereotypical and traditional gender dichotomies. Thus, patterns of consumption and lifestyle emulation can, of course, be played out through career choices, so constituting key elements of a man's identity. Whitehead's (2002) 'heroic male project' is helpful here, and, as has already been noted, can be linked to class: while estate agency carries associations of cool rationality, acumen, judgement and manipulation of others, hairdressing is a skilled manual job associated with creativity and aesthetics. Firefighting holds the most 'traditional' class-based connotations, representing one of the few occupations which celebrate the 'masculine' physical skills formerly associated with manual labour and hard, aggressive, physical proletarian masculinity (Baigent, 2001). Thus, firefighters' 'heroic' physical work has traditionally enabled them to distance themselves from women and other men employed in 'feminised' office labour (Baigent, 2001: 82), by drawing on positive images of hands-on, practical 'working class' masculinity (Cooper, 1995).

For the estate agents of our study, however, class-based identities are evidenced more by patterns of consumption and signifiers of distinction, though these too are manifested in relation to the body. Chapter 8 addresses this through a discussion of how estate agents' bodies represent key sites for the mobilisation and, indeed, reconfiguration of class-based masculine identities in relation to a comparison with their fathers' professions or in a need to alter accents or how a wish to 'dress to impress' meant debt for one man, to enable him to show status through possessions.

In relation to hairdressers, Barber (2008) focuses on the male clients in a Southern California hair salon, as opposed to our focus here where we are particularly concerned with the hairdressers themselves, albeit in relation with a number of diverse significant others, which of course includes the (mainly) female clients in our study. However, significantly, Barber concludes that, while female clients in hair salons are concerned to 'shape perceptions of self and body, as well as form relationships and social networks (Black, 2004; Furman, 1997)' (2008: 457), the male clients of beauty salons 'empty beauty work of its associations with feminised aesthetics and instead construct it as a practice necessary for them to embody a class-based masculinity' (2008: 456) and, as she also finds, a racialised masculinity. Utilising a conception of Fordist industrial production, where masculinity was connected to the doing of 'laborious tasks' she notes the description of working class men's investment in 'the literal sweat and blood of men' (459) as an outward sign of an appropriate performance of masculinity. But it was post war America's economic development with the corresponding increase in white collar jobs which encouraged men to have a new conception of, and relationship with, their bodies. Hence, occupational position is now intimately connected for men with 'looking good'. Or as Clarkson (2005) succinctly puts it 'For the emerging metrosexual, the quest for physical perfection replaces the need for brute force' (239).

Like Barber's (2008) male clients, who enter the gendered space of largely female-dominated salons, our male hairdressers also find ways of imbuing their presence there with an embodied masculine significance in an effort to avoid the feminisation of their identity, especially in the eyes of others, that comes from working in such a feminised space. In Chapter 17 we explore with the data, a need, expressed at times, to display scientific and technological knowledge (see also Robinson et al., 2007). Similarly, the estate agents in our study, who often embodied the meterosexual man's emphasis on appearance and looking good, reflected a class-based performance of masculinity, where to succeed in career terms means wearing the right suit or having the appropriate hairstyle. The fire fighters in our study often embodied an older class-based notion of the masculine embodied identity being correctly performed through manual tasks, where well-honed bodies on display were considered sexy and constituted body capital.

Nordberg's (2005) study of hairdressing included an examination of the particular techniques employed on the client's body; for example, how a person's hair is styled or the cutting techniques used to do this. Through these data, she reveals an embodiment and materialisation of those discourses and values that produce specifically identified subjects. She concludes that the commercialisation of masculinity with the growing interest in men as consumers of fashion and beauty allows opportunities for the hierarchical and polarised gender order to be both reproduced and also transgressed.

Bodies we *have*

The subsequent discussion of the three occupational cultures provides a more detailed overview of the ways in which the body – as something we *have* – might figure within the experience of embodied identity. In other words, what we continue to focus on are the ways in which representations of particular kinds of male bodies play a part in who men think they *are*. This returns us to Leder's (1990) view of the body as the vehicle through which we perceive our surroundings – something which itself 'disappears' in good health. Our data show *other* contexts bringing men's bodies into focus: for example, in reflection on how to hold a client's hair ready for the next cut, on how to shake someone's hand reassuringly or how to navigate the walls of a smoke-filled room. Some circumstances do therefore bring the body powerfully to the fore while others are indeed more 'non-embodied' in an experiential sense. Chapter 8 investigates how such experiences are gendered in that notions of the 'heroic male project' (Whitehead, 2002: 118–9) contextualise them. Thus, 'doing' firefighting enables the living out of a particular *gendered* occupational identity and a broader gendered sense of self as physical, courageous, in control and capable.

That said, firefighting also brings reminders of the body's *fragility*, of the transience of embodied life, in the routine enactment of required tasks. Age, however, makes men aware that they share physical vulnerability with fire and accident victims, and some can develop a distaste for the sharp end of the job. Through our data, Chapter 8 reveals that the materialities of the body *must* be taken into account (see also Hall et al., 2007). Many younger men appear to imagine their youthful bodies to contain endless potential – or at least this is how older men remember their own younger self-perceptions. Once older, and having endured the rigours of the job, the body's unavoidable materiality impinges more firmly on their sense of self and their ability to participate and perform physically as men, in the same way as before.

Having the capacity to transform both the bodies of clients and of themselves, hairdressers' embodied existence might seem to confirm discursive notions of the body as a project with endless possibilities. However, in an industry which privileges youth, pursuing the fleetingly fashionable 'look' makes increasing bodily demands as men age, a reminder of the body's ultimate intractability and of the limitations of purely discursive conceptions of the body. Within each occupational culture, the body men aspire to diverges from the materialities of an embodied life where they grow old, overweight, unfit and potentially injured. Ageing and ill health thus emerge as aspects of men's working lives which bring embodiment powerfully into relief and is explored in Chapter 11.

With this focus, as Jackson asserts, we can use the (ageing) body to specifically assess how boys and men have 'actively turned themselves into masculine subjects' (2003: 71). In an autobiographical examination of different 'moments of the life course', and, in particular, his early teaching career, he examines how 'a fracturing of my heroic performer body/ self created the new conditions for the emergence and re-emergence of my neglected, excluded versions of my masculine self' (2003: 74). Physical and mental breakdown had allowed him to think abut the different ways of becoming masculine which were possible. This fracturing of his sense of an embodied occupational identity finds resonance with the men's experiences across the occupations we examine in this volume. As in the case of Jackson, for example, when an ageing body, or a body which is no longer responsive to the demands placed on it, men in our study might discover themselves unable to live up to either society's or a specific profession's representations of masculinity. However, this also allowed men new ways in which to imagine an embodied self and, through this, different relationships with significant others in their lives, in relation to both public and private spheres.

Furthermore, for Jackson, it was through retirement and the subsequent distancing of himself from paid work that he felt able to explore new and embodied ways of work, for instance, through voluntary work. This is something we explore with men in our study who are facing retirement, or, who may already be semi-retired. But an interesting question we pose is whether and how it is *through* traditionally paid work (albeit not always in traditionally male occupations), that our participants embody different ways of being masculine, especially when the domestic, unpaid work distinction becomes unmanageable or unworkable; for instance, through men being involved in the domestic world more than previously, as a result of increased child care responsibilities. In addition, there can be changes in both working practices and identities as ageing or ill bodies force men to redefine their individual relationships to the world of work and the private sphere. Jackson's view that he can 'learn a great deal from my imperfect body' (2003: 86) informs our concerns here where we go on to discuss the myth of the perfect body.

Conclusion

Our data go on to show how men's *experiences* of their bodies figure within their embodied notions of who they are; whether in terms of age, size, strength, physicality or well-being. This chapter draws on Whitehead's argument that 'many men fail to achieve a seamless, constant, symbiotic relationship between their bodies and dominant discourses of masculinity', yet they still attempt to – and, indeed, their masculine subjectivity is invested in these attempts (2002: 191). It introduced questions as to how those subjectivities emerge within a complex constellation which includes differences of not only gender and age, but also class. Class, as we argued, now reflects a plurality of centres, the result of the dislocations of modernity, in addition to the importance of consumption in marking similarities and differences between men. Notions of the 'heroic male project' (Whitehead, 2002: 118–19), though helpful, require a nuanced perspective which takes account of men's capacity to move between residual identities such as the 'working class hero' and 'self-made man', someone defined through suit, watch and car, rather than simple practical know-how.

In addition, the shifting gendered makeup of particular occupations – as women become firefighters and estate agents and men become hairdressers – has implications for the nature of the relational identities of masculine and feminine. To what extent do 'feminine' practices of care and empathy among hairdressers and estate agents represent a male appropriation of resources once seen as particular to women? Or are we witnessing the feminisation of many of men's embodied working practices across all three occupational cultures? To some extent our contrasting occupational cultures do represent 'scenes of constraint' (Butler, 2004), yet within them individual agency constantly materialises – and our data subsequently evidence gender being not only 'done' but 'undone'. Stereotypes of the well-muscled firefighter; the glib estate agent; and the glamorous hairdresser do resonate with dominant discourses of masculinity which men in these occupations actively engage with. They constitute 'the body' in relation to which men's embodied subjectivities are negotiated. Yet alongside seeking the 'seamless, symbiotic relationship' which Whitehead describes (2002: 191), our data show men performing contradictory masculinities and sometimes highly local processes of inter-subjective negotiation and resistance: the home-handyman hairdresser; the older, yet clear-thinking firefighter; and, among estate agents, a continuing commitment to claiming a 'professional' identity. As we have argued, these examples represent the 'structures of practice' which, in Connell's view, 'respond to particular situations' and are 'generated within definite structures of social relations' (2005: 72). In this chapter we have focussed on their very different – and potentially unexpected – implications for the materialities of men's bodies – and individual men's embodied sense of who they are. Gendered subjectivities, we argue, are generated through men's embodied engagement with prevailing bodies. For as Simpson (2009) argues; 'Bodies matter, not simply because we work with and experience feelings through our bodies, but because bodies carry meanings which have implications for performances of gender (Simpson, 2009: 95).

8
'I'm a Suit Man': Embodying Occupational Masculinities

As Chapter 6 demonstrated, the men we interviewed from all three occupations were able to adopt a reflexive distance from the stereotypes associated with either the muscular, sexually irresistible firefighter, the sharp practice estate agent or the fashion victim hairdresser. Their occupationally grounded masculinity was practiced in ways which, as one might say for the estate agents, 'suited' them. This is not to overlook the pressures and constraints which resulted in a sometimes unwilling conformity, but simply to acknowledge men's capacity for awareness and, at times, choice when it came to 'fitting in' at work. Rapport's (2009) ethnography of hospital portering in Scotland provides examples of how this might occur within a culture of over-determined institutional regulation. As Chapter 2 described, in a case study of a porter he calls Bob Hume, Rapport depicts a man who conforms to neither the regime of the hospital where he works, nor the gym where he bodybuilds: 'As "hospital bodybuilder" Bob compassed or contained a sense of elsewhere within himself, and as such was never contained, alienated or overwritten by the locale in which he found himself – hospital, gym or wherever' (2009: 103).

While we suggest that Rapport's notion of reflexive engagement with available identities speaks to *all* processes of identification, for Bob the Bodybuilder his body itself was a key vehicle within his transitive performances of identity. Not only did its muscularity allow him to perform an over-determined version of the 'aggressiveness, bravado, mateyness, derring-do and devil-may-care attitudes' of other porters (Rapport, 2009: 105), but also, in his erratic conformity to the regimen of working out, drug taking and dieting that body building required, his body represented 'the focus of so much of his attention in the construction of his identity' (Rapport, 2009: 103). In this chapter we show how the men

we interviewed reflected upon the embodiments that were particular
to their occupations, the ways in which they understood and practiced
the bodily styles they saw displayed by other men in the office, the
meeting, the client's small private home, the fire station, the site of
the emergency, the salon. Unlike Bob the Bodybuilder, many of them
were at pains to emulate the ways in which their colleagues managed
their bodies, particularly those colleagues they saw as successful. Yet,
as Whitehead argues, 'the masculinities, as bodily expressions, which
accompany such displays are largely idealized and many if not most
men can sustain them only through effort, if at all' (2002: 190–1). This
chapter asks how men's subjectivities emerge within this complex constellation which includes differences of not only gender and age, but
also of class.

More or less embodied?

While firefighting and hairdressing seems to make obvious demands
upon the body, whether in terms of strength, skill or conformity to
fashion, estate agency might appear to be simply a matter of the right
suit. However, as Morgan (2002) has suggested, we need to reflect critically upon assumptions such as these, for in modern society, he argues,
some men are misleadingly seen as more embodied than others (see
discussion in Chapter 7).

We begin by locating our male participants within the hierarchical
landscapes of masculinity and gender relations referred to in Chapter 7,
taking account of differences not only of occupational status and age,
but also social class. Among estate agents, growing up in families where
local heavy industry provided the main form of employment was not
uncommon and they reflected upon their identities through comparisons with their families of birth. Thus, the theme of the self-made man
recurred in our data, with older men in particular reflecting on their
achievements in class terms. For some, making the transition from
humble beginnings to an affluent lifestyle through skill and hard work
was a longstanding source of pride. During interviews, they noted the
distinction between wages earned from physical labour, on the one
hand, and a profession requiring middle-class styles of speech, thought
and knowledge on the other. One young man compared himself to his
father, who worked with his hands, while he himself was a 'suit man'
who had the gift of the gab.

Making this transition was demanding and, as described in Chapter 3,
Brett Hardwick, an older estate agent, experienced initial discomfort in

an office environment with well-to-do clients when he had grown up on a council estate. He had modified his accent and was aware of changing his voice with different clients. In reflecting on their everyday lives, therefore, men measured themselves against alternative styles of masculine performance. While some estate agents' fathers might seem to have made their living in more 'embodied' ways, how their sons thought, spoke and presented themselves were, nonetheless, dimensions of their embodied being. Thus, as this chapter elaborates, once identification is recognised as a contingent, intersubjective practice, the centrality of comparison with others to knowing who one is – and is not, becomes apparent (Jenkins, 2004).

Opportunities for comparison, then, are a feature of everyday life and indeed of the life course (Hockey and James, 2003). As such, they offer scope for knowing our bodies and indeed ourselves. As Chapter 7 discussed, as human beings we both *have* and *are* bodies (B. S. Turner, 1992). If our bodies are us, as this distinction indicates, then our participation in society cannot be other than as embodied beings. Indeed, our embodiment is not simply something we take *to* our social environments; rather, it is constituted precisely through our ontological status as socially interactive, materially grounded beings. However, as Chapter 7 noted, Leder (1990) describes our bodies as the vehicle through which we perceive our surroundings – something which itself disappears when our health is good. What, then, can the men who participated in our study, who were not in the main unwell, tell us about their embodiment? Are their accounts likely to be restricted to descriptions of the models or stereotypes of the body which pervade their occupational cultures? And if so, what can we infer about men's embodied experiences of their bodies from these models? In Leder's (1990) view, the body enables us to engage with our environment and not with its intrinsic properties; when we stroke the cat we feel its fur, not the workings of the hand we are extending, not unless that hand is arthritic (James and Hockey, 2007). Yet, we suggest, a focus on identification reminds us of the importance of comparison, of the sense of match and mis-match, not only with other people but also our changing circumstances – and such experiences of similarity and difference cannot be other than embodied. It is in this way, then, that we come to know who we are, a form of knowledge which is both in itself embodied *and* enables reflection precisely upon our embodied 'fit' with a dynamic social and material environment. In the data below, we demonstrate that within the workplace, movement between (social) contexts, tasks and activities inevitably involves comparisons – between then and now, me and him. This mobility, we argue, brings men's bodies into focus and in so doing enables reflection that encompasses both the body they *have* and the body they *are*.

Bodies in motion

In this chapter, we prioritise the embodied experiences of estate agents, as members of an occupation where masculinity is not self-evidently associated with a particular kind of embodiment. We locate their experience within the context of the working lives of both firefighters and hairdressers, showing how some circumstances and social encounters can bring the body powerfully to the fore, while others involve subtler engagement with bodily experiences such as style of speech, cut of clothing and choice of posture. All, nonetheless, involve the materialities of human embodiment and bring opportunities for knowing oneself through comparative processes. For firefighters, the adrenaline buzz of responding to fire calls was central to men's enjoyment of their job; indeed to their sense of themselves as a firefighter. Dealing directly with fires could mean sensory overload as smoke and heat had to be managed, and touch and hearing became vital for negotiating buildings. Retired men described missing the thrill of these experiences, yet the routines of a shift pattern can lodge so deeply lodged within the body that one retired firefighter's female partner said it took him three months to stop waking during the night when his watch was on tour (see Chapter 4). Younger men told us they'd resisted promotion because they joined the service *'to ride the wagons'* (fire engines). These experiences are gendered in that notions of the heroic male project (Whitehead, 2002: 118–9) contextualise them, shoring up a broader gendered sense of oneself as physical, courageous, in control and capable. Powerful body-based experiences of this kind can, however, mean exposure to the body's vulnerability. Chapters 2 and 6 make reference to the inevitable comparisons brought about by the ageing process – between one's younger and older embodied self. This kind of awareness can make men aware that, like fire and accident victims, they too are mortal. Older men and their partners described how shift work for an older man can become 'knackering' (as several men put it), each tour requiring a longer recovery period, an embodied experience which throws into relief an earlier time when their bodies seemed to contain endless potential.

Strength and stamina are just two of the body's attributes, ones experienced directly by both young and old firefighters as they respond to the demands and indeed aftermath of emergencies, whether in the form of adrenaline surges or sustained exhaustion. Stamina is also an issue for hairdressers who spend many hours on their feet, working at awkward angles to achieve particular hairstyles. How they *look* as they work has implications for the extent to which they 'fit in' among their colleagues, just as it does for firefighters whose nicknaming practices spotlight distinctive features of the body, such as baldness. However, hairdressers' appearance and bodily style also have a powerful economic dimension. If they are to inspire clients' confidence in the service they are selling, their capacity to transform a client's hair and, by extension, their entire 'look', men needed to style and groom their own bodies in particular ways. As Sam Cartmell (28) said 'yeah clients do like to come in and think oh that looks nice ... they've obviously got a bit of style ... they're gonna be able to create that on me. So, so I think ... you do have to be conscious in a morning to make some kind of effort ... just presentation not kind of like, vain, vanity'. However, in an industry which privileges youth, pursuing the fleetingly fashionable look makes increasing bodily demands as men age. One hairdresser, a confident performer, said men of his age (he admitted to being around 50, refusing further detail) rarely remained on the shop floor. He stressed that he retained the energy to participate in hair shows, enjoying the excitement of his work, attracting many clients and training junior staff. Yet he also revealed anxiety about his appearance and uncertainty about what to wear when clients expected someone younger. His choice of uniformly black clothing was both a fashion statement and a disguise for his paunch. Another hairdresser, in his late thirties, demonstrated almost hyperactive energy and passion for his work, confirming his status through stylish clothes and an expensive convertible car. In addition, while bodily injury might seem to threaten only firefighters, hairdressers' bodywork involves repetitive actions and physical strains which can undermine functional health. One man's wrists were scarred from operations after continual cutting had weakened his tendons.

To what extent are the embodied experiences of firefighters and hairdressers to be discovered among estate agents, an occupation where the client's gaze might be expected to rest on the materialities of bricks and mortar, rather than strong arms or a stylish haircut? As older estate agent Brett Hardwick made apparent, the occupational culture of estate agents does involve forms of body-based self-surveillance, as in the cultivation of a particular accent. Other data show how a broader range of bodily practices are subtly implicated in encounters between estate agents, their clients and their colleagues. In this competitive, individualised profession, constant striving to meet targets can be stressful. Estate agency paradoxically combines the ideals of quality service with maximum profit – and the men labour under their clients' potentially negative preconceptions of them as glib, untrustworthy salesmen. Success therefore depends on cultivating a prospective client's trust, as discussed in Chapter 6. As a young estate agent just starting out on his career noted: 'you are selling yourself".

What the data below indicate, therefore, are the unexpectedly far-reaching implications of estate agency for men's embodiment. In the statement 'I'm a suit man', man and suit are elided in a business world where men can be referred to simply as 'suits', one item of clothing standing for their entire occupational identity. As Chapter 8 described, many of the female partners of estate agents portrayed them behaving 'like children' when they arrived home from work – quite literally tearing off their suits, something they saw as 'a knee-jerk reaction' that allowed them to cast off their work roles and professional 'fronts'. So while strategic body management may become embodied and therefore invisible to the estate agent-at-work, the data below describe ongoing shifts between front- and back-stage behaviour that expose men to comparative, embodied experiences of match and mismatch.

For estate agent valuers, for example, everyday work involves meeting families selling residential homes; landlords seeking investments and developers requiring advice on projects. Observational data show body management's key contribution to successful outcomes, yet this diversity of settings demands flexible practical mastery (Bourdieu, 1977) of winning bodily styles. For example, in meetings with investors and developers, men cultivate an 'impressive' bodily performance, taking up space by crossing their legs above the knee or leaning back with their hands folded behind their heads. Handshakes tend to be strong and eye contact sustained when persuading the investor that here is an agent 'that people think they can do business with'. In addition, agents must look the part and valuers are invariably impeccably turned out in suits and ties, markers of a class-based masculinity which is rooted in patterns of consumption and not production. Evidence of financial acumen can be flagged through possessions, dress and objects: many men wear designer cufflinks, shirts and scarves, and these choices are a focus for bodily self-awareness. One young estate agent we interviewed, new to the profession, incurred debt by ostentatiously cladding himself in designer gear, evidencing the lifestyle he was aiming to sell prospective clients.

While moneyed investors and developers may represent a small section of an agency's client base, residential valuation appointments make up their 'bread and butter work'. Apparently mundane, these appointments involve layers of emotional labour (Hochschild, 1983) that again require bodywork. Since both client and agent are likely to assess one another's motives and trustworthiness, the agent seeks control of this process on first entering the property. Valuations can be tense, particularly when families or individuals have been forced to sell; 'home', with its connotations of family, generalised reciprocity and emotional warmth, contrasts starkly with market connotations of profit, impersonality and exact value. In the vendor's home, valuers must show deference while exuding professional confidence and selling themselves and their agency. The management of bodies in space is important here: seated on vendors' sofas, admiring their gardens/cats/kitchen extensions/dado rails, the agent ingratiates himself through conversational niceties, non-threatening body language and considered advice. One agent said, 'you have to fit in ... be an actor', referring to the agent's need to somehow morph into whomever he imagines the client expects; sympathetic, business-like, authoritative, gentle. Participant observation revealed one unusually tall and impeccably dressed estate agent, visibly and awkwardly compressing himself into someone less imposing, crammed onto the vendor's sofa. Tea-drinking and lengthy domestic rituals can indeed undermine the professional nature of the visit. Afterwards, agents may shift identities and speak disparagingly of the properties and would-be vendors they have engaged with. As men's partners testify, therefore, the embodied effort of impression management later becomes apparent as suits are discarded and men romp around their homes with their children.

Conclusion

This chapter has made the embodied experiences of estate agents its primary focus, comparing these with data drawn from among firefighters and hairdressers. Leder (1990) viewed the body as the vehicle through which we perceive our surroundings – something which itself disappears when our health is good. Yet our data show that other contexts can bring men's bodies into focus as they move between (social) contexts, activities and, indeed, periods of the life course itself. This mobility enables comparative reflections upon dynamic embodied experiences, observations that men were able to articulate. To be a firefighter, we learned, is to thrill to a surge of adrenaline through the body when a fire-call comes in, often after long periods of relative inaction, an enforced spell of anticipation that younger men in particular found disappointing, having entered an occupation they imagined to be physically challenging (see also Chapter 9). In the salon, men could experience a growing mismatch between the reliably robust and stylish body they had cultivated during training and their increasingly heavy, potentially weakened or damaged physicality, a divergence which could, however, be compensated for through interpersonal and technical skills. In the shorter time-frame of an ordinary working day, an estate agent's tall, authoritatively professional body might become awkwardly out of place in tiny, well-worn domestic environment, an incongruity a man might seek to overcome through posture and the management of his limbs. In addition to these moments, or periods of the life course, when the body becomes anything but invisible (Leder, 1990), its capacity to engender belonging remains key: as a focus for colleagues' 'piss-taking' in the fire station mess room, a resource which can be deployed in securing a house buyer or developer's trust, and an ever-changing site of stylish self expression.

This chapter began by citing Whitehead's (2002) argument that bodies which represent or express idealised models of masculinity constitute a potent focus for men's attention and, indeed, investment, regardless of their success in emulating such forms of embodiment. Stereotypes of the muscular firefighter; the glib estate agent and the glamorous hairdresser do resonate with dominant discourses of masculinity that men in these occupations actively engage with. They constitute the body in relation to which men's embodied subjectivities were negotiated. Such negotiations are, however, highly local, inter-subjective processes. The particularities of our participants' situations therefore reveal not a transparent living out of stereotypes, but instead a complex environment of social negotiation. Thus, estate agents might be seen as somehow less embodied than other men – relatively invisible when compared with the hairdresser mirrored around the salon and exposed to passers-by through picture windows. Yet paradoxically, body management emerges as integral to appearing authoritative and securing clients' trust as they negotiate housing market uncertainties in a competitive field. By contrast, firefighting appears a primarily physical job, embodying ideals of the 'last working class hero' (Baigent, 2001) and 'immaculate manhood' (Cooper, 1995). Yet as one firefighter said, tapping his temple, 'it's not enough being macho and all muscle, you have to have it up here'. Notions of the heroic male project (Whitehead, 2002: 118–19), though helpful, require a nuanced perspective which takes account of men's capacity to move *between* residual identities such as the working class hero and the self-made man, someone defined through suit, watch and car, rather than simply practical know-how.

9
The Sociable Body

This chapter examines the bodily basis of masculine belonging and sociability in the particular environment of the fire service. It achieves this by exploring the geography of men's everyday working lives, with a particular focus on their embodied movement between different areas of the fire station and the outside world. Although women are employed as firefighters, they were not members of the watch we worked with. That said, women's bodies were evoked in within our data in ways which reveal the particular gendering of the men's bodies we discuss here. Similarly, while the chapter focuses on occupationally based identity, data also speak to men's domestic lives, showing how each domain shapes and, indeed, intersects with the other; for example, the four days between tours is often used to pursue 'fiddle jobs' which involve skills such as building, plastering and car repair work. Rather than being simply an additional, external occupation, expertise built up in these jobs can be reintegrated into the fire service as men trade favours, helping one another out with DIY projects in the home. Connections between these apparently separate domains of work, sociability and domestic life are therefore evident in the data we consider here.

Spatio-temporal embodiments

Chapter 1 describes the multiple qualitative methods used in the study we draw upon. To make sense of masculinity as an embodied practice, workplace participant observation was key to accessing men's engagement with particular activities and, indeed, with one another – within the geographies of their workplaces and associated locales. We used the method mainly in the fire station itself, partly because fire calls are increasingly less frequent, given developments in building regulations and health and safety provision, and partly because we were prohibited from joining the men on the fire appliances themselves for insurance reasons.

What this work made evident was the importance of *place* for understanding the particular performances of masculinity we observed: when a fire call comes, its impact is felt primarily within the fire station, where staff, their vehicles and their equipment are normally located. In other words, many of the firefighters employed to manage the emergencies anticipated for a particular area are usually grounded within the region's fire stations. While hairdressers and estate agents move from the domestic sphere into a salon or office in order to make a start on their core tasks, firefighters enter the fire station to make themselves *accessible*, should an emergency occur. Accessibility involves the readiness of vehicles and equipment, backed up by the provision of appropriate training. But it is the men themselves who are key to responding to whatever needs are signalled. Thus, we cannot overestimate the distinctiveness of a workplace within which the flow of work is largely unpredictable, where, as fieldnotes describe, men play out a waiting game, drifting between TV room, mess room and gym, moving slowly to required but non-urgent tasks such as checking equipment or fitting smoke alarms in domestic homes. These are, however, their secondary tasks; men are primarily employed to 'wait in the wings', yet with no idea when their 'cue' for making an entrance will actually come. Fieldnotes record first entry to this setting as follows:

> [In the TV room] Suddenly I am confronted with seven men, feet on the table, watching TV, arms crossed. Staring at me ... bemused. 'Do you like drinking tea?' one asks, 'we do a lot of that'.

Two months later, fieldnotes describe the men's return from delivering smoke alarms to domestic properties:

> On the men's return they have a lunch hour. Some wander off to the gym and most trek into the TV room for more tea ... No-one really talks and most men slump in their seats with their feet on the tables, glaze-eyed. At the end of the lunch hour there is a slow return to movement amongst the men as they drag themselves up from their chairs.

Consistently, throughout the four month period of participant observation, similar recordings note: (after checking equipment) 'everyone drifts up to the tea room'; (before breathing apparatus drill) 'Graham and Mark leave (the tea room) first – they will be setting up the drill – and the others slowly follow them'; and 'it feels like another disjointed day with strange faces (relief staff), boredom and listlessness.'

The evening shift, for example, begins with lights, equipment and sirens being checked and the men's leggings set up inside their boots in readiness for a call. After this 'the men wander upstairs for tea'. Someone has brought in a cake and everyone settles to tea and cake in the mess room while one man collects money for the fund from which food is bought for meals. And then there is a fire call and the room rapidly empties of all but two men who have duties in the fire station itself. Ten minutes later 'the rest of the watch are back ... a false alarm ... and they finish their tea and cake'. Then a call from the crew manager comes through the tannoy; the men are due to go out and fit smoke alarms: 'everyone ignores him for a few moments – "we need tea" – and they carry on drinking, before gradually drifting to the kitchen to clean their mugs and wander off'.

It is precisely this rhythm of embodied practices that characterises the men's days and nights. Tea and cake (or indeed any meal) can be abandoned, only returned to in this case because the call was identified as false. Indeed, when a call comes, nothing takes precedence. Fieldnotes record that during a drill that involved men fully kitted out in weighty breathing appliances negotiating a mock-up of a smoke-filled building collapsing during a fire, 'there is an urgent voice from above – fire call. The men disentangle themselves hurriedly ... and shoot upstairs. I follow them all to see the men, half in and half out their yellow overalls, clamber up on the appliance and speed away'.

During a visit undertaken to set up fieldwork, notes record:

[Talking with the Watch Manager] For about two minutes, when a loud ringing starts – a fire call. The Watch Manager jumps up and rushes to the door. On his way out he calls to the younger man to look after me – (the younger man) is on light duties due to a sports injury and is not going out on calls ... he leads me to the appliances ... where men are jumping on board. One of them grabs a printout detailing the nature of the call and the whereabouts, and they are gone.

During a charity event the men staged in the city-centre to raise money for the Firefighter's Benevolent Fund, Greg, a firefighter is described as 'slumped against the pumps (fire appliances) listening for fire calls' while other men chat to the public: 'after ten minutes the watch get a fire call and head off with the sirens and blue lights flashing'. Fieldnotes describing events in the station record men 'whooping with delight' when a fire call comes.

Insights such as these, gleaned through over three months' participant observation, are complemented by men's own accounts of their everyday, embodied lives. Wesley True (46) was very much 'one of the lads' and summed up the difficulty of remaining always at the ready for a physically challenging yet unpredictable and relatively rare demand:

> It can be very boring as a Fireman and if you're left ... you know you have a lot of spare time, not so much now it's getting less and less spare time ... Smoke alarms, yeah, and they're changing, they're trying to bring, drag us into the modern world, so like a normal job but slowly but surely ... but Pete (previous gaffer) realised that if you're just robots walking ... you know, do this, do that, it just gets so boring and mentally it's rubbish. So they used to let us mess about and it used to break the boredom up, keep us happy and I was happy to come to work, I loved it.

This rhythm differs markedly from those we observed among hairdressers and estate agents. While Chapter 4 describes the ragged boundaries between the 'home' and 'working' lives of men in these two categories, hairdressers and estate agents nonetheless accomplish a whole series of tasks sequentially; for example, working through a list of appointments with clients. Nowhere do we find the firefighters' staccato shifts between slow, unfocussed movement and an urgent leaping into action. What we argue, therefore, is that identification occurs within this uneven flow of embodied practices, whether this be the uncomfortable juxtaposition of silent bodies around a meal table when relief staff are present; or the horseplay of physically piling on top of a team member who 'fluffs a ball' during volleyball in the gym.

As we go on to show, therefore, the stark contrast between drifting listlessly between tasks and breaks, as opposed to leaping into leggings and boots, encompasses smaller, subtler shifts within men's working lives more broadly. Sociability, particularly in the form of banter and horseplay, is by no means confined to periods of passivity in the mess room but surfaces in distinctive ways throughout and beyond each tour. Though the two days and nights of a tour involve continuous availability for fire calls, days and nights do, nonetheless, have a structure. Parade at 9 am required men in the new watch to line up by their fire appliances for a few fleeting moments that testified to the military history of a service that still retains elements of its naval past. This was followed by checking and cleaning equipment. Days were likely to include 'drills' when men learned and rehearsed the use of breathing appliances (BA) and decontamination tents, for example. This might involve a staged emergency in the forecourt behind the garage where the appliances were stored, where a training tower allowed men to practice their climbing and rescue techniques. In addition men left the station to fit smoke alarms free in local properties and perform other kinds of fire prevention work; for example, during our spell of participant observation the men went out on the fire appliance to familiarise themselves with the layout and workings of a new hotel in the city.

During their tour men make meals in the school-canteen style kitchen, one man taking charge, helped informally by a couple of friends. Food is bought out of a mess fund which all men pay into, one man taking charge of collecting their contributions. It is eaten in the mess room, everyone clustered around a single table. Tea and snacks are also consumed in the tea room where men stretch their legs on the coffee table and watch TV. Shared sleeping accommodation is also part of the fire station. During breaks, men have alternatives to watching TV: they play cards, they work out in the gym, they play volleyball. Taking part in physical exercise is not only something they tend to welcome; it is also encouraged by management as a way of maintaining physical fitness (Wolkowicz, 2003).

Masculinity and belonging

Key to belonging to a watch is participation: in fire calls, community safety work, drills, maintenance of equipment, cooking, eating, sleeping and playing cards, volleyball or football. The body features strongly within all these social practices. Men become familiar with one another in a physical sense, sharing intimate knowledge as a result of bodily proximity during night shifts and seeing colleagues in tense circumstances, physically drained and exhausted. Whereas sleeping, cooking and eating are almost entirely home-based activities for hairdressers and estate agents, in the fire station home and work are elided; men know which colleagues sleepwalk, snore, dream or talk in their sleep. Personal physical idiosyncrasies become part of the group's store of knowledge and are central to the teasing that defines the group. Jokes about physical appearance can signal acceptance, but also involve testing one another, the key being never to rise to taunts. These practices create the watch as 'family', as men described it - a place where men come to belong and where their work-based identities emerge.

It might seem, therefore, that highly distinctive, materially-grounded experiences of bodies in space – or of embodiment within places, are sufficient as an explanation for the data we are presenting. Yet this would be to neglect the *social* processes through which everyday masculinities are reproduced within this social context, a form of homosociability which echoes Gregory's (2009) discussion of the importance of sport, banter and drinking to the gendering of power within the advertising industry. Vincent Twycross (29) gives some insight into this during a conversation about fitness and sport within the fire service:

> I just ... I've never played football so I haven't got a clue what I'm doing, I played a couple of times, ran myself ragged and gave up, it was just useless. I just get in everyone's way, so I don't usually play football, but yeah, we played cards the other day, the old watch used to all play cards, but really regularly, but there's, because the watch (is) all new and half of them are temporary and nobody knows anybody really, yet, so we're still forming the watch really.

This process of 'forming the watch', we argue, involves embodied practices such as effective team work during a fire and horseplay during drill or in the gym; it also encompasses the body itself as a site of identification. How men look and how they manage their bodies is anything but socially invisible. Rather, their bodies constitute the basis for distinctions between different degrees of belonging that are marked out graphically in the ways in which the men interact as a group. For example, fieldnotes describe Len, a relief firefighter, and the ways in which his unpopularity materialises to position him at the periphery of social space:

> Len is shy and awkward, with a nasally Birmingham accent ... Blue Watch roll their eyes at him a bit and Greg tells me not to get cornered by him. He is quite boring apparently.

John, a member of Blue Watch, explains their response; not only has he had direct of working with Len at another fire station, but Len has a wider reputation for being nervous and jumpy. He is thought to tell lies about his private life, and to conceal his ignorance when, for example, driving the fire appliance. Moreover, he is subservient to gaffers. Rather than oblique comments or back-stabbing, Len's lack of fit with the watch is made visible through eye rolling. Around the meal table, when Len is present, details of his sleepwalking and his swearing and screaming in his sleep are recounted.

It is in settings such as the meal table, therefore, that the watch is 'formed', as Vincent Twycross puts it. When new or cover staff were present, fieldnotes record that: 'round the brunch table, things are a bit strained. The new faces make the personality mix unfamiliar and there is less interaction and joking than usual. Everyone seems a bit unsure what to say. The "bigger personalities" are not around and no-one wants to say anything'

By contrast, on the last night of this particular watch's tour, unflattering stories were told about a former station officer who looked like an unpleasant cartoon character. In underlining the man's lack of fit with the watch, its core members drew together – and fieldnotes record 'It feels quite comfortable around the table – everyone knows one another and seems on good form. There are no tense moments or awkward silences'.

Processes of identification, albeit highly visible, are however subtle in the nature of the distinctions made. Taking the example of bodily fitness, Alec Simpson (41) discussed the extent to which firefighters lived up to their image as strong and sexually alluring. He said that he'd been fit as a younger man but a later period of living alone and 'enjoying life as it came' meant that he had put on weight over the previous five years. The public, he felt, viewed a firefighter as a 'bronzed ... god stood there and they look at the calendars and some of them are very disappointed with some of the fire crews that turn up [laughs], and we all get older and we all get hairier'. Interestingly, though diet and exercise were seen by many men as increasingly important as time passed, the ways in which they were pursued could themselves become a focus for both belonging and exclusion. As such, then, physical fitness did not simply make a man a better firefighter. Excess weight, for example, might belie the physical strength needed to lift heavy equipment. While at one time, a fire station was likely to have a bar where men could drink when not involved in other duties, now a gym takes its place. Yet in terms of belonging, or 'forming the watch', what goes on in the gym has many echoes of the bar. And just as watches will extend their time in the fire station by having a *watch night out* every pay day, so golfing, cycling, running and climbing are activities which men undertake together once they come off duty. Indeed, as Lupton argues:

It should be recognised that health-maintaining practices do not stand alone and above other practices of everyday life, but are incorporated seamlessly into the life-world of the individual, often in ways that submerge any overt "health" associations under other meanings deemed to be more important to the individual's identity.

(1994, cited in Watson, 2000: 61)

Alan Proctor (43), for example, said, 'I wanted to lose a bit of weight and get a bit fitter and I found, doing this job as well, you know, great ... make time, you know so perhaps now, so I wanted to lose a bit of weight, get a bit fitter and save a bit of money, if Tim goes to university, I haven't got any money, you know like, Emma's at university ... and I'm 43, you know ... its easy to put weight on now, so I do, I'd rather be slimmer, you know ... like I say on the Fire Brigade you know, people slag me off if they're looking at [me] ... bit overweight or bald'.

When Alec Simpson (41) was asked whether other watch members would encourage or tease him about taking exercise, however, he said, 'A bit of both, some of the lads think it's a great thing, I got nothing but praise after last year's competition where I did so well, but generally most people take the piss .... 'You fat old git, what you doing that thing for?''

Men therefore differentiate between one another in terms of the nature of their bodies; not only are certain bodies spoken of openly and critically, but whether or not men will be encouraged to change their pattern of diet and exercise reflects their positioning within social space more broadly. Thus Alan Proctor (43) said of Gavin, a similarly aged watch member: 'like Gavin at the moment, have you seen Gavin? He's sixteen stone, he says he's sixteen six, but he must be seventeen stone, he's got like a, he's always had like sort of, big and apparently when he was a teenager he said he was quite fat, but he's got a big arse, so he has, he's got, I mean I think I've got a big, but Gavin's massive, but like he's put some weight on because he's upstairs working. He's like, eats takeaway stuff I think, you know so bad diet really more than, so we've been going running, so dinner times'.

Alongside this drawing up of lines of difference and similarity can be set those other bodies encountered by firefighters. Women firefighters were associated with a 'culture of fear' around political correctness, the men said; for example, images of women's bodies normally found in the fire station on page three of tabloid newspapers had become out of bounds, along with swearing. Yet contact with female members of the public was taken as an opportunity to demonstrate sexualised belonging: for example, the self consciousness of a young firefighter working with the public during the charity event described above was intensified by older men telling him to *'get in there'* when young women passed by. Similarly, the presence of Alex, the female researcher, initially aroused the Assistant Divisional Officer's concerns: 'I want to get some work out of the watch. I don't want them distracted. You're a woman and they're red blooded men'. The relational nature of gender was particularly evident when the men left the fire station: in the hotel where they were being familiarised with the layout, female kitchen and spa staff giggled and smirked and men responded by flirting and making jokes among themselves about massage rooms and saunas.

Being red blooded and demonstrating one's interest in women, for some men, was therefore an important dimension of belonging, one that required the presence of women's bodies, either in public or in the tearoom newspapers. The bodies of women in the fire station itself were, however, seen as potentially problematic – a distraction from work or a constraint on the practices through which watches 'formed'. Similarly, those other bodies which in part define the nature of masculinity among firefighters – those of people who are injured or dead, are routinised dimensions of talk among men in the fire station. Fieldnotes record Steve and Greg recalling incidents they had attended 'where people were burnt to cinders, limbs hanging off, decapitated'. The men are described as 'not exactly making light of these awful things, but are discussing them in quite a routine fashion, as if they were difficult customers in a shop'. Yet this familiarity with the dead was also an aspect of masculinity which had to be managed – along with being 'red blooded'. Thus Sean, another member of the watch, had described 'gory injuries' to school children visiting the station the previous week and the Watch Manager had been concerned about that tales of eyeballs popping out, scalpings and missing limbs, told by a firefighter without parental experience himself, would result in nightmares.

Conclusion

This chapter has shown the distinctiveness of a workplace where men contrive to manage 'the waiting game' which constitutes the major part of their time – to the extent that men in city-centre fire stations differentiated themselves from those working in small suburban fire stations by claiming that these men went about in carpet slippers and were in bed by 10 pm. Unlike hairdressers and estate agents who 'fit in' by virtue of their distinctive style or their capacity to excel where others do less well, for firefighters belonging involves appropriate participation in the processes through which watches are formed. New recruits and temporary staff would find themselves on the periphery of a watch, cautious at the meal table, unable to infiltrate the inner circle at the bar after work. Through a particular style of bodily interaction, where differences and similarities are a continuous focus for attention, the watch forms itself as distinctive personalities discover their individual niches within the collectivity.

As we have argued, firefighters' embodied engagement with their occupational roles takes two radically different forms. Yet despite the profound contrast between these roles, they are separated by a boundary that can be overturned at any point in time. As a result, men are continuously ready to respond to what is an unusually challenging set of circumstances, one where the materialities of collapsing buildings and choking smoke have to be dealt with alongside the damaged, dying or dead bodies of individuals and the terror and loss that fire or accident victims may be experiencing. It is within this context, then, that the homosociability we have been describing takes place. In an environment of unpredictably; long periods of work for which men have little heart, the *social* boundaries of the watch are made to assume a marked stability. Belonging is achieved, not acquired, as new recruits are submitted to scrutiny and the emotional challenges of wind-ups and piss-taking. In the confines of the fire station, there is little scope for privacy and as the watch 'forms', its boundaries become increasingly self-evident, both to those who constitute its 'bigger personalities' and those who find themselves excluded.

10
The Performing Body

This chapter explores embodied identification within the very different spatio-temporal environment of the salon. Unlike firefighters' concern to 'form the watch' through participation in a ruthlessly bounded team, or 'family', hairdressers may adopt not only a critical distance from their occupationally defined masculinity, but also stand back, reflexively, from more pervasive or taken-for-granted dimensions of masculinity itself. We suggest that the following features of the salon can be seen to make it an environment where men reflect upon, resist, or reinvent more hegemonic masculinities: it is a feminised arena; a setting which has associations with homosexuality; and a workplace which makes bodily and indeed emotional transformation its core product or output.

Newton's ([1972] 2002) discussion of the concepts of drag and camp is instructive here, offering both empirical parallels with our own data on men and sexuality, but also, and perhaps more importantly, a set of more generalisable theoretical concepts which have resonance within the salon: theatricality, audience, performance and style. In her work on men's dress, she argues that one item from 'the feminine sartorial system such as earrings, lipstick, high-heeled shoes, a necklace' ([1972] 2002: 441) can undermine the entire masculine system of dress. This is explained as follows: '[t]he superordinate role in a hierarchy is more fragile than the subordinate. Manhood must be achieved and, once achieved, guarded and protected' (Newton, [1972] 2002: 445). What this chapter explores is the extent to which working as a hairdresser and spending one's days in the feminised environment of the salon can be seen as 'the one item' which puts masculinity at risk. As we found during interviews, this environment can provoke reflexivity among men who otherwise and elsewhere might be unlikely to question the specificity of their taken-for-granted masculinity and its associated privileges.

Chapter 3 provided an historical background to hairdressing, arguing that by the beginning of the twentieth century the previous market for male hairdressers who attended wealthy clients in their own homes had given way to more democratic beauty and fashion practices. In the public setting of the 1900s salon, hairdressing's association with elite classes was being overtaken by a feminised workforce who provided services for a much broader range of women. This public bodily engagement of client and practitioner was, arguably, made manageable through employing female hairdressers to work on women's hair (Herzog, 1996). When men enter hairdressing, therefore, they are not only working in a feminised occupational culture; they are also working directly upon women's bodies. As elaborated below, Cox (1999) identifies the specific issue of 'bobbing', rather than simply 'dressing' women's hair, that emerged in the 1920s, arguing that 'camp' provided men trained as barbers with an ambiguous, non-threatening way of doing masculinity within the feminised environment of the salon. Today, men who enter a career in hairdressing engage in bodywork that is located within a spectrum that includes nursing, care work, childcare and professions allied to medicine such as chiropody, occupational therapy, and physiotherapy. Each of these is linked with, but also subordinate to higher status professions such as teaching and surgery; in the former, bodily contact is largely prohibited, in the latter much of the contact is with the anaesthetised body. As this chapter will demonstrate, therefore, male hairdressers are at risk of having a marginalised masculinity imposed upon them by virtue of their occupational identity, yet via particular embodied performances of masculinity, they seek and often succeed in laying claim to more desired identities. The centrality of the salon's orientation towards bodily transformation is, we argue, core to the scope men discover for reinventing masculinities.

Women's work

Academic interest in men who work in female-dominated occupations has grown since the mid 1980s. As Chapter 2 described, feminist analyses note that men may be advantaged in these circumstances by accessing a glass accelerator to promotion (Bradley, 1993; Lupton, 2000), but that men who choose 'non-traditional' careers may find their masculinity and sexuality coming under scrutiny (Lupton, 2000; Sargent, 2000). Lupton (2000) argues that working in a female-dominated occupation may undermine men's capacity to conform to hegemonic masculinity within either the workplace or their lives more broadly. Men risk being both feminised and stigmatised as a result.

In the sphere of hairdressing, Lindsay's (2004) Australian study describes young people's participation in an occupation where 82 per cent of the workforce are female, a workforce that is regarded as trivial, for example within middle class academic circles. Hairdressers are working class service workers, rather than professionals, in this setting – and the job is seen, typically, as something women undertake between leaving school and starting a family. With regard to the implications for masculinity, Lindsay says: 'As hairdressing is an unconventional career choice for men, it feminised work that carries the stigma of male homosexuality, the men may be more accustomed to justifying their work as a serious occupation. By contrast, hairdressing is a straightforward occupational choice for young working class women. Most of the women took their jobs seriously but a job was something that could be put aside and taken up again' (2004: 266–7). Gimlin's (1996) work in a New York salon catering for white middle- and upper-class women provides another perspective on the gendered status of hairdressing as an occupation. In this setting female hairdressers experienced themselves and their work as lower in status than their clients. Rather than living out the stereotype of low status female workers seeking an undemanding filler between school and motherhood, these women 'attempt to position themselves as professionals with specialized knowledge and skills to nullify the real social differences between themselves and their customers' (1996: 507). In this way, they sought to transform their 'job' into a 'calling'.

Lindsay's Australian sample make few references to glamour, fun or trendiness, instead highlighting very poor wages and long hours as their job's key characteristics – yet young men in particular cited its status as a career choice: 'Andre explains, "basically my work is pretty much a large majority of my life"' (2004: 266). Similarly, Brendon, discussing the use of Ecstasy as a leisure pursuit, said: 'But with a casual job you could do it. But when this is what you've set for the rest of your life, as your occupation, you put that before anything. And I do' (2004: 266). As Chapter 2 noted, Bradley's (1993) suggestion that men move across gendered work boundaries 'only in very special circumstances' (cited in Bagilhole and Cross, 2006: 39), belies the fact that feminised occupations can be viewed positively by men: for example, the nurturing dimensions of care work can have a direct appeal, as Bagilhole and Cross's (2006) data evidence.

Our own data show very similar attempts by men to redefine the nature of hairdressing, yet also demonstrate that its opportunities for another kind of masculinity are part of its attraction. Thus, Brendan and Sam, two 'out' gay men employed in a salon where we carried out participant observation, were at pains to stress the *professional* status of hairdressing with its 'masculine' scientific and technical skills. Brendan had an acknowledged reputation as an accomplished stylist; Sam arrived in his present job with a striking array of technical skills that he acquired at college and in his previous salon. Fieldnotes record him expressing the opinion that 'Men are in it more as a profession', then noting that ' he absolutely hates it when people think that hairdressers, by definition, are thick'. Brendan is recorded asserting that reality TV shows set in salons had 'brought up the status of hairdressers in the public eye; i.e. that now more people recognised it is hard work and that there are technical aspects of the job'.

For other men, the feminised nature of the job was seen as a positive attraction and many reported being a 'novelty', or having a 'special position' in the workplace. As Steve London, a hairdresser in his forties recalled:

> Contrary to what you might think, you were really looked after by women it was a really, you know you were, there was, they were, it was just great, just a great atmosphere.

The positive connotations of working as a man among women took several forms. Steve told us that being a straight man among women had beneficial effects for his social and love life. He said:

> Oh it were fantastic, then I didn't I used to use it to my advantage then, you've got to use... Yeah, use it to your advantage ... it were just fantastic but at that time I didn't have that many male friends, all me friends were female, I'd got a big, there were a big crowd of us and I used to just knock about with girls.

Other men reported preferring the company of women. According to Gordon Bristow (65), 'women are, they have a much broader view of life then men, men is all football, sex, cars and basically that's, that's it'.

Transformation, performance and gender

Like the hairdo itself, gender, as a category of identity, is without internal stability. In other words, just as hair must be constantly attended to if a desired style is to be created and sustained, so gender itself is the outcome of performance rather than a fixed property of the individual. This perspective opens up the possibility of reinvention, change or indeed, transformation and, as argued above, the salon emerges as a site where these possibilities are in evidence. As the data below suggest, the bodily transformations which constitute the salon's core business have implications for the performance of masculinities.

To transform the client, then, is the hairdresser's highest aspiration and this concerns not just their hair but also their emotional state ('making them feel special'), their relationships, and their social life (see Gimlin, 1996, for discussion of this process in New York salons). In this respect the salon differs from the barber's shop where, traditionally, the 'short back and sides' was administered as a way of maintaining a particular look and offered little scope for radically *changing* the individual's appearance. Raymond Cartwright, who owned and single-handedly ran a salon in a working-class district, offhandedly refused an appointment to a man who, he said, just wanted a quick chop (making a chopping sound while miming the action with his hands); Raymond identified as a 'proper stylist', not a barber. While clothing can enhance the look of the body, work with hair, a property of the body that admits changes of colour, length, shape and texture, lends itself to particularly profound transformations. It is an element of the body that can be radically altered and, indeed, painlessly detached.

What are the implications of this everyday preoccupation with transformation for men working in hairdressing? As argued above, we can view the social and spatial environment of the salon as a site at which gender identities become open to scrutiny. Claire Dunbar (45), a hairdresser herself, said that male hairdressers are always seen as 'gay or sex mad' and described how her partner, Michael, 'always makes a point with a new client at some of talking about his wife ... think they get it over some way or another ... just subtly in case they are wondering'. Andy Hathaway, a divorced, middle-aged hairdresser said that 'my mother would not let my elder brother become a hairdresser because she thought he's going to be gay'. Context-specific assumptions such as these contrast markedly with a wider social environment where, as Hockey et al. (2007) argue, heterosexuality is the taken-for-granted social identity of individuals who betray no evidence of belonging to a category that is somehow other than 'normal' or 'natural'. Indeed, as Richardson (1996) argues, despite the popular assumption that a word that subsumes 'sexuality' must refer to sexual preferences and practices, heterosexuality has the status of a *social* identity, whereas homosexuality remains a sexual identity. What she is arguing, therefore, is that heterosexual sex is synonymous with 'normal' adult sexual desire and practice, something that merits no special attention. Heterosexuality not only exceeds, but also encompasses taken-for-granted sexuality, concealing it within institutionalised principles of social organisation that systematically privilege those espousing this social identity. By contrast, homosexuality encompasses a form of 'unnatural' sexual desire and practice, undermining the oppositional nature of the gender order itself. As such, then, homosexuality is the 'marked' category, often foregrounded through comparison with the invisibility of heterosexuality.

As the data already presented indicate, working in the salon exposes masculine identity to scrutiny. Not only can men feel that the privileges and status of masculinity have been undermined by entering an occupation that is on a par with low-grade working-class 'jobs', but in taking on what is in practice 'women's work' they have become aligned with the subordinate half of the gender hierarchy that Newton ([1972] 2002) refers to. In addition, however, *sexual* identities are at stake in that the customary assumption of heterosexuality is likely to be suspended. What we find within our data are a variety of responses on the part of men.

We begin with hairdressing's traditional association with camp, the UK 1950s celebrity hairdresser, Mr Teasie Weasie, epitomising this stereotype. As noted, Cox (1999) argues that when women began to bob their hair in the 1920s, barbers rather than hairdressers were the only class of professional skilled in cutting rather than 'dressing' hair. However, their associations with masculinity deterred women's use of their skills – and a new class of camp hairdresser emerged, someone with the cutting techniques of the barber yet whose phoney French accent and 'effeminate' style reassured women about the status of their otherwise threatening masculinity.

Here, we use the concept of camp also for its theoretical as well as empirical relevance in making sense of an environment where hegemonic masculinity comes under scrutiny and where men discover scope for re-negoiating or re-inventing their gendered identities. Newton argues that camp is 'concerned with a *philosophy* of transformation and incongruity' (italics added, [1972] 2002: 442), whereas drag is more directly associated with masculine/feminine transformation. None of the men we observed or interviewed in any way presented themselves as men in (metaphoric) women's clothing. Yet many of them played with or appropriated aspects of femininity. While some of the older hairdressers did display a style readily identifiable as 'camp', the *concept* of camp has a broader sphere of relevance in the salon than simply these men's behaviour. What Newton argues is that incongruity, theatricality and humour are characteristics of camp: 'incongruity is the subject matter of camp, theatricality its style, and humor its strategy' ([1972] 2002: 442). As already argued, hairdressing, as a low status, feminised occupation, is at odds with traditional hegemonic masculinity. In these terms, then, the man in the salon is an incongruity, someone who incurs the risk of gender transgression. Of the theatricality of camp, Newton says: 'camp is style. Importance tends to shift from what a thing *is* to how it *looks*, from *what* is done to *how* it is done' ([1972] 2002: 443). The camp, she says, is a performer with an audience, 'this is its structure' ([1972] 2002: 443). It is 'suffused with the perception of "being as playing a role" and "life as theatre"' ([1972] 2002: 444). And finally, with respect to humour, she says 'camp is for fun: the aim of camp is to make an audience laugh' ([1972] 2002: 445).

In the three ways indicated below we can see how the technologies of camp were deployed within the salon as men reflected upon the incongruity of their presence in the salon, drawing on strategies of theatricality, audience, performance and style to engender the fun and sociability they anticipated on entering the salon every day – elements of the job they were unwilling to sacrifice for the security of managing or owning a salon.

Performing femininity

The work of a hairdresser was likened by many men (and women) in our study to a performance, a feeling exacerbated by the heavily scrutinised aesthetics of the salon. As Chapter 6 argued, for hairdressers being at work involved adopting a sociable, chatty and positive demeanour, whatever their underlying mood. Gordon Bristow (64), said 'you've got to perform for them as well. Part of my kind of character in hairdressing is making a women feel extremely comfortable'. The requirement for outgoing empathic responsiveness to women was seen by some participants to make men 'more feminine'. Maurice Lloyd (50), said:

> You spend your life working with women every day, you take on far more feminine characteristics, because you can relate to women, if you're working with women ... because even the straight men are very, very effeminate... You spend your life working with women, every day, you take on far more feminine characteristics.

Rex Tucker (41), married to Pauline, said 'I do admit I have a feminine side around certain peers of mine I do feel quite feminine but I don't let that bother me, they obviously don't mind the way I am with them,

I'm not saying I go into you know camp mode but they do make me feel quite feminine'. Asked what he meant by 'a feminine side', he replied, 'I don't do football, I've never done football so I don't know the first thing about football so I've got loads of friends who know about football and they all sit together chatting about football and this, that and other and, and I think what, you know I do cleaning at home they don't know what the meaning of the word is so, yeah, so it's, it's quite a weird sensation but I don't let it bother me, I think it did to start of with, I thought is it me what am I doing?'

This perspective was echoed by Ronnie Sheldon (63), married to Eileen, who said:

> I've got friends who are very friendly, who are probably more friendly than me and I'm not frightened of flirting with them, you know male friends, it's fine, they're comfortable with it, I'm comfortable with it, Eileen's comfortable with it, it's just, you know comfortable with the way that I am I suppose... I've never really been frightened about my feminine side, I suppose you can't go into hairdressing in the first place if you are, you can't be a butch hairdresser it's impossible, if you saw me doing shampoo and set, giving all this, you just can't do it you can't be a butch hairdresser there's no such thing, you can drink and womanise as much as you want but at the end of the day basically when you're working you are feminine.

As these and previous data indicate, then, becoming more 'feminised' is largely seen as a positive thing by hairdressers. The ability to relate to women, as both clients and colleagues, is felt to enable them to be more successful hairdressers, and more integrated socially into the salon environment. Furthermore, this feminisation of subjectivity can be experienced as a pleasurable and enjoyable experience. It would seem that for them, 'becoming' feminine, in the course of their everyday work and the social interactions this involves, was viewed as no threat to their self-identity as a man. These findings suggest that hairdressing does, indeed, seem to open spaces re-working the rules of what it means to be a man.

Performing camp

Data deriving from three months' participant observation in Raymond Cartwright's salon show him engaged in complex, contradictory, performances of masculinity, a style that exemplified Newton's definition of camp as 'a *philosophy* of transformation and incongruity' (italics added, 2002: 442). As its eponymous owner, Raymond was in his late fifties and his older female clientele were gradually dying off. His 'one-man' business was set in a row of shops in a working class area. With other local traders losing business, Raymond noted wistfully that, 'we're like Last of the Summer Wine here'. A colourful character amidst the greyness of the immediate locale, Raymond made frequent, fond references to his wife while holding court among his long-term clientele, for whom he 'did' a self-parodying camp masculinity that involved exaggerated gestures, hand flourishes and rolling of his eyes, and formed a focus for knowing banter between Raymond and his clients, even as he sustained it. Bemoaning his mother's choice of his name, Raymond said it made people think he was a 'puff', though 'nothing could be further from the truth'. 'Of course', his clientele would chorus, smiling knowingly at one another.

Conversation between Raymond and these women usually encompassed feminised topics such as food, body shape, diets and local gossip. However, when the male chiropodist who rented a room at the back of the salon (since his business too was in decline) met up with Raymond in quieter moments, the talk was all of garages, sinks, DIY, the repair of lean-tos and cars. Raymond thus contextually swapped between conversation and action that emphasised femininity, and 'manly' talk, so demonstrating a fluid conformity with, and subversion of, gendered boundaries.

For these older women, then, Raymond's 'camp' masculinity was outdated, a residue of an earlier era when public, cross-gender bodily proximity might require a boundary-making resource such as medical training or an alternative form of masculinity; a time when these women were young, perhaps unmarried, and close contact with a man might represent a more charged encounter. Yet, like Raymond, they now played upon the ambiguities of his everyday performances. To complicate such interactions further, Raymond's identity encompassed that of a carer for these women. For example, he would help older female clients into and out of the salon, and often undertook handyman activities in their homes. This 'care-work' addendum to his hairdressing role might draw on traditionally masculine electrical and DIY skills, yet took on more feminised dimensions in the salon where he removed women's coats, helped them into chairs, bought their lottery tickets and cigarettes and made their coffee. Through these practices, Raymond was able to assert himself, so enhancing his self-worth and status. In addition, his intentionally playful camp performances acted to transform the traditionally feminised activities of care into sources of power and control. Older women listened faithfully, if knowingly, to endless repeats of the same jokes; they indulged his anecdotes, flattered him and emphasised his importance by admitting their own reliance and need. 'What a treasure he is. What would we do without him?' they said, 'A service to the community is Raymond'.

Precarious performances

In contrast with Raymond Cartwright, Steve London (48) described shifting between the 'acts' he maintained for different clients. He said, 'if I'd got a right tasty twenty-one-year-old blonde in, I'd be completely, I'd be completely different to how I would be if I got a seventy-year-old biddy with no teeth in'. When asked whether his colleagues were aware of his shifting performances of masculinity, he said, 'Oh yeah, because they can see me face change, body language is completely different.'

Fieldnotes record Steve's slightly camp, stylised movements and conversational tone: his hand movements were flourishes, his walk was stereotypically 'mincing', and his voice full of gossip, innuendo and laughter. Female colleagues described him as very feminine in his choice of conversation: 'the way he talks he's like a woman in some ways, you know like, I don't mean the way he speaks as in his voice, I mean he likes a good gossip and a chat about everything and not a lot of men do that, they're not very open'.

That said, Steve found that his performances could undermine his heterosexual status in ways that he found problematic and as a result he would 'go the other way':

> But when I worked in salon I started getting guys coming in and asking me out. And then I'd go out and if I went out with a couple of mates I'd have guys coming up and asking, blokes coming up and talking to me because if they'd found out I was in hairdressing and because I'd got blonde hair and yeah, it did, it perturbed me a bit and that's, I thought, no, I'm not doing it, that's not me and I've never done it since in fact I'll go the other way ... I'll be more, not necessarily in salon, but I act more rough or macho and even when I go out now, me friends know that if anybody comes up to me or a girl comes up who I've never been introduced to I never tell them what I do... you get fed up with them saying well what should I do with my hair?

Conclusion

In this environment where, as participants put it, 'it's how you look and the whole visual', both masculinity and heterosexuality are exposed for scrutiny, making this a setting where, as our data suggest, men resist, appropriate and reinvent historically specific ways of 'doing' masculinity. 'Camp' constituted an important dimension of the emergence of hairdressing as an occupation where men have found employment. As Cox (1999) argues, as a response to modernity's re-formulation of femininity and the trend towards a pared-down aesthetic, 'camp' enabled women to 'bob' their hair without entering into problematic cross-gender bodily proximities. Lindsay's (2004) Australian data revealed hairdressing as a low status, working class occupation, undertaken predominantly by young women prior to marriage and parenthood, and by young men yet to settle into a profession. However, where her data and ours intersect is in accounts of particular younger men who frame hairdressing as a technical skill to be developed and embraced, an identity they define in opposition to contemporary stereotypes of the 'party-animal' hairdresser. Gender then meshes with class differences, the cult of the celebrity (male) hairdresser, initiated by camp, media personalities, such as Mr Teasie Weasie, now being fostered internationally by men such as Nicky Clarke and John Barrett, for whom that particular performance of masculinity is no longer relevant. However, for less ambitious men, hairdressing brings the benefits of an enjoyably social environment where status differences are less evident, yet where physical stamina and long-term economic stability are always at potential risk, where differences of class are less likely to be transcended.

11
Embodying Mundane and Life Course Transitions

This chapter brings together the issues raised in Chapters 8–10, drawing on theoretical models of transition which allow its embodied implications for identity to be highlighted. In his work on rites of passage, Van Gennep ([1908] 1960) offered the schema of a three-stage process which enables changes to take place within an otherwise stable 'society'. Written from a functionalist perspective, his schema nonetheless enabled subsequent work on the liminal or middle stage of a rite of passage, a time and place within which identities can be ritually dismantled and others formed (Turner, 1969, 1974). The concept of liminality has been used to illuminate less obviously 'ritual' processes, but the spatio-temporal positioning of the body, in both a material and social sense, remains core to the scope of this model to explain identity transitions and the ways in which distinctions between individuals, as members of different social categories, come into being (Billington et al., 1998: 58–83; Hockey and James, 2003).

Data from work among men in all three occupational categories show the strategic creation of spatio-temporal distances, buffer zones and solitude, which can be seen to enable the transition between work and home-based identities. Described by men as a way of sustaining a sense of oneself as an individual, these liminal or buffer times and places are also key to a man's 'mobility', his capacity to 'fit into' different social environments. Moreover, as the later sections of this chapter describe, his capacity to manage embodied transitions into different age-based social categories. Time, place and the body are therefore key to identification. However, as the data presented here reveal, it is in relation to embodied others – partners, children, work colleagues of different ages – that spatio-temporal materialities come to resource mundane and life course transitions.

Home/work

Chapters 3 and 4 introduced discussion of the relationship between home and work as apparently separate environments – Chapter 4 highlighting the ragged nature of the boundary between them, along with men and women's attempts to bring a lived boundary into line with the home/work relationship as imagined. Here we develop these themes, drawing on data to show how understandings of the nature of home and work inform the embodiment of gendered identities. As our participants described, time and space were important resources in managing their twin identities, as either hairdressers, estate agents or firefighters – *and* members of a family or friendship group. Relationality and autonomy are important considerations here, elements of identification lived out in embodied, spatio-temporal contexts. Here, distances between home and work might constitute a liminal period within the passage between home and work-based identities; and differences between people, whether one's colleagues or one's own remembered self, informed the process of identification.

We can begin by noting that men's entanglements with colleagues, partners, children, friends and other family members were by no means circumscribed by the boundaries between home and work. Men in hairdressing, for example, both young and old, often worked alongside a female partner in the salon. Giving the client exclusive attention was important for the potential transformation they might achieve (see Chapter 10) and this required distance between partners – or, indeed, friends. Pauline Tucker who worked alongside her partner Rex (41), explained how this might operate in practice:

> we one-to-one with us clients really. Sometimes if he's at side of me and we're working, we'll all have a bit of a banter, and sometimes it can get a little bit domestic, you know and, you know and sometimes the clients don't help because the clients'll wind it up a little bit more.

Other entanglements were evidenced in the complex interleaving of partners' timetables. Ceri Treadwell, lawyer and partner of firefighter Dominic Treadwell (44), was anticipating that her work would involve:

> night time call out and evenings and weekends … and with Pete's shifts … it's just going to be like boot camp … you know Lucy, the baby you know calendar in and out, in and out you know so we don't see much of each other really when I'm working.

Rather than childcare arrangements, Nigel Saltash (50), a firefighter nearing retirement, discussed attempts to integrate the couple's divergent leisure timetables:

> We try, we try and go out for a meal once a week. But quite a lot you can't because she, and she goes dancing on a Wednesday night, so I'm Tuesday and Thursday, well Tuesday, Wednesday, Thursday's out and if it just happens that I'm on nights Friday and Saturday.

Relationality thus bound partners in ways that transcended the boundary between home and work, sometimes in ways they welcomed – for example, when shift work and part-time work combined to give each of them time to enjoy home and leisure on their own; sometimes, as these data indicate, more problematically as domestic and work-related agendas collided. This brings us to identification's other aspect, the contribution of spatio-temporal *distance* to men's transitions between identities. Here, relationships are suspended as participants sought time and space out with the categories of, for example, 'hairdresser', 'husband' or 'father'. Thus, many men described creating episodes which they experienced as neither work nor home time – important liminal periods during which they made transitions between different dimensions of their identities. As the data indicate, we can understand the creation of these spatio-temporal buffer zones as themselves constitutive of the living out of masculinity. In other words, these periods do not simply allow masculinity to be produced or inhabited; they are, themselves, intrinsic to its reproduction in that men had the resources to spend time alone in a pub or to wander the farther reaches of the large gardens they had been able to purchase.

Perry Sanford, for example, a 45-year-old salon owner, did enjoy being known throughout the city for his success as a hairdresser:

> to my peers yes, because it gives me some credibility, because I always knew that whatever I was going to do, I wanted to be bloody good at it and so the only way you can judge that is by how busy you are with the general public and the, how your peers perceive you.

However, he went on to say:

> [B]ut outside of, outside of the hairdressing world, when I'm outside of the salon, I like the anonymity ... a lot of hairdresser would probably go, if they were going for a drink they would probably go to bars, I will go to the Bass pub ... I'll go there and sit quietly because I just

want, I want to be somewhere that's good but not the mass appeal, I just want to sit, bit of quiet time, if I want to talk I will do, I don't, I don't want to have ... I think it's a consequence of the job ... at the end of the day when there's so many people pulling and one or two ... it's an automatic situation to feel that you're drained, just go and recharge as we all do, so I think it's a consequence of the job, on a daily basis as opposed to perhaps another job where you may not be involved with the public.

Perry went on to say that his previous failure to distance himself from work had contributed to two divorces, events he very much regretted.

Patrick Valentine (28) owns the salon that he and his partner work in. They have young children and he finds the limited time he has with them frustrating. That said, he still generates time that is neither work nor home time when he is finding the business difficult:

Usually if it's a really, really bad problem and I feel really anxious about it, I'll, I'd go out first anyway after work, I won't go straight home, I mean I don't go drinking lager, I do, I'd go for a coffee and then I'd go, I'd go home and usually I've had time to you know that extra half an hour forty five minutes gives me enough time to chill out a bit because I am on, I'm working on this like speed right up until I leave work so when I get home I have to have at least half an hour to calm down anyway .. And Anna's the same when she's been working, 'cos you talk that much all day I haven't got anything else to say you know.

The importance of time apart from both work and home was also evident in Patrick's description of his leisure pursuit, scuba diving:

It's a nice way of relaxing you know, even though it's an adventure sport it's, you can't hear anybody, you know it's so peaceful under water.

Firefighter John Smith (26) spoke similarly of one of his leisure pursuits, climbing:

Climbing is brilliant out on the rocks and stuff, its good inside for training, because you can do a lot more of it, get fit but its brilliant just to get out I just like to cycle up there ... get away from it all. It's nice.

For Mickey Smith (26), the importance of non-relational time was also evident in the boundary time he claimed between home and work. Prior to a shift he would retreat from everyone around him for 'Mickey chill time'. His partner, Chloe, explained:

> He'll sometimes cycle up to Staunton Clough and climb by himself which I think is, one, highly dangerous in case he falls off and two, quite it must be a Mickey time thing ... did he tell you about Mickey chill time? Before a shift say if he's got a day before he starts a night and he could've been doing nothing all day, he could've been watching the television all day, come four o'clock 'Mickey chill time', everything stops and he'll just watch some more television in that case but if he's been out with his friends and the group finds it, like all our friends and it's a phrase that's used, 'oh I need some Mickey chill time', even if he's been doing something like having a drink round somebody's house, 'I've got to go, I've got to go, four o'clock Mickey chill time' because he needs that space between the end of his life and start of his work. He needs that hour where he does nothing and mentally prepares himself.

Comparing Mickey and Chloe's accounts reveals that for him coupledom was somewhat problematic. 'I do just like my own time', he said, describing her need for company compared with his fulfilment of this need among fellow firefighters. Tension between them surfaces when, albeit humorously, Chloe describes 'Mickey chill time' as 'an absolute farce'. Mickey, perhaps as result of teasing from Chloe and his friends, made no mention of 'Mickey chill time' in his interview.

Like Perry Sanford and Patrick Valentine, Chrissie Hardwick, partner of 58-year-old estate agent, Brett Hardwick, described the pressures of running a business. Again a man uses a spatio-temporal resource he owned, in order to create a betwixt and between, liminal period. Chrissie said:

> There's lots of pressures aren't there when you're running a business for someone else ... uptight and frazzled ... he'd come in and have to go out in the garden and stroll round and do something to let off steam, had an argument or you know because you're, you know what you want to do is not always what other people want to do and there's just conflicts.

Forty-one-year old estate agent Phil Cruikshank's partner, Nicola, described Phil undertaking a similar, albeit temporally brief, strategy for moving between identities. While she preferred not to discuss her work problems at home, if she did raise something she found that:

> he really annoys me that when he comes home, [laughs] he's like, he just walks straight past us and I'll just be in the middle of telling him something and he walks upstairs and he takes off his suit.

Only when Phil has made his transition from estate agent to partner will he engage in appropriate interaction with Nicola.

The removal of the suit was key to many estate agents' identity transitions. For example, semi-retired Tony Flatt (54) said:

> I had to get out of my suit the second I came in through the door, reaching for gin glass, [laughs] you know the drive home was part of the process and the getting out of the suit, the gin and tonic and then finally relaxing.

His boundary setting was, however, fragile and he went on:

> But very often I would wake up in the night and write notes to myself, which is pathetic but I couldn't go to sleep not knowing there was a note pad and a pen beside the bed, so if I woke up I could write notes.

These data show the ways in which embodied, spatio-temporally located practices can constitute a liminal or buffer period between home and work. In some cases this concerns the transition between work and home, the shedding of work-related preoccupations; in others it enables men to actively draw together the resources which coalesce in their work-based identity. In some cases this kind of distance can be difficult to achieve, for example, when a couple live and work together, and, as Chapter 4 demonstrated, the home/work boundary can itself prove hard to establish and sustain. In particular, however, it is striking that these men were not describing a relatively passive participation in shared, after-work leisure; instead their agency is evident as they actively sought opportunities to re-create themselves in ways that then enabled an altered identity to be lived out. Solitude was often embraced before a new sociality was entered into.

Life course transitions

This section develops the themes of relationality and distance as ways of intepreting men's experience of transition. Alongside the spatio-temporal transitions described in the previous section, we address men's embodied transitions between age-based identities across the life course. First, we consider how participants' understandings and experience of their bodies can be made sense of in terms of relations of similarity and difference within processes of identification. In addition, however, we examine men's responses to what they described as the paradoxical *inevitability* of exercise and diet which they must, nonetheless, exercise agency in pursuing. Thus, while men may, for example, exercise with friends or partners, their efforts were directed towards distancing or protecting themselves from what they otherwise see as the intractable toll of genetic legacies and work-related bodily stresses. In these processes of relatedness and distancing, the workplace and the family emerge as key resources mobilised by men in managing life course transitions.

When hairdresser Brendan Amies (37) described how he viewed his appearance as he grew into his 30s, he said:

> I'm probably a lot wackier and you know striving for a bit of individualism, but not being too like out there [laughs].

This *individualism* was, however, within the context of:

> young, creative people coming through and getting a name for themselves and I suppose even though if you grow older with your clients, you know they're growing old with you, you're getting older you've still got that mentally in your head, you would still have that young artistic flow coming through and you're ... thinking that if you get older, people might stop coming to you and go to the new younger stylist that's around so, whether mentally you try and to keep yourself looking younger whereby wearing trendier clothes that probably are too trendy for your age really but you just want to keep yourself with a younger look generally.

Sue Hodges, the long-term landlady of Andy Hathaway (50), also cited the pressure of a younger cohort who contributed to a hairdresser's sense of growing older:

> [For] an older hairdresser like Andy, it's very difficult and will be as time goes on ... the public perception is to come into a salon and find all these glitzy young people who are waiting on your every client and do your hair.

Gordon Bristow (64) similarly referred to the youth-oriented nature of his business, pointing out that:

> I mean at 64 and still having young girls come to me, to me that's just amazing, I honestly thought that come 40, nobody would ever want to.

While he described *dressing* far more soberly now that he was older, he expressed ambivalence when it came to ageing and hairstyles, saying:

> I've never changed my image, never, in my eyes, regarding this changing of images, you're expected indirectly to represent the fashion at the moment, short back and sides, I mean I've still got my droopy seventies moustache and my long Mick Jagger hair.

Key to the status of these data are the words *in my eyes*, a phrase which suggests some mismatch between Gordon's more private experience of embodiment and his awareness of its public perception.

While younger colleagues and clients were key to the relational dimensions of growing older, both work and family could be resources mobilised as rationalisations for current or future concerns about ageing, illness and death for men of all ages. Ceri Treadwell, partner of firefighter Dominic Treadwell (44) said:

> It really bothers him because he's got he's quite arthritic in his knees and his feet and his mum's very arthritic and he gets very down about it, because he'll says you know, I'm going to be just like my mum.

Young firefighter Mickey Smith (26) cited his father's sudden death as already a source of personal anxiety:

> He was a big strong bloke as well, never had any health problems in his life and then he just gets took out, its weird ... I live reasonably healthy anyway, I mean I started trying to cook more fruit and veg and stuff like that, eat less rubbish, but he worked, he worked in the steelworks for most of his life, well a lot of it and apparently worked with some really nasty material ... so in a way I'm worried because he did die young, but I don't think its genetic necessarily, I think it could have been his circumstances at work.

Another firefighter, Wesley True (46), reflected on workplace exposure to death and its intersection with one's own ageing process:

> when you're younger it doesn't bother you as much, as you get older it bothers you more ... because when you're young you think you're, well nothing can hurt you, you know you're immortal type thing, that'll never happen to me, I'm not bothered about that, bit macho, as you get older and you've got children you see things and things happen to other people and you think well it could happen to me, and when you see it's somebody's family, it hurts more.

Occupational exposure to death was not confined to firefighters. Talking of the importance of making the best of mid-life, estate agent Patrick Thompson (57) recollected:

> I had a house to sell, 69-year-old chap, stayed at home, looked after his 90 plus year old mother for God knows how many years, he liked travel and he liked photography, very keen amateur photographer and the mother died, 'oh, I can travel at long last', within six months, gallstones and he dropped dead.

In these examples, then, relationality operates as a mechanism through which men generate a sense of their embodied health status, their vulnerability to accident or sudden death. Whether through engagement with family members or those encountered at work, other people play a key role within an individual's sense of identity across time.

To distance oneself from threats of these kinds, indeed, to disrupt the ageing process itself, men exercised agency. Pauline Tucker said of her partner, hairdresser Rex (41):

> He does go to the gym, he works out three times a week ... I think that's come really after he was forty, I think you know to most people you hit 40 and you think I need to be doing something'

Through swimming, older estate agent, Patrick Thompson (57), actively took on the challenge he perceived in younger people, saying:

> [W]hat's pleasing I get in that pool and much younger blokes than me get in there and they think 'Ah, I'm going to thrash this old bastard', you know ... up one length, and then five lengths later I'm still

going strong and there they are lingering down in the shallow end or whatever, I've overhauled them.

Firefighter Brian Underwood (41) was similarly forthright about his commitment to cycling: 'I'm a complete fitness freak', he asserted. Brian envisaged a future which would always include cycling because of its *low impact* upon the body:

> I can't see there ever becoming a point (when he would give up cycling), I'll be a doddering old fool you know ... I've been to France and I've seen guys that you know when you drive past them you look at them and my God he's looks about 90 and he's still on a bike, but there's no reason why not, you know.

Conclusion

This chapter has explored the scope of a rites of passage schema (Van Gennep [1908] 1960; Turner, 1969) to help think theoretically about the implications for identity of transitions between home and work and between different phases of the life course. Two dimensions of this process have been explored: first, the centrality of relationality to apparently individual negotiations of time and place, expressed in the ways in which relationships transcend but also inform the boundary between domestic and occupational spheres; second, the temporary suspension of relationships which bind men into occupational and domestic identities. By subsequently considering the elements of relationality and autonomy with respect to life course transitions, the chapter has shown how other people inform men's perceptions of their own embodied experience, both present and future – and, importantly, how men exercise agency in overcoming what might seem to be the inevitabilities of family patterns of illness or the arbitrariness of sudden death.

Part III
Emotionality, Masculinity and Gender

12
Masculinity and Emotionality

Introduction

In Chapter 7 we focused on the body, but made it clear that bodies and emotions cannot, for various reasons, be separated, despite the persistence of post-Enlightenment dualistic models of the mind/body split. As Hockey et al. (2007) argue, for example, their interviewees often used *either* a romantic *or* a carnal discourse of heterosexual sex. The separation of bodily life from emotional subjectivity can thus be seen as a persistent but false dichotomy, since the body and emotions are inextricably linked. Lupton (1998) observes that physical manifestations of an unbalanced emotional state are not a modern concern, but can be dated back to the Early Modern period. During that period, there was little social pressure for self-restraint, and emotional imbalances were believed to lead to illness or certain personality traits, hence the use of leeches, for example, to balance 'humoral' fluids, black bile, yellow bile, blood and phlegm.

From the sixteenth century onwards, however, there came increasing pressure to regulate and civilise the body. Lupton observes that 'there emerged a conflation of bodily discipline with the disciplined self: without disciplining the body, the self would become unruly' (1998: 75). The Enlightenment, thus, heralded a period during which emotions were seen as irrational and the enemy of reason. This is reflected later, in the horror of the nineteenth century, Victorian bourgeoisie when presented with the bodies of the working classes, the sick and the 'fallen' whose boundaries were not well contained (Walkowitz, 1980). Although 'Body McCarthyism', the fear of contamination through bodily contact with those defined as 'Other', persists, particularly following the advent of HIV/AIDS and the consequent preoccupation with bodily fluids and potential damage to our immune systems, the situation regarding our emotional selves is rather more complex (Lupton, 1998: 86).

Within contemporary society, to be 'in touch' with one's emotions is seen to be important, but perhaps even more crucial is the ability to *manage* our emotions effectively, preventing them from becoming troublesome in our everyday lives. As Seidler (2006) argues, therapeutic models which adopt a 'confessional' approach to the disclosure and acknowledgement of emotions have become popularised, the focus being to ensure that once issues are addressed, emotions are appropriately managed, 'tied off' and made 'safe'. Indeed, as Hubbard (2005) argues, this kind of emotional self management has become an aspect of the processes through which selfhood is constructed, gender being one of the socio-cultural circumstances he cites as important: 'it has often been noted that men and women manage their emotional selves very differently, with men encouraged to repress particular emotions that are associated with vulnerability rather than strength' (Hubbard, 2005: 121). In relation to our concerns here, therefore, we were interested in finding out whether, in practice, men did attempt to manage and control their emotions, both within and across different public and private spheres, and if their diverse experiences confounded or confirmed notions of the 'unemotional' or 'inarticulate male' as someone who lacks emotional resources and skills.

In addressing these questions, this section provides a unique contribution to these debates in a discussion of new empirical evidence presented in Chapters 13–16. Together they detail the changes (or their lack) in relation to men's emotional lives at home and at work. We therefore ask what such evidence reveals about the everyday practices of men engaged in emotional labour, for example, in sharing intimacies within familial, romantic and peer relationships, as well as in friendships and with work colleagues. This chapter now goes on to review work in general on men, masculinity and the emotions. It is followed by a section on the heterosexual 'couple' in relation to their emotional lives specifically, given that heterosexuality is a key organizing principle for many of the men (and women) in our study, and this leads into a section on men and emotions in the workplace. Finally, the chapter provides a discussion of intimacy, trust and vulnerability and of male friendships in a specific leisure context, that of the 'extreme' sport of rock climbing, which sheds light on the data we use in subsequent chapters in this section.

Men and emotions

What exactly do we know about men's intimate, personal lives, especially, for our purposes, those in relation to their occupations and domestic, family lives? Indeed, how do men conceive of their own, emotional working and private life? As we have previously argued (Hockey et al., 2007), popular and gendered assumptions about 'men's emotional inarticulacy' (Rutherford, 1992; Lupton, 1998) can be seen to be reflected in the lack of sociological attention given to the emotional dimensions of men's experiences of heterosexuality. In a wider context, it has been identified that, in general terms, masculinity has been seen recently as 'troubled': men have lost their traditional occupational identities and, therefore, a 'breadwinner' role within households (Connell, 2005). Seidler (1989, 1992) has stressed that men have had to deal with the consequences of their emotional alienation from themselves. He has also noted their painful struggle for a suitable 'emotional language'.

However, some theorists are sceptical of the idea or even existence of the notion of a 'masculinity crisis' which theorists such as Horrocks (1994) contend. For others, the scope for change represented by such a crisis is doubtful. McMahon (1999), for example, has asked why gender relations appear resistant to change, despite the apparent feminisation of men in the public sphere and, indeed, the widespread enthusiasm for such a shift. He argues that women continue to care for men, both in body and soul, and that the notion that men have fundamentally changed is very much exaggerated. The emotionally inarticulate male may now be asked to take more emotional responsibility for himself and others, but despite this, there are authors who have felt that 'Men's deafening silence about their own sexuality as opposed to the objects of their desire continues' (Middleton, 1992). Indeed, elsewhere, (Robinson, 1996), it was argued that men can emphasise the 'male wounded psyche' at the expense of analysing male power and privilege.

Traditionally, men have been seen in masculine ways: to 'master' and control fear in an instrumental fashion, or, to manage socially unacceptable and unruly emotions. As noted, Seidler (2007), for example, argues: 'Through an identification of masculinity with "self-control" within diverse cultural settings, men learn to relate to particular emotions as signs of weakness and so as threats to their male identities' (2007, 9). In earlier work, Seidler (1992) posits that men learn to leave their emotional histories behind them and, therefore, run the risk of being unwittingly controlled by a history that many of them have not yet come to terms with. Men strive for control, in work, in relationships, as fathers, for example, but such satisfaction is always only partial and short lived. Seidler (2009) also asserts that different masculinities mean men have very diverse ways of relating to emotional lives. Men learn to control their emotions so as not to show vulnerability, and many men 'perform' masculinity to hide any inner turmoil they may be facing, from other people. Their masculinity may be, then, all they have as a way of claiming self-esteem. Nonetheless Seidler (1998) and Williams (2001) describe men's increasing propensity to take responsibility for, and, we would add, reflect publically on their emotional lives, as the men in our study have done.

Moreover, Whitehead (2002) argues that we need to move beyond the dualism we describe, one which sees emotion, or its acceptance at least, as exclusively a female preserve, and men as being emotionally incompetent or even repressed. This is not least because such a view stereotypes women as being associated with irrationality and emotion, not reason and rationality. However, we also need to go beyond a consideration of men and emotion which has emerged, in large part, from the literature defined as 'pro-feminist' men's accounts of the repressed male psyche (see Robinson, 1996, for a discussion of this tendency and the implications of men taking such a position for feminism and gendered relationships). As Whitehead notes, 'Despite the overwhelming evidence of many men's emotional blockages, it would be both simplistic and misleading to assume that all men are either lacking the emotional depths apparently available to women or are overly emotional when it comes to aggressive and violent expression. In short, as Hearn puts it, "we should not presume men to be either too much in control or too much out of control of themselves"' (2002, p. 177).

Furthermore, while authors such as Williams (2001) have pointed to such research which represents men as relatively unemotional and incapable of making inter-subjective connections, Hearn (1993) in contrast, has argued that sites such as the male-dominated workplace are emotionalised through the controlling of other people's emotions – and the emotion of controlling 'emotional labour' (Hochschild, 1983). Alternatively, in Robinson et al. (2007), we have argued that many forms of masculinity can now, at one level, be seen to constitute emotional expressiveness. Witness, for example, the public tears of sportsmen or the raw anger of campaigners for organisations such as 'Fathers 4 Justice' in the UK. In terms of 'undoing' gender, then, should this be seen as a chosen form of feminisation, or as Boscagli (1992) argues, evidence of men's power and a symptom of anxiety in a time of crisis?

Such analyses have led a number of theorists, including Connell (2000, 2005), to argue that a consideration of emotional relations in the context of masculinity, is a fundamentally new direction in theory and research. Seidler (2009), for instance, argues that the male identities which have emerged from diasporic and transnational migrations mean we need new ways of thinking about the relationship between men, bodies and emotional lives and the complex male identities which have thus emerged. Also, he critiques Connell's notion that, in relation to hegemonic masculinity, women's oppression is structural but men's 'pain' is simply personal. This, he says, creates too general a gendered distinction and does not allow for an examination of men's emotional lives being structured through relations of power, that operate through class, race, ethnic and sexual differences. This mirrors the recent interest in emotion in social theory more generally and the insights of feminism in connecting heterosexuality to men's position of social dominance. With Hockey et al. (2007), we conclude that we still, vitally, need empirical evidence in detailing the changes (or even lack of them), in relation to the supposedly natural, intimate and hidden character of gendered, heterosexual relationships.

Specifically here, in the context of public and private masculinities, what does our empirical evidence reveal about the everyday practices of men, such as fire fighters, who are engaged in activities where emotions such as fear and trust are necessarily, at times, managed and controlled in 'extreme' situations? Further, how are issues of intimacy dealt with in male friendships? What then does this reveal about how their emotions are handled in more 'mundane' contexts, for instance in terms of their everyday heterosexual relationships, and indeed, over the life course? Seidler (2009) has argued that a post modern culture recognizes that the fragmentation of identities can open up 'new spaces' but that these identities are not easily constructed and further, that we need question the view that 'conflicts between different spheres of life are easily handled' (2007, 12). It is this issue of men 'handling' different spheres of both public and private life, particularly in relation to their emotional and intimate lives, that we examine in the rest of this chapter.

Intimacy and emotion in private

In relation to the private sphere, and where, in our study, many of our participants had a long-term heterosexual partner, we were interested in the way men dealt with their emotions and intimacy in that sphere, and particularly in terms of their transitioning each day from the public world of work into families and relationships in their roles as fathers and partners. Bringing a feminist perspective to bear on Giddens' (1992) notion of the pure relationship, Jamieson (1998), in her own empirical study of gendered relationships, takes a historical view, and, further, does not assume either the nature or the desirability of intimacy. She argues that though some change is occurring in this respect, the 'doing' of intimacy is not the central organising axis in women's and men's private lives (see Hockey et al., 2007).

Another argument is put forward by Kerfoot (1999) who, in suggesting that men cannot 'let go' in relationships, also contends that men cannot connect with others. Whitehead (2002), in turn, writes '[w]ays of being a man and exhibiting masculinity intrude into men's experiences and displays of intimacy, potentially rendering it synthetic, strategic or to be avoided' (2002: 173). Men, from this perspective, are seen to *manage* rather than fully experience emotional situations, a perspective which can be extended to the question of their relationships and friendships with other men. Additionally, as Whitehead notes, a number of writers on masculinity have argued that men both fear and avoid the unscripted response and uncontrollable situation: 'In seeking to control the uncertainty that might be generated by emotional intimacy, many men – consciously or otherwise – reach for conventional practices and behaviours of stereotypical masculinity. Here, masculinity becomes a means of rendering social relations manageable, not a means for disclosing intimacies' (2002: 174).

The development of new family forms, such as step-families, single parent and same sex families, are important here and have led to claims that the late twentieth century has seen the democratisation of the personal domain (Hockey et al., 2007). Arguably, this has produced shifts in the way family and relationships have been theorised in terms of intimacy and the emotions, yet while the practical and economic dimensions of heterosexual relationships have been prioritised within sociological studies of marriage and the family (VanEvery, 1996: 40), the emotional experience of contemporary heterosexuality still remains opaque (Jackson, 1999). Nonetheless, work is starting to emerge on these aspects of heterosexuality; for example, Johnson and Lawler (2005) present arguments surrounding the interaction of romantic love and class in heterosexual relationships and Johnson (2005) addresses debates around heterosexuality as identity and practice in relation to love relationships. In contrast with psychologists and psychiatrists for whom the psyche has been a privileged domain, sociologists have drawn more on social constructionist theories of emotion. This tendency is being re-addressed more recently in work on emotion. For example, Lupton (1998) explores the cultural discourses of emotion which see men's and women's affective lives as different, and looks at the new models of masculinity that men have adopted.

Asserting the emergence of radical shifts in intimate relations, Giddens (1992) maintains that these result from the coming together of diverse social processes, including those between couples and within families. The notion that the self now constitutes a 'reflexive project' is key to these arguments. This, in Giddens' view, enables more democratic relations in the private sphere. However, alongside the critique that Giddens ignores the reflexivity of much earlier generations (Jenkins, 2004), feminists have problematised his broad brush approaches to gender relations; Jamieson, for example, argues that 'Giddens's vision of a possible future draws selectively from the range of available evidence and only briefly discusses aspects of the wider context which perpetuate inequalities between men and women' (1998: 40).

Jamieson (1998), nonetheless, views the post/modern family as an increasingly self-contained unit, relying less and less upon the wider kinship and support networks that had characterised pre-industrial life. The implications for women have, therefore, been quite pronounced in that they have become increasingly isolated within their relationships. Arguably, such isolation has been buttressed to some degree by the emergence of the 'pure relationship' (Giddens, 1992) and the growing emphasis on 'disclosing intimacy' (Jamieson, 1998) which focuses the attention of the couple on each other as both confidante and friend, creating expectations of empathy, communication and understanding. These are phenomena most closely associated with the post-1960s period, a time associated with rising divorce rates. Mansfield and Collard (1988), in their study of 60 newly-wed couples reveal that the heady experience of 'falling in love' soon gives way to the cold reality that couples often seek incompatible goals in marriage. They observe: '[m]ost (though not all men) seek a *life in common* with their wives, a home life, a physical and psychological base; somewhere to set out from and return to' while wives sought *a common life* with an empathetic partner ... a close exchange of intimacy which would make them feel valued as a person not just a wife' (1988: 178–9).

Duncombe and Marsden similarly observe that:

> there is various evidence to suggest that conflict arises because individuals' capacities to express emotion are socially regulated or 'managed' in such a way that men and women have a differing ability or

willingness to think and talk in terms of 'love' and 'intimacy' and to make the emotional effort which appears (to many women at least) necessary to sustain close heterosexual relationships.

(1993: 221)

Consequently, they question how far men can and should change emotionally in the ways that many women now appear to demand.

No longer a somewhat peripheral aspect of heterosexual relations, emotions; their management and their expression of them therefore, emerge as central to the contemporary institution of heterosexuality. The more emotional, intimate aspects of heterosexuality as currently lived or aspired to, thus require urgent investigation by sociologists tuned to the inter-subjective nature of social institutions such as 'family', 'coupledom' or 'marriage'. And these issues find resonance in our data, in that men are seen to be able to perform in the public sphere, in their chosen occupation, sometimes because of the domestic tasks women still continue to undertake. These may sometimes occur alongside tasks undertaken on behalf of their partner's work, for example, 'balancing the books' or accompanying them on trips to suppliers, but also because of the emotional labour undertaken by women regarding children and their own and other family relationships, for example.

In relation to the private sphere and its interaction with work, Seidler (2007) also points out that '[w]ithin the disciplines of a globalized economy men can no longer expect to identify with work as a lifetime career' (16). As well as working long hours, thus producing tension in the private sphere of relationships and the family, this can lead to a gendered emotional distance in the domestic sphere between couples. But this realization also entails, as we are doing here, 'theoretically engaging in new ways with issues of masculinities and emotional lives' (2007: 17).

Specifically in relation to the transition of men's emotional lives across spheres, and the pervasiveness of a feminised model of what emotionality is, or should be about, Whitehead (2002) explores issues around men, masculinities, intimacy and the emotions through focusing on a problematization of the public/private divide, particularly in relation to work in comparison to home life. He concludes that feelings of love and anxiety are not easily abandoned as men move between home and work. Similarly, intimate relations are not produced solely in the private world. However, he notes that this public/private dualism has not been that much explored in relation to areas such as leisure, something that is addressed later in the chapter in relation to research that has been carried out by Robinson (2008) on the 'extreme' sport of rock climbing. This examines issues common to men in sporting, home and work contexts, that is, those of trust, vulnerability and male friendships. Before that, however, we consider how men at work, with respect to their emotional performances and conduct, have been theorised.

Men, emotion and work

Jackson (2003), in relation to his previous occupation, describes how the shattering of a dream of being a star academic performer led to his physical and emotional breakdown: 'In this rawer, more exposed state, I could no longer go on hiding my emotional distress in workaholic habits and running away from my pain' (Jackson, 2003: p. 74).

Relationships such as this, between emotion, its management and the workplace, have attracted considerable sociological attention, as we go on to outline. Hearn (1993) has argued that male-dominated workplaces are emotionalised through the controlling of others' emotions and the emotion of controlling emotion labour. This is to sideline occupations which are arguably becoming more feminised, such as estate agency, and those which are already feminised, like hairdressing. Bagilhole and Cross (2006) show that, for some men, traditionally feminine traits such as the ability to show emotion are also aspects of their working lives which they value: 'you learn, you talk about your soap operas, your family a bit more' p. 43 (psychiatric nurse). We therefore ask whether this should this be seen as a chosen form of feminisation, or, as Boscagli (1992) asserts, evidence of men's power and a symptom of male anxiety in a time of crisis? It is too simplistic to assume that men's 'feminisation' of their emotions in occupational contexts (and beyond) is either about a new way of exerting power over women, or making money in the capitalist marketplace by manipulating emotions. It could be argued that many men feel more comfortable showing their emotions, encountering less stigma in doing so, and it could also be argued that men have always showed emotion, but in ways that have not been directly comparable with women. As a result, these expressions have been sidelined in that emotionality has gradually become feminised. As the case of Raymond, our hairdresser, shows, the relationship between masculinity, emotion and care crystallises in unexpected ways (Chapter 10).

The emotional aspects of men's work performances have also emerged in our research with estate agents and firefighters. Among estate agents, the careful management of clients' emotions and the cultivation of good personal rapport are key resources for securing business. As Chapter 8 describes, estate agents invest emotional labour in communicating, providing services or listening to a client's problems, subtly altering their demeanour for different types of client. This effort takes place in a gendered context where power relations are still present, and where emotions can be manipulated to produce advantage. There is a common perception among estate agents that this emotional work is something that woman are better at, and that this 'explains' women's rise in the profession. Similarly, male firefighters will note that women can shine in certain aspects of the job, usually those requiring 'feminine' empathy for victims and a caring touch. Despite these stereotyped perceptions about men, women and emotion, estate agents and firefighters are daily engaged in the application of emotion to work tasks and their success at the job would appear to partly rest on this. As Walker (1994) discusses in her work on men's friendship, men may articulate the belief that women are better at emotion and inter-personal relationships, while still displaying proficiency in securing intimacy within friendship. Our chosen methods and data suggest that looking at actual practice can reveal a far more subtle picture than interviews alone would suggest.

As we discuss in Chapters 8, 9, 13 and 14, being a fire-fighter, for example, involves experiencing and managing a range of emotions such as excitement, nervousness and disgust, while also actively excluding, or containing, certain emotions, such as empathy. Many fire-fighters report that seeing victims or fatalities of fires and accidents is not always upsetting; not knowing the victims personally means that men and women are able to disengage themselves to get the job done. However, emotionally distancing oneself from victims is a technique that does not always work, and many men have reported attending incidents that have stayed with them, or which have upset them more than usual. The emotional 'fallout' from incidents is often managed as a group, with many watches resorting to black humour and in-depth discussion after the event to comes to terms with distressing experiences. Some men also rely on their partners to talk over upsetting incidents, perhaps more than they admit to their colleagues (and this is where our interviews with female partners have been revealing). Our methodological stance, which looks at men at work and at home, and which takes into account a female perspective on their lives, has thus allowed us to get behind some of the established discourses surrounding men and their jobs, and beyond what men say themselves. This has revealed the men we have studied as more rounded individuals.

The literature concerning men in feminised occupations, introduced in Chapter 2, has pointed out that men, as well as accessing possible advantages, may also experience ambivalence in negotiating a masculine identity in a 'woman's world'. What Simpson (2005) calls 'role strain', can emerge from internal and external negative perceptions. It would appear that common discourses about the gendered nature of certain occupations and their work practices form a framework within which men must reflect upon their individual role and status and negotiate a masculine sense of self. As Lupton (2000) argues, this process may involve drawing on the positive feminised aspects of the work to create a sense of self, or downplaying masculinity's traditional association with domination and control. As Simpson (2005) shows, men may manage 'role strain' by giving out selective representations of what their work entails, highlighting its masculinised elements. What these arguments show is that 'men's reasoning about female-dominated work is multi-faceted and at times contradictory' (Bagilhole and Cross, 2006: p. 46).

For example, our data suggest that men working as hairdressers must negotiate sets of gendered expectations to create a viable masculine identity with an emphasis on their professionalism, their technical skill and prowess, as well as conforming with the aesthetic standards associated with the profession. This raises problems as they age, as we examine in Chapter 11. Similarly, in Chapter 10, we show how Raymond, a hairdresser, subverts a more traditional performance of masculinity in his working environment in ways that, nonetheless, grant him prominence among his clientele of older women. However, less expected, caring aspects of his work complicate the assumption that men are controllers and manipulators of emotion at work.

Emotion work at work

The concept of emotional labour, in recent years, has been seen as key to debates on work, and for our purposes here, to understanding men at work. In particular, recent work has focused on masculinities, emotional labour and aesthetic labour in relation to men working in service work (see Nickson and Korczynski, 2009). As these authors point out, Hochschild's influential work *The Managed Heart: Commercialization of Human Feeling* (1983) first introduced the concept of emotional labour, which she defines as the management of employees' feelings during the social interaction inherent in the work process. This concept continues to shape current work, even now, on how front-line staff manage the emotional work needed to carry out their jobs. Though Nickson and Korczynski (2009) also note that theorists such as Lopez

(2006) problematise this work by arguing that the conception of emotional labour is too heavily predicated on Hochschild's initial assumptions that the service worker is subordinated to both management
rules and the paying customer. It is a critique, of course, that focus on
men in feminized occupations brings into sharp relief in terms of how
hegemonic masculinity can still serve the ends of men in feminized
occupations (see Simpson, 2009).

Recent work from Nixon (2009) comments on how the 'service
economy' has paralleled the detachment from the labour market of
low-skilled men and how a conventional gendering of emotion and
emotional labour is implicated in this. He concludes, with respect to
the 35 unemployed low-skilled men he interviews, that they reject low-
skilled, customer orientated interactive service jobs, due the fact that
such work calls for emotional skills which are markedly out of place
in a male, working-class habitus: 'The men rejected female-dominated
interactive service occupations that involved high amounts of emotional labour because they struggled to manage their emotions and
be passive and deferential within the service encounter and because
such work denied them the opportunity to relieve their stress in their
usual ways – through shouting, swearing, taking the piss and having a
laugh' (2009, 318–39). Nonetheless, as Nickson and Korczynski (2009)
point out, though there is some evidence that middle-class men seem
to be more at ease working in feminised occupations, there is both
no simple explanation for this, and thus the comparison should not
be overstated, as we explore through our data on estate agents in
Chapters 8 and 16.

More generally, emotional labour can be seen as gendered on
different levels. Simpson (2009) explains the emergence of this
gendering in terms of men's historical links to the public world of work
and production, and women's to the private sphere, where their role of
nurturer is located and so has been viewed as the 'natural' home of the
emotions; women are thus seen as the 'natural' keepers of the emotions
and of care. Also, gender and emotional labour has been constructed as
a performance, and she cites Hall (1993) and Williams (2003) who, for
her, argue that 'giving good service through emotional labour is "doing"
gender, involving for example the performance of culturally defined
and gendered scripts' (2009: 66).

In contrast, however, Simpson (2009) also contends that men's identities are very much caught up in both emotions and how visible those
emotions are in the workplace. For instance, men may gain status from
their emotional labour, but, on the other hand, their inferior status

(in respect of service work) may cause them to have unhealthy, negative emotions towards other, higher status men. Identity, Simpson (2009) argues, is therefore constructed through both positive and negative emotional responses to their working environment and the experiences that they encounter there. Men, she asserts, are sometimes also in positions where they have to exert their emotions in a traditional sense, for instance, through being authoritative, and so display a masculine embodied emotional identity. Our firefighters are interesting here, in that they sometimes need, in the course of their work, to exhibit a traditional male emotional response, by disciplining their emotions, as for instance, when they are confronted with a burns victim. Some of them, however, have also spoken of struggling with that level of self-containment that they feel is part of just 'doing their job'.

More recent arguments in relation to emotional labour have examined sexualised work, or how, in interactive services, employees become 'sexualised labour'. With reference to work which they describe as 'not inherently sexual but can be imbued with sexuality', Warhurst and Nickson argue that we need to shift from a focus on emotional labour to aesthetic and sexualised labour, where we can therefore see how important bodily displays are in emotional labour and ' how emotional labour can feature sexiness' (2009: p. 386). Aesthetic labour is seen to foreground embodiment, showing how corporeality, as well as the emotions of employees are appropriated for profit. In this sense, being 'good looking' or having 'the right look' is intended to appeal to customers thus 'creating affective service-interaction' (Warhurst and Nickson, 2009: p. 386). And such a focus on employees' looks, they argue, can be extended to the issue of sexualised labour 'to demonstrate how selling the service becomes selling sexuality' (Warhurst and Nickson, 2009: 386). In this way, they argue, both employees' corporeality and their sexualisation can be better understood.

Walls (2007) in research done on service sector industry is concerned with emotional and aesthetic labour at work and in the private sphere, how this 'escapes' the workplace, when staff continued their work role in the private sphere. Aesthetic capital, he argues, was a central reason in why male employees got, or kept, their job in fashion retail. As well, using the phrase 'emotions all hours' – workers continue with their work role in the private sphere, for example, with customers they meet socially. On the one hand, this emotional labour could have negative repercussions, for example, customers may be difficult in future encounters, or, staff could use the situation to their advantage, in the getting of regular customers, for instance. So they are exposed to certain 'risks' but also can accrue benefits from this as evidenced with our hairdresser Raymond, who ran his own salon, and did odd jobs for customers in their own homes, partly for altruistic reasons, but, nevertheless, benefitted by ensuring that his elderly clients remained loyal to him and his business. This exemplifies Wall's (2007) view that in the workplace, the emotional and aesthetic labour that is available to the employees as workers is both gendered and sexualised through their body language, how they communicate verbally and the physical space that they may occupy. This then leads to advantages/disadvantages in the workplace.

As discussed in Chapter 7, Simpson (2009) argues that all workplaces are characterised by varying levels of embodiment and disembodiment in that particular gendered bodies mesh more seamlessly – 'fit in' – with those that surround them, and so become less conspicuous or 'visible' (see Leder, 1990). In relation to this, she cites Morgan et al.'s (2005) argument that we experience both the pleasure and pain of work, as well as interpreting the emotional responses of others, both in and through the body. Thus, emotions and bodies are intimately linked in the workplace, and in complex ways. Simpson (2009) particularly notes this in relation to how emotional labour is performed in service work, for instance, with nursing where facial and body displays are fundamental to the performance of emotional labour. This was evident in our hairdresser's careful insistence on focusing exclusively on a client when cutting their hair and making them feel special, as if there was only two of them present in the hectic, fast-paced world of the salon (see Chapters 11, 13). This could also be seen in the estate agents' appreciation of a potential vendor's home, the deliberate smile designed to signify approval at a client's choice of home decoration, for instance.

Also, both the estate agents and the hairdressers in the study could be seen to exemplify Simpson's (2009) argument that those involved in service work, albeit of different kinds here, could mobilise 'feminine' emotions and, therefore, men could derive status and power from this. For example, Raymond, the 'camp' hairdresser, with his very explicit attending to of the female client's needs that go beyond the mere dressing of their hair, witnessed in the constant cups of coffee he made for them, or the extension of his emotional and physical labour into their homes, where he did DIY jobs for some (see Chapter 10) could retain clients' loyalty. As Simpson also notes, 'By appropriating emotions and bringing them into the masculine domain, associated skills and aptitudes can be divorced from essentialized and devalued notions of femininity. Equally, men can position themselves favourably against traditional notions of masculinity in their avowed capacity for nurturance and care. This supports the notion of a deferential and gendered division of emotional labour which may have positive identity implications for men' (2009: p. 161).

Though debates have often focused around service work in relation to emotional labour and masculinity, Nickson and Korczynski (2009) call for still more work on how men experience front line service work, in particular on how class and gender interact in how men experience such work. However, as our research reveals, we also need to think how the concepts of aesthetic and emotional labour inform a more nuanced understanding of how men perform emotionally, both within and across spheres and in different occupations, for example, where men dominate such as in firefighting or where a profession is more gender neutral, such as with estate agency.

Trust, vulnerability and male friendships

As noted, Whitehead (2002) argues that the public/private dichotomy, which is central to our work here, has not been much investigated in respect to aspects of men's lives such as leisure. Seidler suggests, in relation to men's emotional selves, that men are preoccupied with sustaining control of themselves to avoid feeling vulnerable through a loss of self control, and, furthermore to 'ward off threats to our male identity that come with our vulnerability' (1992: 2). And so, to control this vulnerability, men 'often move into activities' (1992: 2).

However, Robinson's (2008) qualitative research, on the 'extreme' sport of rock climbing reveals how such assumptions may be true for some men, while not for others. Her study concerned male identity across the life course, the everyday, mundane lives of men, and their connection to the 'extraordinary' world of a high-risk leisure pursuit. This included the way sporting masculinities were configured in the sport itself, but also in relation to being fathers, friends, in heterosexual relationships, and at work. A number of the climbers' accounts revealed that these men moved into the sport, at times, to avoid controlling others, if not themselves. In addition, by taking part in the pursuit of rock climbing, some of these men did not avoid feelings of vulnerability. Moreover, this consideration of male emotions, and control of these, can also shed light on the dynamics of gendered relations and how they are implicated at an everyday level in constructing masculinities.

Whitehead (2002) argues that to trust, one must let go of fear and the desire to control, but here in Robinson's research, to the contrary, emotional control does not have to be about maintaining an image of macho masculinity, but can be seen as something important to the climbing task at hand and the desire to avoid danger, and possibly injury or death. Neither does keeping control preclude displaying emotion in front of other men. Whitehead (2002) has also suggested that some discourses and narratives of masculinity allow greater trust between men. This is demonstrated in rock climbers' management of fear and vulnerability (Robinson, 2008). Such displays of emotion will usually take place in front of a climbing partner, often, another male. In effect, the management of fear is only possible because of the trust these climbers place in their climbing partners. Vulnerability can be shown in an extreme situation and the fear involved, depending on how it is managed and performed, seen as acceptable.

However, it is the public management of such emotions which often concerns these climbers. Therefore, to show such feelings on a low-grade climb, or a climb seen as well within one's limits, can be met with derision and thus be perceived as a sense of failure to keep composure. It is not just that trust, or the lack of it, is a key factor in facilitating or disrupting the possibilities of climbing success and well-being for the climbers interviewed, but so too is the fact that men can 'manage' intimacy by engaging in conventional masculine practices and in so doing, therefore avoid intimacy at a deeper level (see also Kerfoot, 2001). Robinson's data on sporting masculinities reveals that we need to think in a more complex and inter-related way regarding how the issues of emotional control, trust and displays of vulnerability interact; that is, across the generations and in relation to how the same man can display control in one context, but not in another, as we do in our study here more generally.

Robinson (2008) also argued that a focus on male friendships in the context of an extreme sport can expand on the relatively limited theorising of the emotions and intimacy in the context of masculinities that has been carried out in sociology more generally. While Davidson et al. (2003) point out that a number of theorists have argued that women and men 'do' friendships differently, they also draw upon Webster (1995), who argues that for men, identity is seen to precede intimacy, while for women these aspects are coincidental. Moreover, Miller (1983) has asserted that most men are disappointed in their male friendships which are defined by men as being 'thin' or insincere. Further, Davidson et al. use qualitative data to conclude that 'men, throughout their life course, may have had reduced opportunity to pursue intimate relationships' (2003: 174). They also argue that over the life course, men's friendships are generally forged and maintained in the workplace. Outside of work, friendships are made through social clubs, sports and other leisure situations, which are characterised by 'side-by-side sociability, focusing on activity and often on competitive pursuits' (Davidson et al., 2003: 182).

Robinson's interviewees' accounts of their climbing friendships support Messner's (2001) view, that the claim that men in sporting situations bond without any intimacy is not substantiated. Further, men's subjective sense of self can be seen to be wrapped up in their climbing friendships, and, therefore, the possibility of change to their subjectivities through a connection to others must be seen as a possibility. In addition, the idea that men are emotionally inarticulate is not borne out by those interviewees either. One climber in his 40s, when asked if he took up the sport because it offered opportunities to compete or the chance of encountering danger or risk, replied, 'It wasn't, no. It was mainly the friendship and the, you know, being part of a group.' This attitude is contrary to ideas that sport is a place where hegemonic masculinities are constructed and performed through a celebration of danger, risk and competition as our male participants revealed, in diverse ways, across the three occupational groups.

How, then, does the extreme sport of climbing afford men a space to reveal sides to their character they may not be comfortable doing in more 'ordinary' situations. As we have already established in this chapter, a number of theorists have argued that men don't 'do' friendships in the same way that women do. However, as with the idea of men not being able to be as intimate with others or show emotions such as vulnerability, we must be careful not to confuse the ideology with reality – or, indeed, fail to problematise the ideology itself as gendered. And these realisations are explored in the following chapters. Lastly, it is worth bearing in mind that Pahl's (2000) and Whitehead's (2002) suggestion that it is friendship, not coupledom, which will come to provide the most constancy for people's relationships, has some purchase for men's friendships across spheres, Thus, in this context, the evidence in our project supports Whitehead's argument, that, 'Whether based around straight, gay, white or black identities, men's friendships with other men can be seen to be crucially important in sustaining masculine subjectivities and men's sense of identity as men. In addition, recognizing this does not take us very far from the earlier point made by Seidler that men's same-sex friendships very rarely provide the possibilities for social transformations between women and men' (Whitehead, 2002:158–9).

Conclusion

In the following chapters in this section on masculinities and emotions, we flesh out some of the theoretical ideas initially introduced here. Furthermore, through our data, we can recognise both differences between our three occupations, as well as similarities. For example, with our hairdressers, there was often a need to perform emotional labour in both public and private spheres, for example, in the salon, but also at all hours if men were cutting friend's/family's hair in the domestic space. Often, though the public image of firefighters is one of the iconic hero, and further, one who is fully in control of their emotions, we see men struggling with this in the course of their everyday working practices, and sometimes failing to live up to this stereotype. For estate agents, the gradual feminisation of their emotional working space, over time, meant that they, sometimes knowingly and strategically, used this shift in advancing their careers. Thus, across all the occupational groups we were concerned with, men showed themselves capable of using emotional intelligence and emotional management to their advantage, for instance, when cultivating client relationships. Equally, at other times, the strain of (sometimes competing) emotional performances across public and private spheres was too great, and relationships suffered, as female partners sometimes attested to.

In Chapter 13, we examine the issue of emotional labour on oneself and how emotional labour can be deployed to resist or sustain hegemonic masculinity. Here, we show how emotional labour in the work place, rewards, but can also reinforce traditional gender hierarchies, specifically for our purposes, gendered power relations. Chapter 13 also further unpacks the term 'emotional labour', as relevant within different occupational contexts. In Chapter 14, emotional labour within the wider landscape – the home/work boundary – is investigated to see if emotions are contained, or if emotional distancing *constitutes* this boundary. Here, we see if work can be a haven after the trials of the life course as well as investigate how emotional sharing can resource or destabilise masculinity, and how gendered shifts in occupations may be refused, resisted or appropriated through emotional practices. Chapter 15 is concerned with emotion and friendships, something we have raised already in more general detail here in relation to leisure. Finally, Chapter 16 looks at emotions and the research process and we ask, in doing this, how reflection on this process can problematise understandings of masculinity.

13
Emotional Labour Revisited

As Chapter 12 explains, the extent to which traditional stereotypes of men's emotional inarticulacy hold true within contemporary Western societies has been a focus for debate rather than a matter of consensus. This chapter brings an empirical perspective to bear on this question through three occupationally located case study examples of feelings rules (Hochschild 1979, 1983). In so doing, it considers not only the forms of gendered interaction through which rules are communicated and held in place, but also the spaces and tasks through which they are played out. For Hochschild, feelings rules are 'the side of ideology that deals with emotion and feeling' (1979: 551), a perspective which highlights the way *social* factors affect what one feels, and what the individual thinks and does about their feelings. While Hochschild concerned herself with the ways in which human beings' capacity to reflect and act upon their emotionality could serve the ends of capitalism, here gender power is our focus. Thus, we explore the ways in which feelings rules inform men's and women's orientations to their own emotions, and to those of other people. Gender, we argue, is an aspect of these rules; how our participants made sense of what each other were feeling and how they felt able to express their emotions were informed by their understandings of what a man or woman might be expected to feel and do in any particular context.

The data we present reveal the influence on men of a relatively recent feelings rule: the belief that emotional expressivity fosters well-being, and that emotional 'control' brings risks and dangers, not only to the individual but also their relationships (Lupton, 1998). In addition, data indicate broader cultural shifts within different organisations' willingness to support emotional expressivity and give space to men's emotional needs, both through formal structures such as counselling services as well as informally through emotional care within peer groups. Yet echoing McMahon's (1999) suggestion that gender relations appear resistant to change, despite trends towards the feminisation of men in the public sphere and their expressed enthusiasm for such a shift, our data also evidence apparently traditional strategies of emotional regulation and control undertaken by men, in relation to clients and members of the public, their colleagues and indeed themselves.

To explore this contradiction the chapter undertakes comparative work across different occupations, exploring the contextual nature of emotionality. In so doing it treats emotionality as contingent, rather than 'essential', contextualising it within occupational cultures and the materialities of workplace environments. In this we follow Bondi et al.'s call for 'a non-objectifying view of emotions as relational flows, fluxes or currents, in-between people and places rather than "things" or "objects" to be studied or measured' (2005: 3). The notion of feeling rules used in this chapter also draws attention to social as opposed to psychological dimensions of emotionality. However, the notion of feelings rules has been criticised for assuming that human beings 'contain' genuine feelings or an authentic self which are then vulnerable to constraint or distortion as the individual passively conforms to external sets of rules, a critique that also calls for more attention to individual agency (Lupton, 1998: 20–1; see also Chapter 12). While drawing upon the sociological insights offered by Hochschild's (1983) feelings rules, then, we treat emotions as both intersubjective and spatio-temporally located.

'I don't even hide it very well'

Across all three ages and occupational cultures where data were gathered, men spoke of emotions and emotional expressivity as appropriate responses to difficult situations; indeed, some men represented themselves as emotionally labile while others saw themselves as problematically over-controlled emotionally.

Wayne Steade, a 29-year-old firefighter, said 'I'm one of the more caring ones of the bunch ... I'm a bit of a softie, a lot of a softie really, I don't even hide it very well.' And his partner Trudie affirmed this statement, describing how tears would well up in his eyes if a conversation touched on something sad. She could read him like a book, emotionally, she said.

Martin Cos, a 54-year-old estate agent, compared himself with a former business partner in order to underline his own emotionality: 'I was much more of the creative side, he was the logical ... what I do comes from the heart, what he does comes from the head.' In his view, this meant that he lacked the doggedness necessary for success in business: 'You have to be something which I'm not, which, because I can take it personally if I'm turned down by somebody.' In response to rejection, he said, 'I'd never shout at anybody but it would eat me up ... I probably would dwell on it, yes.'

If Wayne and Martin fairly readily described their emotional responsiveness, men who saw themselves 'bottling up' their feelings were concerned about the consequences of this approach. Kevin Kirkpatrick, a 42-year-old firefighter, said: 'I don't think I talk about it ... to anybody ... I do some things but ... this is probably a fault of mine, I should talk about things a lot more than I do but I don't tend to. It's probably more healthy to discuss things and to, I don't know ...', he continued.

Joe White, a 24-year-old estate agent, echoed this view when describing how emotion is defused in the shared office he works in: 'You can't have a serious conversation with them ... and that's how they cope with things, they just try and laugh it off.' Acknowledging that he adopts a similar approach, he expressed reservations: 'I always keep things to myself, I think that's my undoing sometimes.'

When talking about other men's emotions, some participants said they saw all men as vulnerable to potentially powerful distress. Nigel Saltash, a 50-year-old firefighter, described a colleague who had left the service with a nervous breakdown after a very difficult emergency: 'I know this lad and I still know him ... and that was genuine ... he had his breaking point and everybody's got it but I've, I've just not reached it yet.' The notion of 'genuine' emotion revealed his model of emotionality as either innate and therefore genuine, or faked, possibly with an eye to early retirement. When asked if colleagues were critical of the man who left, Nigel said: 'No, because everybody knew that he were genuine.'

Along with a notion of 'genuine' emotion sits a reflective comment on the embodied or sensory nature of emotive memories; Clive Bell, a 53-year-old, recently retired fire fighter recalled a particularly difficult emergency that went 'straight into my memory bank because I came home smelling of death.'

Marcus Holdsworth, a 64-year-old estate agent, similarly acknowledged men's emotional vulnerability when he said: 'There are an awful lot of surveyors and estate agents in the city who've had nervous breakdowns.' Just as Nigel Saltash spoke of every man having his breaking point, Nigel felt that men could not always be expected to be in control of how they felt or what they did: 'I mean statistically over the course of a forty year career, you can't always get it right can you?'

These beliefs, that men's vulnerability to emotional distress was to be expected, were expressed forcefully by Alec Simpson, a 41-year-old Watch Manager in the fire service. He saw encouraging men to seek emotional support as part of his job: 'I've told people before, "you want to go and have a word with ...", we've got our own occupational therapist at headquarters.' Alec had used the service himself: 'I've spoken to them about problems I've had with the kids ... it looked like it was affecting me, you know. That's what they're there for, phone them up, find out what, can you help me?' When asked whether there was stigma attached to seeking emotional help, he said, 'There's a little bit, there is a little but the only way you can get rid of that sort of stigma is by using the services, that's what they're there for.'

'Water off a duck's back'

These data suggest a model of emotionality – and indeed emotional styles – which does not differ markedly from those associated with women. Younger men seem to have espoused a pervasive cultural orientation that pathologises emotional control; older men draw on many years' experience when attesting to men's emotional vulnerability. Yet, as Lupton argues, the capacity to 'feel' has become the hallmark of the new man – 'I feel, therefore I am' (1998: 134), to the extent that when men do cry publically, this can endow them with a higher social status. In parallel with re-definitions of emotional expressivity as a resource that men can appropriate, however, much of our data also make reference to men's persistent capacity and, indeed, commitment to regulating their own feelings and those of colleagues. Among estate agents, a number of men described being able to distance themselves from demanding or distressed clients: 'like water off a duck's back'. Similarly, some hairdressers said they avoided anything but a non-committal response to clients when they recounted personal problems. Derek French, 58, put this succinctly: 'Diplomatic and quiet, zip'. Karl Innis, 59, included exposure to clients' problems among the stresses of hairdressing, saying 'I've got friends ... what had to pack in because they couldn't cope with it ... they don't know how I've done it, but I've got a strong willpower'.

This capacity to regulate one's personal feelings has parallels in the way men resist responding to the 'wind-ups' and 'piss-taking' to which they are subjected as new firefighters (see also Gregory, 2009;

Chapter 9). Emotional control is learned the hard way. When asked whether some men got upset by 'piss-taking', Richard Shawcross, 23, said 'if they do, they just get it even more though so, you can't show signs of weakness, if you see a chink in chain that's it, you'll get torn down'. Equally, piss-taking can be an expression almost of fondness, an indicator that a man is trusted to take a joke in good humour, and is an accepted member of the watch.

As argued, making sense of this apparent contradiction in men's understandings and experiences of emotionality requires attention to their everyday environments, an approach which treats emotionality as an embodied, intersubjective dimension of working life. Below we examine case study situations within different occupational cultures, identifying key themes which transcend divisions between them, yet still find expression in context-specific ways.

'You can turn into a counsellor'

Making the materialities of the salon and the temporalities of hair-dresser/client interactions a focus reveals the distinctive ways in which broader patterns of reinvented or feminised masculine emotionality are realised within everyday life. As Chapter 10 discusses, men may experience the salon as a feminised workspace where they 'fit in' to an environment where women and women's emotionality are privileged. In this setting, emotional labour (Hochschild, 1983) means regulating one's own emotions and those of a client, the former allowing the latter to be achieved in ways which suit the professional agendas of the hair-dresser. This can occur before feelings surface, or after they have been experienced, and includes 'faking' an emotion one does not feel.

Fashionable, city-centre salons constitute shared workspaces where mirrors militate against privacy for staff and clients. Yet within the open-plan salon, a client enters a spatially and temporally bounded, social micro-environment. This occurs via the hairdresser's capacity to give them undivided attention, to undertake both the practice of hairstyling and the emotional labour of making them feel 'special'. Patrick Valentine, 28, said 'It's nice, it's because you get a rapport and you don't usually sit down with somebody on a one to one for an hour, we have hour appointments here, I wouldn't go into a bar and sit next to somebody for an hour I wouldn't do, but this I can do quite easily, I think.'

In small salons in working-class areas a single hairdresser often works across several clients' hair simultaneously, his emotional labour oriented towards fostering humour or dramatic interest among a sociable cluster of clients. Derek French, who for many years had run a small salon with Joyce, his wife, knew intimate, sometimes scandalous information about their long-term clients, sometimes cutting the hair of three generations within the same family. He would enter into reciprocal, caring relationships with them: if he had a problem he would seek advice from a client with relevant professional expertise. Plants, given by clients, would be redistributed in the form of cuttings, particularly among his older customers: 'it's more like a greengrocers shop than a barbers', said Joyce.

Within the hairdresser/client dyad, therefore, clients may reveal emotionally charged personal information. As noted, some men develop strategies for distancing themselves from its emotional impact – or indeed the caring role of counsellor. 'Like a psychiatrist, you listen to the same stuff all the time', said Karl Innis, 59. Patrick Valentine, 28, managed the hairdresser/client with care. While he enjoyed building rapport, as noted, he resisted the demands of giving emotional support: 'you can turn into a counsellor', he said, indicating his view of this as a transition into another role, rather than an elaboration of his professional and personal style. 'I don't really get involved in ... I don't really get that deep into it, they can tell me about it but I'm not going to, I don't want to be a counsellor ... you might come out with the wrong thing' he said, implying that emotional support required professional expertise, rather than being a dimension of 'rapport'. 'No I wouldn't want to go down that route', he concluded.

He can be compared with Joyce French, who said 'you're more like a counsellor in a lot of things'. Speaking alongside Derek, her husband and business partner, who saw clients as a potential source of professional advice, she highlighted the emotional dimensions of such relationships: 'you know my dad had accident, a few years ago, he was knocked down by a drunken motorcyclist'. Derek took up the thread: 'I mean even now the customers, every time they come in – "how's the old fella?"'. 'They're ever so kind', said Joyce, 'you know if anything, if anything goes off ... and they'd help you out, wouldn't they?' 'Majority of them would, you know they'd do anything to help you if they could', replied Derek. Here, then, within this heterosexual couple's talk, emotionality, practical advice and plant exchange merged. As Chapter 10 noted, men in fashionable salons might take on feminine conversational styles, revealing personal information and gossip; here within a small, working-class salon, a man assumes a familial emotional style associated with heterosexuality.

'We do have to console the clients'

Among hairdressers, in both city-centre and more working-class salons, relationships with clients could be enduring, nurtured across years and family generations. Within them, emotional reciprocity was evident. This raises questions about the limits of 'emotional labour' as a concept, work-based theories having tended to highlight its uni-directional nature. We can consider the argument that within a feminised environment such as hairdressing, two-way emotional labour is perhaps more in evidence. Professional/client relationships in hairdressing can be compared with those in estate agency where the vendor/estate agent encounter is more likely to be one-off. Indeed, buying and selling houses can be associated with painful life course transitions such as job loss, divorce or widowhood. Brad Charrier, 41, and partner in Saddleworths, one of the city's major estate agencies, spoke about this, hesitatingly but at length:

> Erm you know we, we deal with people who are in matrimonial break-ups, who are very you know highly emotional and they need to be erm, you know nurtured and, and carefully dealt with, erm to reach the right conclusion. We, we move people around the country, you know with job moves, its very, you know, it's a very, very stressful time for them and so you do have to be able to er relate to people and, help them through the whole process ... the nature of the business is that it can be very stressful, because you are dealing with clients ... erm who can be in quite a, a, a frenzied emotional state er and you know however hard you are, and unfeeling that you are, that does come across, you know you do, you do get caught up in that a little bit ... and you, its very difficult to remain totally dispassionate about situations where, where people are very upset and er, and you know that in itself can be quite stressful.

What he describes is clearly a form of emotional labour. 'The right conclusion', is likely to be one that is profitable for the agent, as well as satisfactory for the client. Yet Brad's hesitant style of referring to the emotional costs for the estate agent demonstrates the need to exercise emotional labour upon oneself, Brad's reputation as a tough negotiator being a source of his esteem among younger men. Men described slamming down the phone and swearing when a client was demanding, learning to 'switch off' at 5.30 pm, play sport, watch TV or listen to music as ways of 'letting off steam'. Others saw emotional detachment as a more pervasive aspect of their personalities, a stance with which they felt comfortable in this challenging business environment, despite the new status attributed to men's emotional expressivity. While hairdressers enjoy and take pride in the practical and emotional task of making the client feel 'special', for estate agents the emotionality of their clients was an unfortunate if understandable by-product of buying and selling bricks and mortar. Phil Cruikshank, 41, described his work as fraught because:

> we do get people coming, barging into the office, demanding this and that and they're going to take their property off the market and there are tears and there are strong words and … it's very stressful time for the, see people wanting to move on into the new house and if the chain breaks and falls to pieces, it's … we do have to console the clients I guess.

'Hard work to take in'

Chapter 9 discussed the taunting banter to which new firefighters are exposed in a rite of passage into an occupation where encounters between men and the victims of fires and accidents are more stressful still, potentially. As their data indicate repeatedly, it is not people who have died in these incidents who carry the most powerful emotional impact, but those who are dying or bereaved. So complex are the procedures for dealing with dangerous environments that concentration on these tasks can eclipse emotional responses. Peta Dunmore, partner of 28-year-old Harvey Machin, said he'd been exposed to videos of fatalities during training. However, as she said, 'I think they were more bothered that when they got there they wouldn't remember how to do everything, that was the biggest fear I think.' Daniel Armstrong, 25, described an actual fatality and although seeing someone badly burnt was disturbing, he said 'I think there's that much happening around you and you're worrying about other people and you're worrying about where you're putting your feet so you don't disturb evidence because of what's happened, I don't know, you just blank it out kind of thing'.

Commitment to institutionalised, team practices can thus, at times, take precedence over the emotive power of fatalities. Yet such feelings can nonetheless be seen to have a kind of agency, to circumvent attention-switching modes, when firefighters experience personal identification with the victim. This can transform the victim from the object of complex procedures to a subject whose emotionality is perceptible in some way. As Bondi et al. argue, in practice emotions are not containable and instead need to be understood as 'relational flows, fluxes or currents, in-between people and places' (2005: 3). Dominic Treadwell, 44, recalled the experience of rescuing a young man from a fire: 'trying to give him some oxygen but I knew he was going to die, he looked at me and I looked at him and I knew he was going to die and he did do ... and yeah that really upsets me'. In addition to this moment of identification, Dominic also discovered the difficulty of containing feelings within the work environment, experiencing them quite literally as a flow between people and places: 'when I come home and it's Tina's birthday and you know her granddad's and her mum's like saying "Open the presents, open the presents now" and I'm having to open these presents and I've just seen somebody dying, you know a couple of hours ago'. Identification can also connect firefighters with bereaved people who are sometimes involved in the same incident. Richard Shawcross, 23, had first encountered a fatality when two teenagers died in a violent road traffic accident and although it had not upset him, he had returned to the spot repeatedly because 'it were just, hard work to take in'. What had been more difficult, however, was that 'you could see families at bottom of road and they were ... that probably upset me more, seeing them at bottom of road'. Dominic Treadwell, 44, said that 'the worst thing I've ever had to do, is not somebody who was injured, it was a boy who was trapped in a car, a twelve-year-old with his mother and his mother was dead next to him ... there wasn't much left of her to be quite honest. And the kid just sat there but strangely enough because of the crash he couldn't see his mother ... as we were trying to get the kid out because he was actually unhurt ... the worst thing was he looked at me and ... he said "How's my mother?"'. Through extreme situations such as this, firefighters' capacity to distance themselves emotionally was challenged. Stanley Pye, 55, said 'the only things that really upset were kids ... when a lad fell off a tree and went onto a railings and ... they cut the railing around him ... and he was saying "Am I going to be alright?" They were saying "You're going to be alright" and yeah, "I'm going to be alright" ... and then he died'.

These data have been included at some length; they not only reveal the ways in which men made sense of their own emotions and those of colleagues and victims of fires and accidents, but also testify to the feelings stimulated in the course of offering these reflections. Noteworthy is the repeated emphasis on the exchange of eye contact between victim and firefighter, an identification which transcended a 'them' and 'us' distinction which otherwise inured firefighters to their own, embodied vulnerability. All participants attested to the subsequent emotional support they received from colleagues and superiors, noting that this might challenge gender stereotypes; Mickey Smith, 26, describing the aftermath of a fatality said 'my first gaffer ... he's just like a massive bear of a bloke and like really rough but even he checked that I was alright like ...so I was impressed ... they've got this tough man image but it's alright'.

Conclusion

From across all three occupations, these data show men engaged in emotional labour, managing the painful feelings of those undergoing both the distress of a life-threatening incident and the stress of house buying and selling, or assimilating the everyday worries of a client they are trying to make feel 'special'. In engaging such forms of labour, men's own emotional lives took shape, sometimes in ways they found difficult. As a result, *self*-management was an associated labour that many attested to. In a number of cases, we see men reassessing gender-specific feelings rules as, for example, when 'a massive bear of a bloke' attends to the emotional undoing of those he is required to lead. And alongside the gendering – and re-gendering – of feelings rules, we find men's conceptions of their occupational identities becoming a source of emotional boundaries, for example, when hairdressers desist from offering counselling. That said, such conceptions can be yardsticks against which men measure themselves – and experience a sense of failure. As John Durrant, a 54-year-old estate agent said, 'You have to be something which I'm not'.

14
Sharing Emotion: Men's Experience of Vulnerability

This chapter develops the theme of emotional labour introduced in Chapter 13, focussing more directly on the intersubjective nature of emotionality. The extent to which men confide both work-related and personal worry and stress to their female partners, colleagues and one another; and the ways in which others respond to them is our primary concern here. Thus, our data show how relationships between men and their female partners become sites for reproducing or resisting a traditional, gendered division of emotional labour, sites that are implicated in transitions between work and home, and any associated shifts in masculine identification. In addition the chapter addresses the implications of heteronormativity, the normative status of heterosexuality, for the emotional dimensions of men's relationships with one another: for example, it can render homosexual relationships a potential source of distress that can distance men emotionally from both parents and work colleagues; equally, heteronormativity can legitimate men's mutual exchange of negative feelings towards female partners, so helping sustain male homosociality.

As Chapter 12 noted, for men in many occupations, home and work are divided from one another by spatial – and temporal – boundaries, yet emotion is fluid and can transgress these boundaries. Feelings such as 'stress' can carry in either direction, despite men's efforts to contain them. Equally the different spatial and social environments of the home and the workplace can provide refuges from one another – or indeed independent sources of support. As the data presented in this chapter indicate, however, while the workplace can be a refuge or escape from domestic problems, it may not be a site within which emotional difficulties can be expressed and support given. Alongside issues associated with the notion of home and workplace as divided from one another by particular spatial distances and timetables, we can also consider the notion of emotionality as constitutive of, rather than simply influenced by a home/work boundary. In Chapter 4 we discussed the idea of home and work as mutually generative, the material boundaries between them having a productive rather than simply classificatory role. To this argument, then, we can add the notion that shifts in emotional focus and style can help create those spaces that men understand as 'home', 'office', 'salon' or 'fire station'.

These concerns contextualise this chapter's engagement with specific questions about men's emotionality and the gendering of affect. It asks, for example, whether socio-economic shifts in the nature of hairdressing, estate agency and firefighting have a gendered dimension which might have implications for men's emotional lives. As data indicate, love and money can intersect in problematic ways and in so doing reveal the relationship between feelings rules and social hierarchies grounded in gender, class and occupational status. Related to this, how might the workplace and its relationship with home offer men ways of 'doing' emotion which challenge a traditional gendered division of emotional labour?

Keepers of the heart?

Discussing the history of a gendered construction of emotionality, Lupton says that, with the growth of a separation between domestic space and an industrialised world of work in the nineteenth century, '[m]others were expected to regulate their male children and produce them as rational, dispassionate citizens, even as they themselves were portrayed as irrational and emotional' (1998: 111). In that our project involved interviewing women who featured within men's domestic lives, a partner's orientation towards a man's emotional life was an important dimension of our data. Women's interviews showed that a capacity for empathic warmth, a commitment to emotional expressivity, and a felt concern at the prospect of any threat to a man's emotional well-being were seen, by women, and men, as desirable and indeed necessary qualities that were intrinsic to femininity.

For example, Chloe Rowbottom said that her partner, 26-year-old firefighter, Mickey Smith, 'tells me about every job, he comes home and tells me about every single job'. More problematic, in her view, was the fact that 'if obviously he's seen dead bodies and quite recently he's had an incident with a fatality, I really don't think it, obviously it bothers him, but he's got a mechanism of shutting it out'. As she put it, 'he'll happily talk about it in a very factual way'. Mickey's potential exposure to emotionally distressing experiences was not something she felt able to relegate to his workplace persona. Instead, she assumed some kind of personal responsibility for the potentially deleterious effects of Mickey 'shutting it out'. As Chapter 13 indicated, firefighters can become emotionally haunted by victims who were very obviously aware of the seriousness of their condition, whose lives they 'saved', but only for a while. In these circumstances men identified with victims' suffering and Chloe demonstrated her concern, saying that if Mickey had to face this situation, rather than simply removing a corpse, 'he would reflect but I just hope that that situation never comes really because it will be a horrible, he's not cold he, you know, he would, he'd feel things and I think he would probably say'. Chloe's worry over potential threats to Mickey's emotional well-being was born out by Yvonne Kirkpatrick, partner of firefighter Kevin Kirkpatrick (42). Describing his capacity for moody withdrawal, she indicated her sense of obligation towards managing his feelings: 'I would say "what's the matter?" and try getting it out of him but he wouldn't, he doesn't talk about stuff like that he's just very, very typically male in that. Doesn't really speak from the heart, I have to ask, I have to probe, push'.

These data therefore not only suggest a traditional gendered division of emotional labour but also reveal women's reflexivity with regard to their *gendered* role in sustaining it. In some ways they shore up the notion of women as more vulnerable to distress, less capable of controlling their feelings. However, as Lupton argues, the traditional casting of women in the role of 'keepers of the heart' (Brownmiller cited in Lupton, 1998: 107) involves more than soft-hearted empathy; in their role as mothers, women were also expected to *regulate* men's emotional upbringing, to 'produce rational, dispassionate citizens' (1998: 11). Again, among the female partners of firefighters, this dimension of a gendered division of emotional labour was evident. Thus, Trudie Steade, partner of 29-year-old Wayne Steade, said:

> If he comes home and I think he's going to start ... being a bit sort of maudlin ... start dwelling on something too much, that's when I turn round and say 'well that's, you know that's your job you've trained to do you've got to get on with it', kind of thing which I know sounds harsh. But its true as well, yeah, and I think coming from a nursing family ... I've been brought with that 'you've just got to get on with it' mentality and I think Wayne's had to sort of accept that and learn that as well a little bit ... you've got to start rationalising it somehow haven't you, I think?

This dualism – of empathy and emotional regulation – was not confined to the management of highly charged situations among firefighters. Daisy Chalfont, partner of 27-year-old estate agent Curtis Manford, described a kind of emotional economy where access to empathy was to an extent commoditised, each partner weighing their willingness to listen against what the other was prepared to offer: 'he'll come home and tell me but sometimes I have to kind of say "Right, enough" … (and he'll say) "I'll just tell you this one more thing" and then he will and that will be it and he'll shut up'. Asked in her interview whether she brought her own work problems home, she said: 'Yeah, I do tell him stuff and I'm not sure whether he listens or not … yeah, he kind of gets it a bit back from me as well I suppose'. What is striking about these data is the 'rational' approach to managing Curtis' emotional needs that Daisy reveals: 'I'll sit and I'll say "Right, it's half past ten, you've got to stop talking about work now"'. Managing the time allocated to Jonathon for receiving empathy was therefore carefully considered. As Louise explained, 'I don't mind him telling me things … because I know that …if he doesn't he'll just dwell on it and he'll be laid in bed and he'll be like wide awake … but then if he sits there and he talks about it for an hour then that seems to kind of make things better'. Sharing a bed, Daisy clearly benefits from ensuring that he sleeps soundly. Her agency as an emotional 'manager', rather than a passive, empathetic 'shoulder to cry on' comes through strongly in her interview. Similarly, Moira Chisholm, wife of Derek, a 43-year-old partner in the estate agency where they both work, regulated the expression of her own work-based emotional vulnerability as a way of generating a distance between the relationship she had with Derek at work – as his employee, and at home – as his wife. She said: 'Well I do go back now, I'll do that "oh I'm blooming sick of such and such today, because of A, B and C" and I'll say "leave it at that, don't worry I just needed to say it"'.

Emotion in context

The data presented above show conformity to many dimensions of a traditional gendered division of labour, one that also reflects heterosexuality's pervasive role as an organising principle (Hockey et al., 2007). However, when emotional expressiveness and support are examined from a life course perspective it becomes apparent that different interpersonal connections are in play at different ages. That said, participants clearly had a sense of who could appropriately be approached with what kind of emotional need, whether or not they felt their own lives actually conformed to this model. Among young hairdressers, establishing long-term heterosexual relationships and buying into their material expression in home ownership and parenthood was not particularly common. Many of them had continued living with parents until they were in their thirties. In some cases these were men who at some point had come out as gay; others were simply committed to what one described as a *'nomadic'* life, retaining a base with parents yet spending a considerable part of the week with friends, particularly those who had already established homes of some kind. In these circumstances many men perceived parents as a key source of emotional support. However, for gay men, emotional closeness to parents could make coming out to them even more difficult in that they empathised with a parent's potential distress. For others, however, both gay and heterosexual, parents had been entirely supportive, continuing to offer living and storage space as they gradually established an independent life.

Cathy Thornton, friend of hairdresser Brendan Amies (37), described her disappointment when she heard that he had come out as gay to someone other than her. She used a family metaphor to explain her closeness to him: 'a brother, yes brother, friend … he's godparent to my eldest daughter'. Brendan reciprocated, saying that for him Cathy was like a sister, shoring up his statement through reference to having a brother and therefore being able to recognise a sibling relationship when it was offered. Interviewed together, Cathy and Brendan agreed that although Cathy had been upset that he hadn't confided in her, it was, as he said, 'because of my, like, closeness to Cathy it was, like, people who were closest to me, it was the hardest to speak to'. Subsequently Cathy had urged him to come out to his parents, offering to talk to them alongside him. These data do show the complexity of the relationship between home and work, emotionality shifting fluidly between them in some circumstances. Thus Brendan had experienced considerable distress that his sexuality remained secret: 'it's kind of built up and built up to me, at one point I thought my head were gonna explode … I thought I were gonna have a ner .., a breakdown, you know, but I tried to hold myself together and being that, that same person at work'. Eventually he did 'break down' at work and another female colleague cancelled the staff's night out and spent two hours talking to him in a local café. These data show the elision of work and home, as metaphors drawn from the domestic world of the family are used to characterise workplace relationships. For Brendan, it was not only a colleague who was first to provide emotional support, but also his clients, as his friend, colleague and 'sister' Cathy related: 'clients have been fantastic as well haven't they ...you know female clients ... sent cards to you didn't they ... you know "Be your lovely self"'.

Thus, despite the pervasiveness of heterosexuality as an organising principle reflected in practices around emotional expressiveness and well-being, other kinds of relationships might take precedence, either in the absence of a heterosexual partner, or alongside that relationship. As exemplified in Cathy 's reference to her status as 'friend/sister', however, participants adhered to specific, sometimes hierarchical models as to who should be confided in. Associated with these models are a related set of ideas as to who should *not* be confided in, in the sense of valued relationships which participants felt would be put at risk if an individual's emotional vulnerability became apparent. When 28-year-old estate agent Paul Lewis was asked whether his emotional style would vary with different people, family, friends, colleagues, he said:

> Yeah, absolutely, yeah, with your friends you want to come across as, as not a wimp really don't you? You want to come across more masculine, you want to, you wouldn't tell them about any soppy problems that you might have, I suppose that's what you talk to your girlfriend about, not soppy problems but minor things that might get on your nerves, probably with my girlfriend or, or Mum and Dad, you wouldn't do that with your friends, no.

What Paul defined as 'soppy problems' was not, however, clearly defined and his subsequent comments suggested that it was the *style* rather than the content which might vary when problems were articulated to others. While hairdresser Brendan described the intense feeling that 'his head might explode' with difficulties he had surrounding intimate relationships with other men, young heterosexual men described taking the opportunity to 'moan' and 'whinge' to one another about their difficulties with a female partner. Thus, estate agent Paul Lewis said: 'you go out for a moan with your lads, the lads, don't you, about your girlfriend sometimes ... someone I play snooker with, quite often we always do that, have a bit of a whinge ... (girlfriends) wanting more commitment than you sometimes, a lot of the time, and we have the same sort of problems ... it's always, always seems to be a problem with women, that you get to the stage where they do want more commitment than the man'.

Emotions, then, constitute not only a source of vulnerability and risk but also a resource to be deployed in fostering homosocial connections through the identification of shared problems with 'women' (see Messner, 2001; Haywood and Mac an Ghaill, 2003; Gregory, 2009).

Gendered differences in emotional styles, and in the ways in which men interact with other men, as opposed to women, is summed up for estate agent Simon Pulling (52) in a distinction between 'chatting' and 'talking': 'I've always had female company, you know always liked to be, but I've always like the matey football side, the laugh and the chat and you know, the banter that goes with that as well, sort of thing, so, which is a bit like it, because it's, you can have a chat with the lads or you can go up and talk to the ladies'.

Love and money

When Cathy described the closeness of her relationship with Brendan, she identified the economic relationship between herself and Brendan as important. This aspect of emotionality is often downplayed in a pervasive opposition between love and money expressed in the persistent social censuring of paid child and elder care, and the stigmatising of paid sex (Finch and Groves, 1983; Sanders et al., 2009). Yet as participants described the shifting profiles of their emotional lives, the implications of financial and related materialities were often discussed. For Cathy, Brendan's status as an independent hairdresser who rented a chair in her salon helped minimise sources of tension between them. By comparison, her friendship with another woman which had involved a business *partnership* was troubled by mutual resentment over imbalances in their respective contributions and resulting financial benefits.

The importance of financial aspects of emotionality was particularly evident among hairdressers where small businesses might become vulnerable as a result of a costly divorce settlement. Equally, heavy financial and emotional investment in such businesses could introduce considerable stress within a couple's relationship, whether that business was shared or not. Andy Hathaway (50), for example, said that he and his former wife should never have worked together as hairdressers, that the contact at home and work was too much: 'As soon as we had our own business, the business troubles then come into your home life and when I was married we had a big house and everything else, and when we got divorced I now live in someone's attic, you know.'

Steve London (48), another hairdresser, described the financial as well as emotional fallout when his wife left him after 18 years of marriage. He said, 'my initial plan was to retire around about fifty-five but then unfortunately me wife left me and I had to pay her quite a substantial amount of money and that I had to cash every, every penny that I'd invested in and saved ... and re-mortgage because I had no mortgage ... so it left me back to square one again ... so now I have no money saved, no investment, I haven't even got a pension plan ... I now live for today and that's all.'

Partner in Saddleworths estate agency, Geoff Pym (50) had married and divorced twice. Known at work for his confrontational style, he made the interview an opportunity to reveal a more emotionally vulnerable rather than aggressive aspect of his identity. Describing the impact of his commitment to working life upon both his marriages, he said that his first wife:

> used to struggle with Saddleworths as, you know I think my second wife as well struggled to a degree with Saddleworths because I think probably in many respects and probably if you ask Todd's ex-wife and maybe Andy's, you know they would, maybe would say the same things, that in many respects, Saddleworths has been such an important part of our lives that they might have thought at times that they were secondary to, to Saddleworths. And I think that was probably looking back, with hindsight, that was probably the case, not that I deliberately did that, it was, as I said. You know I wasn't one that was ambitious but I couldn't not take my work home with me mentally and so I couldn't just switch off, so if something had happened at work during the day, I found it very difficult not to think about it.

When Geoff left his first wife, his personal decision meshed very unfavourably with the global economic recession of the late 1980s and early 1990s:

> There was times as well when the business, when I got divorced when I was in financial settlement, you know it was '91, '90, '91, and the business, you know we were that close to going under ... because it was when the housing market had crashed. You know interest rates had gone up to fifteen percent, you know it was just a nightmare and the bank were calling in, just about ready to call in the overdraft ... I look back now and I think how did I get through that period ... it was touch and go, it was only because my mum bailed me out financially that I was able to remain a partner in Saddleworths really.

Conclusion

This chapter shows that, among heterosexual couples, emotional openness and mutual support was an expectation, even if it was practised reciprocally with difficulty at times, a traditional gendered division of labour tending to emerge as a fall-back position. As indicated above, emotional withdrawal was seen by more than one woman as 'a male trait', something to be expected, if regretted. What our data also show is the way in which styles of emotional expression, or talk, help constitute the domains of home and work and contribute to the doing of particular kinds of masculinity and femininity. By working across occupational and domestic cultures, and the often permeable boundaries between them, we have been able to identify the ways in which different kinds of relatedness inform ideas about how and what can be expressed. In addition, the contingent nature of social relatedness, as an element of gendered emotionality, has materially grounded dimensions which, for example, express themselves in financial and ownership issues which are not only particular to, but also transcend the boundary between work and home.

15
Men and Friendship

In his work on acquaintanceship, Morgan (2009) explores its linkages with friendship and considers the ways in which sociologists have examined informal relationships in the workplace. This chapter develops our similar focus on emotionality and connection in men's lives at work and at home, paying attention to its gendered, intersubjective nature. As Chapters 13 and 14 demonstrated, home and workplace may not only offer different scope for emotionality and its expression, but arguably are constituted through context-specific gendered emotional practices. In addition, however, we saw how the fluidity and flux of feelings meant that they could not always be contained within one or the other sphere, sometimes leaking across the boundary in problematic ways, sometimes being expressed or managed in settings which had not initially stimulated them, yet where support could be offered, potentially in unpredictable ways. We now move on to consider relationships which may transcend not only the boundary *between* home and work, but also cross boundaries which separate home and work from wider collectivities, such as the extended family, the neighbourhood, clubs and other organisations. In other words, we need to attend to forms of social engagement such as the role of relatives, friends and acquaintances from outside the workplace in fostering business, for example; or the meshing of the domains of leisure, work and family when male colleagues meet up for an evening out which includes their female partners.

Acquaintanceship according to Morgan is ill-defined, noting that friendship itself, that supposedly closer and more tangible connection, was itself a concept that people might use in a whole variety of ways. How the men we worked with understood or imagined friendship was therefore something we could not assume but instead explored in interviews. The interactionist perspective which underpins Morgan's work helpfully reminds us that selves are constructed through connections of different kind being made *between* people – and a focus on friendship thus gives us yet another lens through which to examine masculinity and its relational, processual dimensions as 'being a man' emerges in yet another intersubjective context.

As Chapter 12 describes, Messner ([1992] 2001) offered a critique of the notion that there is a clear, gendered distinction between men's and women's friendships, one which reflects another pervasive argument: that men are emotionally inarticulate when compared with women. While the male athletes among whom Messner worked, in the US, anchored their friendships in an external activity, particularly a form of sport, so securing 'closeness without intimacy', he argues that the presence of this kind of 'doing' relationships should not be unreflexively compared with talk-based friendships between women where self-disclosure was seen as a hallmark of intimacy. When such comparisons are uncritically made, as Messner argues, a 'consensus' emerges that '[w]omen have deep, intimate, meaningful, and lasting friendships, while men have a number of shallow, superficial, and unsatisfying 'aquaintances' (2001: 253). What Messner suggests, instead, is that we recognise the gendered nature of the categories through which we appraise same-sex friendships. In his view, a feminised model of friendship and, indeed, intimacy is in play here. As Jamieson (1998) has shown, the self-revealing, talk-based interaction that we 'know' as intimacy is highly context-specific when examined from historical and cross-cultural perspectives. Her perspective remains important as we engage with our own, more recent study in the discussion below.

Mates not friends?

Sociological studies of workplace relationships draw attention to the diversity of occupations and how this influences relationships with home (Morgan, 2009), a key feature of our own study. Where a particular occupation dominated a locale, with almost all of those living nearby being employed within that setting – such as mining and fishing communities (see Dennis et al., 1956, cited in Morgan, 2009: 36), work-based relationships would spill out into occupationally specific leisure environments, such as the Miners' Welfare Hall. In addition, they were likely to encompass family relationships, particularly between fathers, sons, uncles and brothers. Other studies, however, such as Roethlisberger and Dickson's (1939) work on factories, where formal management strategies and informal practices were compared, have stressed the looser connections between fellow workers, focussing more on the role of those relationships within the workings of the factory overall (cited in Morgan, 2009: 35–6). Goldthorpe et al.'s (1968) study of car workers brought out the distinctive nature of these looser connections that were bounded by life in the factory, describing men's distinctions between 'mates' and 'friends'.

To what extent, we ask, does this distinction hold within the environments we have been engaged with? As our data indicate, workplace relationships can extend into leisure activities – as was particularly the case among hairdressers. Indeed, among hairdressers and estate agents, some men were working with other family members, particularly partners, sometimes as joint owners of a business. As Morgan points out, Goldthorpe et al.'s (1968) findings have been interpreted as evidence of the separateness of work and family, of work's more emotionally constrained, rational instrumental culture. This view of the workplace has subsequently been challenged, both by studies which have made informal, emotional exchange in the workplace their focus (Hearn, 1993; Collinson and Hearn, 1996), and those which highlight the importance of work as a site within which individuals generate their 'social life' and indeed find a partner with whom to establish a shared domestic life.

It was apparent among the men we interviewed that their work-related relationships were experienced within a broader life course perspective which might well encompass friendships generated much earlier in life. In other words, not only was the workplace a source of friends, but for men who had been born and educated locally, these might blend into a larger friendship group of men drawn from both sources. Many of the firefighters had lived in the area all their lives and Richard Shawcross (23), said:

> half of lads that I hang about with now I've known since I were like three or four … when I started working away I didn't hang about with them as much, they got jobs and they were working a lot and I were working a lot … we didn't really see as much of each other through probably secondary school to like seventeen-year-old sort of thing we didn't really hang about as much. And then when I started going out drinking locally and things like that, they were out so obviously like we got back in together.

Being a part of a group with a long-shared history then formed a basis for developing further friendships:

> And then there's a few … other half of lads that come out they're a year and two years below me [at school] but they've always lived in

Shale ... they've started coming out drinking ... I didn't know them before but like you're just in boozer and you get to know people and we've all become best mates and we all, like last five years, we've all gone away together, twenty of us gone away, loads, couples as well, loads. Greece mainly, Gran Canaria, Kos, Falaraki, somewhere like that.

Richard's notion of 'best mates' is therefore a capacious category, one which might be compared with feminised notion of a 'best friend' as someone with whom a close, dyadic relationship is maintained, a relationship which in many ways resembles heterosexual monogamy (see also Miller, 1983; Pahl, 2000; Davidson et al., 2003). Richard's mates are clearly male, though he made very brief mention of the fact that when they went away in a large group it was 'couples as well'.

Phil Cruikshank (41), an estate agent, said he counted the people he worked with as 'friends': 'friends with them, yes I ... each other after work for a drink. That's not very regular. But there's probably one person I see more than anybody who we meet up with, his wife, go out for a meal, occasionally, things like that, so yeah'. As opposed to the large, pub-based group of 'best mates' that 23-year-old Richard Shawcross describes, 41-year-old Phil pursues friendship less avidly and, it appears, more explicitly within the context of shared heterosexual coupledom. Nonetheless when socialising with a colleague and both their female partners, it becomes apparent that there are contradictions in what he finds 'interesting' subject matter for conversation. When asked if a shared meal meant talking about work, he said: 'I think the, it does come up but eventually it withers away and we talk about interesting things, but it does crop up because it's so many interesting stuff that's happened during the day, just have to call and chat about you know'.

Simon Pulling (52), a mortgage consultant at Saddleworths, described himself as 'Local through and through and I know the city, like the back of my hand'. However, largely as a result of two marriages and divorces, he now lived in a city about 20 miles away from the one he worked in. For him, friendship was muted, even though he 'knew' a lot people. When asked about his friends, he said: 'most of mine are like what from football or things like that, then, I don't make lots of friends, I, I know a lot of people but I don't get close to many people, so like I say I've always known people, chatted to people, can go out but I don't live in anybody's pocket'.

In the interview Simon was asked whether friendship for him involved sharing workplace or marital problems. He answered: 'No, never, never dream of ... I'm quite private in that ... I just sort it out myself and what I tend to do, I do a lot of running'. His response raises the question of what it is that constitutes the currency of friendship and our data suggest that to an extent the workplace itself – and the work undertaken there – provides a repertoire of friendship styles and values which challenge any easy gendered distinction between 'closeness without intimacy' and 'talk-based self revelatory friendship'. Robinson's (2008) account of friendship between male climbers similarly shows that intimacy can be fostered within extreme situations of danger, mundane activities of sharing a ledge while waiting for others to complete their climb *and* self-revelatory talk. As one climber said of his climbing friends: ' we talk far more about how we are and what's going on in our relationships than I ever do with any of my other mates ... my mates that are not climbers, definitely are not actually very good at talking normally about their emotions' (Robinson, 2008: 109).

Among firefighters, risk and adrenaline spikes lay at the heart of the job, something now anticipated across an increasingly large number of days spent in the fire station, or out on community work. In this context of wearisome and indeed stressful routine, the challenge and potential sting of banter and piss-taking was a key expression of sociality. Moreover, those individuals whose company was most relished were described through metaphors drawn from the domain of madness. Mickey Smith (26) said of his watch: 'its quality because you just constantly working with people that are having loads of fun, they're mental at this station ... are a lot crazier than they were at Hazlinghurst but, Gaz and Jack are off their heads, and Pete, I think Pete should probably be sectioned'.

They can be compared with young hairdressers whose professional lives are as much about extended one-to-one conversations with clients, as the technologies of cutting and colouring hair. As Patrick Valentine, 28, noted 'you don't usually sit down with somebody on a one to one for an hour ... I wouldn't go into a bar and sit next to somebody for an hour' (see also Chapter 13). Sustaining that relationship across years was something that hairdressers saw as important, a point made by older hairdressers in particular who owned small salons in working-class areas. This elision of the client/hairdresser relationship and that which binds hairdressers themselves was evident when Gary Highgate (32) said: 'most of my clients have been coming to me for quite a long time, so it's like seeing friends'.

Hairdresser Sam Cartmell (28) explained that the good atmosphere in the upmarket, city-centre salon where he worked was a result of the longevity and closeness of relationships among staff

> years of, of knowing each other ... I think as hairdressers ... you're so used to talking to people that ... sometimes you possibly are a little too honest ... you're so used to dealing with people, so once you get on to a social level with your friends ... you're not scared to say what you think, or do what you think ... and so obviously you, you become friends and then you know after years of working with people who are ... like your family er you know that much about them, you can be nothing but honest. So we're all that close now, and we've been through that much together, that we are bound together ... even if we, we split up ... as a group, you know, tomorrow ... they'll have had, they've had such an effect on each others lives that, they're always gonna be there.

Sam went on to compare hairdressing with 'other professions' where he felt people were likely to be less happy in their work. He said: 'you wake up in the morning, you think well actually I am quite lucky. I get on with everybody who I work with, you know they're all my friends ... at end of day, you know that you, you all love each other and stuff'.

Like firefighter Richard Shawcross's notion of 'all best mates', Sam's concept of friendship is broad and inclusive, yet its core currency is honesty and openness, rather than daring, craziness and humour. This point was also echoed by Gary Highgate (32) when asked about his domestic relationships, particularly those with his mother. Were there aspects of his life that he wouldn't confide in her? ' No,' he said, 'not anymore, I've been pretty, pretty open with my mum over the past few years. I think you kind of like have to lay your cards on the table so they know who you are'. Not only does Gary claim honesty; he expresses it as a value: 'I've been pretty good at just being able to be honest with her'.

These data highlight the contingent nature of friendship and the meanings, values and practices which constitute it. Gender alone cannot be used as an explanation, however; rather, the nature of work and its everyday practices provides a model for relating to other people, and in particular, sustaining friendship.

When we consider friendship among estate agents, 52-year-old Simon Pulling's model of 'knowing a lot of people' without getting 'close to many people' was not uncommon, as a style of friendship.

Indeed, it echoed the breadth of many men's professional contacts – even though the people they 'knew' were not necessarily all from their working lives, instead being fellow members of sports clubs and other leisure environments. As Chapter 8 described, some of the estate agents we interviewed had shifted across boundaries of social class, modifying their accents and acknowledging the differences between their own and their working-class fathers' identities in terms of their clothing: they had become 'suit men'. More than that, however, 'selling yourself', which was how one young estate agent described his approach to clients, required the capacity to adopt an appropriate persona, depending upon the kind of client or professional contact he was engaged with. Though professional networks among developers and solicitors were important, the individuals who were key to many estate agents' everyday lives were vendors and purchasers. They might only be encountered once, albeit with potential intensity at they moved between homes and perhaps relationships and identities. In this sense they resembled the fire and rescue victims encountered by firefighters, rather than the long-haul clients of hairdressers. For estate agents, then, friendship was more a matter of carefully bounded one-to-one friendships, within the context of a wide range of what Morgan would call acquaintances, in that they 'lie somewhere between intimates and strangers' and that the level of reciprocity between acquaintances can vary from 'high to low or possibly absent' (2009: 108).

Chrissie Hardwick, partner of Brett Hardwick (58) said:

> We have quite a lot of social functions that we sort of do things, occasionally sort of dinner at someone's house, we have friends through Brett's business, we're going to a wedding tomorrow, which is a business friend of Brett's who I know now and his wife, we're going to their son's wedding tomorrow so, a lot of our friends are sort of joint friends and then Brett has a, he knows so many people ... from business, because he's been in Maidstone for sort of thirty odd years, he's just got such a wide circle of people that he knows.

However, like Simon Pulling, Chrissie says that Brett has 'only got a few what I'd call close friends'. Similarly Stephanie Holdsworth, wife of 64-year-old Marcus Holdsworth, said that although they had many friends, if things were not going well for Marcus, he would talk to 'probably his accountant [laughs] no, he's, he's, you know, a good chum of

Marcus, I mean he would you know obviously talk to me about these things but not really, no, I think he's sort of very, very much a private sort of person, in that respect'. And Sarah Ward, partner of 28-year-old Paul Lewis, referred to Paul having quite a large group of friends who, to some extent, he sees on his own. However, when it comes to closeness she says that ' I think more, more one friend than out of them all, he'd probably talk to about personal stuff but the others a bit more, that would be a bit more social'.

Conclusion

Messner urges caution about assuming that friendship between men is about 'bonding without intimacy' (2001: 254). He says that, on the contrary, the athletes among whom he worked felt 'a depth of affection' for one another. Citing Swain (1991), Messner argues that men's friendships should be viewed through their own eyes, rather than the lens of a 'feminine model'. This perspective allows us to recognise the importance of a 'covert style of intimacy' and Messner refers to his own interview material from among athletes, one of whom says of his friendship with a team mate, 'We didn't *have* to talk about everything; We just *knew* we were on the same page' (2001: 254). In a similar vein, firefighter Daniel Armstrong (25) said that among the men on his watch 'I genuinely would say I get on well with Gaz and Jack out of most just because we have a good laugh, same wavelength and that we have a, well we take piss all time basically'.

In sum, learning a particular style of friendship – practising it not only among work colleagues but *as* a member of particular occupational culture, enabled men to generate 'covert intimacy', whether through the craziness of the watch, the loyalty and honesty which bound many hairdressers, or the exclusivity of estate agents' relatively fewer close friends, often among whom was their female partner. Thus, for firefighters, friendship was in part constituted through team work in the risky, if thrilling, conditions of a fire or accident. This practice was complemented by the provision of mutual support, whether explicitly directed towards emotional distress, or more obliquely expressive of that distress through humour, along with the gauging of an appropriate level of challenging wit and banter. Among hairdressers, the longstanding, and at least superficially 'confessional' relationships engendered with clients, were mirrored in the valuing of open, talk-based sociality between colleagues, one that often extended into a social life that merged with the relationships forged within the salon itself. For estate agents, however, the competitive and individualistic nature of their workplace relationships, and the centrality of formal and informal social contacts, gave friendship quite a specific nature, one that combined privacy and exclusivity with the cultivation of a diversity of 'people' who are 'known'.

16
Emotionality and the Research Process

In the three previous chapters we have explored the ways in which the men and women interviewed described the place of emotion within their everyday lives. In so doing, we explained their models of emotionality and their 'feelings rules' for practices such as 'getting over' negative feelings, 'being honest' about emotional difficulties, 'not letting on' when teasing stimulated anger. Alongside these reflective data, we have also placed observational material deriving from time spent among men at work. These show feelings being *expressed* – fear, laughter, warmth, embarrassment, irritation, etc. What this chapter addresses is the place of emotion within the research process itself and we explore three aspects of its contribution to understanding: emotionality as a source of information about participants which might help explain other dimensions of their working and domestic lives; as a strategy for securing access to the relationships and rapport without which data cannot be gathered; and as a means of participating in the flow of everyday lives rather than simply observing them.

This list does not indicate whose feelings we are talking about for we are treating emotion as intersubjective. Here we draw on the work of Holmes (2010) who argues that *reading* emotion is an inevitably uncertain process, one which she nonetheless describes as increasingly central to contemporary social life where traditional sources of authority – or indeed traditions – are less accessible as sources of certainty. Holmes suggests that reflexivity – the capacity to alter one's life in response to knowledge about one's circumstances – is emotionally informed in ways that more rational or cognitive models of reflexivity neglect. While her primary focus is not reflexivity within research practice, she does offer useful pointers when making sense of reflexivity-in-action as observed among our research participants. She critiques a conception of emotions as 'inner individual events that are then socially expressed or managed', instead arguing that '[e]motions are produced within relationships and their associated social and linguistic practices' (2010: 145). In our own work, we similarly consider interactions between participants and researchers as intersubjective, embodied, *emotionalized* encounters.

When presenting our study of masculinities to academic audiences before empirical work had begun, we were often told that men's working environments were inaccessible to women – or at least those associated with stereotypically 'hard', working-class masculinity. Robinson (2008), for example, notes that her access to 'elite' climbers was possible only because of her 'insider' status within the climbing community. When we subsequently produced data from these settings, some audiences were sceptical of their status, claiming that men would amend their speech and behaviour out of secrecy, chivalry or embarrassment. Yet as Robinson (2008) goes on to argue, gender and 'insiderhood' are aspects of research relationships that are anything but straightforward. Indeed, the comments we received as part of the current study were useful in helping us develop our awareness of the gendered nature of our interactions with the men and women whose working lives we participated in and whose narratives we recorded. As critiques, however, they represent a focus on the rational or cognitive dimensions of reflexivity – for example, a considered decision to block access or to 'fake' what is said or done when the researcher is present. By contrast, this chapter is concerned with the *emotional* dimensions of accessing and building relationships between ourselves and those among whom we worked. Thus, we show how embodied engagement with participants drew us into the gendered emotional practices through which our participants and we undertook intersubjective, emotionalised reflexivity (Holmes, 2010). The data we explore derive from fieldnotes made during participant observation among estate agents where relatedness, intersubjectivity and the uncertain status of emotion were evident in particularly telling ways.

Getting to know you

Building on our concern with emotion as relational – a view of emotions as 'felt and done within relations to other people and things' (Holmes, 2010: 145), we begin with discussion of the importance of *personal* relationships as both a route into estate agency, one of our occupational environments, and the stuff of men's working lives within that environment. When Alex Hall secured access to two estate agents, it was through the personal contacts of the two other members of the research team who were more familiar with the area chosen for the study. Moreover, from the beginning of her work with this occupational group, she was participating in the practices of a profession where personal contacts were the stock-in-trade of successful business. Here, in fieldnotes, she describes Todd Saddleworth, the eponymous head of a high profile company, at work:

> [As we leave a potential vendor's home] He reflects to me that he carefully turned the conversation around to someone they both knew in the village. He says 'you have to get your good bits in', implying that tracing mutual acquaintances is a good way of establishing trust and reputation ... he knows so many people in the area; this is a very good technique.

> [At the next potential vendor's property] It turns out that [the client's] fiancé plays golf at a club Todd knows and is friendly with someone Todd knows, as well as knowing Michael Vaughan.

During this visit, Todd repeatedly took calls on his mobile phone, rolling his eyes to demonstrate what a nuisance he found them, a practice which gave substance to his claims to being so widely connected.

Later, as Todd and Alex visit another potential vendor, 'a woman shoots out of her house, hugs Todd and greets him like an old friend. Todd later tells me she is a man-eater, is currently with a judge and she was after him a while back. He certainly seems to know everyone'. When Alex finally completed the day with Todd he recommended an Indian restaurant in town and told her the owner knew him and she should mention his name.

Trust, established through social networks and reputation, through feelings of good will, were thus critical in a business which was volatile and uncertain, and where property and wealth were entangled with emotional dimensions of home, family and privacy. Personal contacts were thus a route to participation in the occupational lives of estate agents. Once access was in place, relationships with individuals were key to generating data. Not only was emotional interaction an important dimension of building such relationships, but in carrying out this 'emotion work' (Hochschild, 1983), an understanding of the nature of everyday gendered social relations could be developed.

For example, during Alex's initial meeting with John Sargent, who had set up Timpkins estate agency, the emotional stances they both adopted, and the feelings this encounter inspired in Alex, revealed much about the nature of both the business itself and the doing of masculinity in this setting. In fieldnotes she says, 'John asked if I was Alex, and we shook hands (strong, "dominant", business-like, lots of eye contact). He motioned me to follow him upstairs ... (after opening conversation) he was keen to be seen as knowledgeable, keen to give his opinions about things, keen to talk. I liked him – he had a sense of humour and enjoyed a bit of light-hearted banter. He appreciated someone to joke with'.

John, therefore, made his impression upon Alex rapidly, both through what he said, his embodied engagement with her, and his humour. As a newcomer to this environment she was reassured through a practiced emotional style which implied feelings of confidence, warmth and authority on the part of John.

When she arrived on the first day of participant observation, however, she encountered a different performance of masculinity, one which suggested a difficult emotional reflexivity on the part of a very junior male member of staff who worked alongside John's practised confidence. On entry to the office, she records, she was asked if she was '"here to watch Tim". Tim himself is sitting at the back of the office – looking a bit wary by now. He is in his late twenties to early thirties. He is slightly nerdy-looking. He has glasses and looks and acts older than he is. He is also quite serious – he doesn't seem very "charming" or gregarious, but perhaps a little shy, or awkward'.

If we examine the recording of this first encounter with Tim, it becomes apparent how Alex, as an experienced researcher, then carried out the emotion work necessary to pursue her professional agenda, just as John had demonstrated his professional skills upon initially meeting her:

> (on first engaging with Tim) I explain a bit about the project and what I want to do. He seems a bit easier with me after a little while – I am careful to ask him a few chatty and sociable questions about his girlfriend, his home, etc. He relaxes visibly and seems ok with me just sitting watching him. I am sat at a desk behind Tracey who works at the branch ... she makes a few witty remarks at the expense of Tim – perhaps he is seen as the office 'geek'? It's hard to tell at this stage how the politics of the office work out. Sally (another member of staff) and Tracey seem quite close. They talk about holiday plans and nights out. They go off to a valuation after a while, and Tim remarks quietly to me that 'it doesn't need to take two of them to go and do it'. The implication is that they are friendly but he is often left to do all the work.

Compared with firefighters, men in estate agency enter a fiercely hierarchical occupation where those in the most powerful positions – usually the company's partners – represent a confident, authoritative style of masculinity which can both inspire but also undermine younger men (see Chapter 5). As Alex continued her period of fieldwork she observed Tim's frequent periods of anxious, emotionalised reflexivity as he 'ruminated' about dealings with clients which had left him feeling less than competent. The fear of professional scrutiny via a 'mystery shopper' was pervasive.

Office tactics

In her account of meeting John and Tim, Alex describes two kinds of gendered interaction, the first where she, a woman, required the approval of a man, John, who was in a position to refuse her. In securing this approval, she drew from him a performance of his style of 'professional' masculinity. In the second interaction, a younger man, Tim, inspired a sense of concern on the part of Alex, a woman, and in showing empathy she established a relationship of trust. This resulted in him giving her an insight into the class and gendered hierarchy of office politics. Her emotional empathy was therefore the currency which secured her the data which she wanted to gather. It might seem, therefore, that as researchers we are every bit as disingenuous as the men who manage a public identity as 'glib, untrustworthy salesmen' (Hall et al., 2007). This perception, however, returns us to the model of emotion as an internal event that may be expressed publicly with varying degrees of accuracy. Indeed, the distinction between 'authentic' and 'pretend' emotion (Denzin, cited in Lupton, 1998: 24) can be seen as key to contemporary cultural constructions of 'emotion', as our data have shown. Instead, however, what we are concerned with here is the workplace (of both the participant and the researcher), and the home, as constitutive of embodied, *intersubjective* emotionality. As such, we therefore pay attention to emotionalized intersubjectivities of various kinds, ones, we argue, that must include that which connects the participants and the researcher.

As Alex experienced the discomfort of being an ambiguous newcomer in both Timpkins and Saddleworths estate agencies, she wrote reflexively about issues of emotional authenticity. Her entry into new territories of emotional expression and practice effectively alerted her to the presence of occupationally specific feelings rules and the uncertainties of their emotional interpretation. As Denzin argues, 'emotional practices make people problematic objects to themselves. The emotional practice radiates through the person's body and streams of experience, giving emotional coloration to thoughts, feelings, and actions' (cited in Lupton, 1998: 24).

On her first day at Saddleworths, Alex noted that staff 'display signs of the "emotional labour" and the "professional performance" of their type of work – that is, the forced politeness and cheery manners are obviously and openly acknowledged as a front. Phone calls are ended with rude comments and complaints about customers, expletives and eye rolling at perceived awkwardness'.

While Alex used theoretical concepts such as 'emotional labour' and 'professional performance', it is clear that her interpretation of the situation was not simply grounded in sociological concepts. She says, 'Everyone seems quite friendly, though I am aware of their "gossipy" character – I get the distinct feeling I am being discussed behind my back. They seem to do it with all the clients, and I am no different'. Through participant observation, then, Alex located herself in territory which for her had a hybrid status. She was 'behind the scenes', witnessing what is concealed from the public; yet she was not 'one of them' and as such found herself experiencing what the public experiences – while being confronted with what the public do not witness, thereby positioning herself on both sides of the fence simultaneously. She understood this position in part through the emotional atmosphere which she was also participating in, as she experienced 'embarrassment', and times when she felt 'awkward but not too excruciating'. At Timpkins, she observed Tim, the young male member of staff, using what she identified as *an* 'understated and straightforward' telephone manner – and was aware that she 'much prefers his telephone manner to the cheery falseness of Saddleworths'.

When Alex recorded – and we read – examples such as those which follow, we may feel an emotionally grounded sense of unease as we gain powerful insight into relations of power grounded in the paradox of someone making the concealment of negative feelings from one person deliberately visible to others. For example, when a vendor angered office staff by making what they deemed an unreasonable request and later re-entered the office with a mortgage consultant, Ivor (who had refused the request), Alex witnessed the following: 'Sharon (receptionist) exchanges a look with me and with Dave – keeping down a giggle. Dave smirks and rolls his eyes slightly. He is hovering around the woman and flashes what I think is a sinister kind of smile – a bit 'put on' and not very genuine – every time she turns his way'.

At Timpkins, Alex observed a similarly skilful performance whereby the concealment of negative emotion from one person was made visible to others. Tracey, a member of the office staff, had cleaned the Perspex display holders in the window. Later a client entered with a child who hid behind the display, putting his hands all over it. When they left the mother told the child to say goodbye to everyone and 'Tracey joins in with a cheery 'Bye ...!" and, without missing a beat, continues on with "...and get a fucking cloth" when the woman is just outside the door. Everyone laughs.'

Like Alex we may feel uneasy when we read these examples. We may find Sharon and Tracey very unpleasant. We may become aware of our own vulnerability whenever we engage with a service industry of some kind, a vulnerability we might fear extends even to encounters with our family and friends. We may feel guilt or embarrassment over times when we too made it evident to others that we were concealing our feelings from someone. Not only Alex, in her proximity to these practices, but also we, the readers of her fieldnotes, participate in the emotional processes unfolding within two estate agents' offices. Among theorists of emotion, some challenge the notion of 'real' and 'fake' feelings (see Lupton, 1998). Holmes, for example, refers to 'avoiding the idea of a "real" self and "real" emotions which must be uncovered' (2010: 148). As Lupton details, the 'strong' thesis of a social constructionist approach to emotion is that it is 'an intersubjective rather than an individual phenomenon, constituted in relations between people' (1998: 16). On the one hand, then, if we become aware of an emotional response as we read these data, we can interpret what we are feeling as an intersubjective phenomenon which links us to the data. Equally, in experiencing these feelings we too participate in an environment where a distinction between 'real' and 'fake' emotion is driving the power relations in play between estate agency staff and their clients. Being able to 'fake', and stimulate laughter through 'faking', rests upon a shared belief in the internal location of 'true' feelings and the possibility of a self-aggrandising management of those feelings in order to fit in with prevailing practices, or impress colleagues with one's bravado. If we feel emotionally uneasy when we read about these practices, this reveals our own commitment to this distinction as members of a shared culture. And it is here that our enquiry into emotionality among estate agents begins, since alongside data generated within the study, we have discovered within ourselves the feelings rules (Hochschild, 1979) which govern men's and women's interactions and aspirations within this setting. These are the data we then engage with.

Conclusion

This section of the book has explored the importance of emotional control among firefighters, where the capacity to contain anger inspired by teasing was key to membership of the watch; and the centrality of sustaining a form of emotional intimacy across both hour-long hairdressing appointments and extended hairdresser–client relationships. In this chapter we have looked in some detail at reflexive fieldnotes generated through participant observation among estate agents. This example was chosen because it is in this environment that paradoxes surrounding the nature of 'emotion' are most evident. For firefighters, emotions were seen as intrinsic, an aspect of the embodied self which, just like the body, were vulnerable to the unpredictable turn of events while responding to a call. For example, in Chapter 13 we described an older firefighter saying of a younger colleague's nervous breakdown: 'I know this lad and I still know him ... and that was genuine ... he had his breaking point and everybody's got it but I've, I've just not reached it yet.'

Even though estate agents shared a model of emotion as intrinsic to the individual, and also reported stress-induced nervous breakdowns, they perceived the nature of emotionality as somehow more complex. As Chapter 6 described, when an established estate agent was discussing his capacity to establish feelings of trust in the client he said of himself, 'I shouldn't have to make an effort, it should be natural ... I shouldn't have to put on an act, for them to trust me.' Yet when another estate agent was asked 'do you actually need to be genuine or do you just need to be able to inspire the appearance of genuine?' and he replied 'I think that's quite correct and I think that's a sales skill that some people don't have because they're, they don't actually project'. Thus, discussions of the importance of sounding 'genuine' in dealings with clients highlighted men's belief in a distinction between 'real' and 'achieved' feelings; and their awareness of the paradox that if 'real' emotions are not actively 'projected' then feelings of trust are not inspired in clients.

The fieldnotes explored in this chapter therefore demonstrate a belief in the distinction between 'real' and 'fake' emotion being played out in interactions between staff and clients; such that it is a resource through which occupational identities are built. Where clients are engaged in the emotionally charged activity of buying and selling their homes, possibly at a time of personal loss and change, after divorce or bereavement, an 'us' and 'them' boundary, constituted through undercover aggression and abuse, distances the estate agency staff from those among whom they seek business. Moreover, in a highly competitive business where considerable wealth and status are held out as rewards, 'awkward customers' are emotionally threatening, not only in an immediate, interactive sense, but also in terms of disappointment and diminished status if deals do not 'reach the right conclusion', as Brad Charrier put it (Chapter 13). By locating herself within this environment as a participant observer, Alex not only gained access to emotional interplays of this kind, but also experienced the sometimes unpleasant intersubjective relations of power made possible through a particular understanding and expression of emotion. As data, her fieldnotes extend the scope of this intersubjectivity, including not only other members of the research team, but also the readers of these reflexive accounts. And by engaging with this material, emotionally, we too 'feel' our way into the processes of gendered identification in play within this particular occupational environment.

17
Undoing Gender/Gender Undone

In this concluding chapter we ask what has been achieved through both the project drawn upon throughout the book and the book itself. What we have set out to understand is the potential fluidity of gendered subjectivities as individuals move between social environments, an enquiry which reflects broader and more profound questions about the nature of human subjectivity itself, and how the quality of individual experience comes into being. To pursue this enquiry we drew on theories of identity – and in particular gendered identity – which treat it as an outcome of socially and materially grounded practice. This is not, however, to dismiss the importance of discourses and representations within the making and remaking of gender. Rather, we think in terms of discursive practices, that is to say the ways in which frameworks of ideas not only serve as a set of criteria against which we are measured, and measure ourselves, the mechanisms of gender accountability (West and Zimmerman, 1987), but also as a repertoire of possibilities which are drawn upon by individuals as they encounter and interact within the social world. Moreover, we understand that it is through practice that historically and culturally specific norms, beliefs and values become persuasive, gaining rhetorical power as 'knowledge' about the nature of masculinity and femininity. As social and material contexts change, however, so practice alters, and being a man or woman is achieved differently. Indeed, we would argue, one becomes a somewhat different kind of man or woman.

We began with an emic, or 'folk' theory about the failure of marriages and family life, a breakdown in heterosexual coupledom. According to this theory, being a firefighter involves gendered practices, and opportunities for practice, which are incompatible with those through which heterosexual coupledom is achieved. While our data do not support this theory in any straightforward way, the theory, in itself, merits examination. To varying extents, firefighters live up to the stereotype of being 'the last working class hero' (Baigent, 2001); they are members of an occupation grounded in military discipline which requires physically and emotionally challenging team work that binds men together for shifts – or tours – of two days and two nights. It might seem, therefore, that their scope for an unequivocally masculine identity would mesh well with the markedly oppositional framing of gender that traditional heterosexual coupledom shores up (Richardson, 1996). Yet, as shown in our accounts of men's vulnerability and the emotional economy negotiated between men and women living as a couple (Chapter 14), heterosexuality is not simply a juxtaposition of gender identities marked out by difference rather than similarity. Rather, it is a site at which both femininity and masculinity emerge as the outcome of intersubjective processes which serve to both regulate and empower one another. What we describe in Chapter 14, then, has roots in nineteenth century expectations, such as the requirement that mothers 'regulate their male children and produce them as rational, dispassionate citizens' (Lupton, 1998: 111). In other words, it is through participation and engagement that particular kinds of difference and similarity are actively produced, rather than simply colliding in an externally generated encounter. Holland et al.'s (1998) work on heterosexual practice among young men and women, for example, argues that through shared participation in dating and sex a particular kind of masculinity is produced and reproduced, a set of values and beliefs which are internalised and upheld by both young men and young women.

In addition, the notion that firefighters cannot accommodate to the culture of home attributes identity with a kind of elastic quality. In other words, identification, as a fluid process, can stretch, but only so far. After that one is not simply 'identifying' – 'doing' gender as a fluid process – one has somehow become another person in that the way one appears to others is radically out of kilter with how one experiences oneself. Subjective and objective selves are therefore so far apart that the individual cannot identify, or 'do' gender, adequately. One feels a fraud and fools no one. The ongoing external–internal dialectic, the meshing of personal and social identity, has juddered to a halt. Such a process resembles what Goffman (1968) describes as 'passing' where a deliberate mismatch between external and internal identification is achieved.

What then do we mean when we speak of 'doing' gender, or when we use the term identification rather than identity to signal a process rather than a state? Kelan (2010) discusses the emancipatory argument that if we can figure out how gender is actually 'done', then we can 'undo' it and so overcome forms of gender oppression at both ideological and material levels. What she problematises, however, are assumptions about what 'undoing' gender might mean. What, she asks, might it require and how will we recognise it if it happens. For example, undoing gender might mean rising above gender to create contexts where it is an irrelevance. Associated with this is the supposition that in some contexts, other dimensions of identity – such as ethnicity or class – might be more relevant than gender. This, she is not persuaded by, arguing that the notion of intersectionality draws attention to the inevitable enmeshment of these dimensions of identity; class and ethnicity, for example, cannot but be gendered. In addition, she argues that many attempts to 'undo' gender implicitly concern themselves with 'doing' gender differently, becoming a different kind of man or woman, yet leaving gender itself, as a binary, in place. This she suggests is not 'undoing' anything for, as Halberstam (1998) argues, 'gender's very flexibility and seeming fluidity is precisely what allows dimorphic gender to hold sway' (cited in Kelan, 2010: 188). Nonetheless, doing gender differently, so creating a multiplicity of gendered possibilities renders a binary model less symbolically efficacious. A potentially generative project is underway and the resulting multiplicity of forms or practices may become increasingly less orderly, to the extent that they stray across a gender divide, muddying the track as they go.

One theoretical resource that Kelan (2010) posits is Halberstam's notion of female masculinity (1998, cited in Kelan, 2010: 188). This, Kelan argues, 'disturbs the gender binary as it shows that female bodies can perform something that is readable as masculinity. The position is part of the gender binary yet creates a new reading which problematizes it' (2010: 188). This possibility is expressed most clearly in the notion that the gender binary 'masculine/feminine' can be deployed, through embodied practice, to undo the gender binary 'man/woman'.

If we consider the data presented in this book, drawing on the inverse of Halberstam's female masculinity to consider the possibility of male femininity, that is embodied performances of 'femininity', or particular elements of it, by a man, we can ask questions about the undoing of gender which help make sense of the transitions which lie at the heart of our enquiry. Cox's reference to nineteenth-century homophobia, for example, where she cites a writer's assertion that 'it *only* requires five hairpins and a petticoat for a hairdresser to be a woman' (our emphasis added) is indicative of the symbolic potency of something we might call male femininity.

The unitary self?

Before proceeding, however, we ask further questions about the nature of 'the self' and 'selfhood' in order to clarify how we might understand concepts such as female masculinity or male femininity. To what extent can we think of human beings as composites of different identities, the 'bits' model, as Jenkins (2004) describes it? We begin by drawing, one more time, on theoretical perspectives we have derived from an emic theory that occupational identities override or disrupt marital, familial or domestic identities among firefighters; for example, the notion of 'mobile masculinities' that treats identity as a process and gender as the outcome of context-specific practice. What model of the self are we referencing and contributing to when we theorise in this way? As argued above, the notion of identity as elastic, something which can stretch between contexts, up to a point, suggests the possibility of a unitary self. Yet, as Jenkins describes, authors such as Freud, Mead and Berne have posited what he describes as a 'bits' model (2004: 44), one within which performance and practice are the outcome of internal conversations, albeit fuelled by externally derived information.

As we follow an older hairdresser such as Gordon Bristow, or Dominic Treadwell, a young firefighter, Brad Charrier, a highly successful estate agent, between their workplace and home, how do we understand the processual dimension of their identification? And if masculinity and its potential for mutability, or indeed undoing, is our focus, then how we understand the process of identification is crucial. The 'bits' model is one that Jenkins (2004) takes issue with. Yet it has a surprisingly wide currency. Montaigne, for example, said that 'We are all patchwork, and so shapeless and diverse in composition that each bit, each moment, plays its own game. And there is as much difference between us and ourselves as between us and others' (cited in Mercier, 2008: front matter). Pessoa, the Spanish poet, published under literary personas whose biographies and religious and political views he mapped so carefully that they became hetero – rather than pseudo –nyms. He said 'Each of us is several, is many, is a profusion of selves. So that the self who disdains his surroundings is not the same as the self who suffers or takes joy in them. In the vast colony of our being there are many species of people who think and feel in different ways' (cited in Mercier, 2008: front matter).

The notion that self and other can be subsumed within a 'bits' model has also been used to reflect on another binary, good/evil. In *The Strange Case of Dr Jekyll and Mr Hyde*, Robert Louis Stevenson ([1886] 1987) opened 'Henry Jekyll's Full Statement of the Case', his character's rationale for medically inducing his transformation to Mr Hyde, with a discussion of the contradictions he already felt were co-existing within himself: 'Hence it came about that I concealed my pleasures; and that when I reached years of reflection, and began to look round me, and take stock of my progress and position in the world, I stood already committed to a profound duplicity of life' ([1886] 1987: 60).

When we compare hairdressers, who move between the feminised worlds of the salon and the home (for however 'male' a home might appear, it remains accountable to feminised concepts of comfort and cleanliness), with firefighters whose occupational culture is markedly masculinised, are we exploring the extent to which that transition requires the adoption almost of a different persona? How can we explain almost a preoccupation with the concept of multiplicity within the self in many areas of Western culture, both literary and more popular? In Geertz's (1983) account of selfhood in three different societies, Java, Bali and Morocco, he describes being disconcerted by encounters with very different notions what it meant to be a person: the effacement of individuality in Java, the individual as a character with a prescribed part to play within Balinese society and the contextually defined and therefore multiple selfhood aspired to in Morocco. He says, '[t]he Western conception of the person as a bounded, unique, more or less integrated motivational and cognitive universe, a dynamic center of awareness, emotion, judgment, and action organized into a distinctive whole and set contrastively both against other such wholes and against its social and natural background, is, however incorrigible it may seem to us, a rather peculiar idea within the context of the world's cultures (1983: 59).

It would seem, therefore, that for many Westerners, a felt lack of internal coherence, a capacity to behave differently in different contexts, is somehow at odds with the values such as 'honesty' and 'sincerity', rendering the statement made by Stevenson's Henry Jekyll a confession of deviance. This, in effect, is what Atkinson and Silverman (1997) refer to as 'a stubbornly persistent Romantic impulse' towards a discoverable interior self whose authenticity is grounded in revealed experience. If we return to Jenkins' (2004) response to Freud, Mead and Berne, however, and his focus on the embodied nature of selfhood, we do find a helpful model. While this problematises the internal diversity which engages Montaigne, Pessoa and Henry Jekyll, it does constitute a resource for understanding identification as a fluid process through which identity – and its associations with sameness, consistency and continuity – comes into being. Thus, Jenkins describes selfhood as 'a rich amalgam of knowledge and feelings, both individual and collective, and thoroughly interconnected and interdependent' (2004: 45). He goes on to cite embodiment, emotionality, sensory knowledge, creativity and imagination, tacit embodied competences and memory as constitutive of 'human nature', a set of capacities which enable 'the processual character of selfhood', as opposed to the reified notion of 'the self' (2004: 51).

This dynamic model thus allows us to consider how a traditional, hierarchical gender binary might be resilient, despite its multiplicity of performances, yet still, potentially, be undoable. To return to the question raised at the beginning of this chapter – of what this book and its underpinning project have achieved, our work has engaged with men and women's embodied capacity to reflect upon themselves and their lives.

This is a capacity shared with others and realised intersubjectively, as 'emotionality, sensory knowledge, creativity and imagination, tacit embodied competencies and memory' (Jenkins, 2004: 51) come into play. And alongside Jenkins (2004), we can place Rapport's (2009) call for more attention to be paid to the processes of living out particular identities, the achievement of integrity despite powerful external requirements to conform to institutional values and practices. As Chapters 2, 7 and 8 described, the hospital porter, Bob the Bodybuilder, had the capacity to distance himself from both the hospital and the gym where he undertook body-building regimes, a capacity that gave him control over his own identity. Bob, Rapport argues, achieved this 'through a bodily focus by which he came to contain multitudes ... within himself: weightlifter, porter, luxurist' (2009: 103). For Rapport then, 'human beings are never cognitively imprisoned by pre-ordained and per-determining schemata of cultural classification and social structuration; they everywhere experience the relativity and contingency of cultural truths, the ambiguity, malleability and mutability of social rules and realities' (2009: 104). Rapport is not, however, positing a 'bits' model when he refers to 'multitudes'; rather he is calling attention to a unitary self which has the capacity to 'author' its own life, to appraise the institutions and interactions which constitute everyday life, and to adopt particular positions vis à vis them.

Masculinities in transition?

By bringing together a broad range of established and more recent theoretical and empirical materials in Chapters 2, 7 and 12, we have provided a context within which to examine the everyday and life course experiences of men in three different occupations. Within the masculinities literature, as noted, there is uncertainty as to whether masculinity is in crisis or transition. Certainly, many of men's traditional forms of employment in heavy industry, and their associated male-dominated leisure activities, have ceased to lie at the heart of working-class communities (Dennis et al., 1956). D. D. Jackson's (2009) poem, *Men without Work*, describes them relocated to the domestic sphere, indeed to its periphery, where they become invisible, 'fiddling around in sheds', 'aliens in the slippery worlds of MP3'. This is, without doubt, masculinity in crisis. While D. Jackson's 'men without work' 'get under their wives' feet' and push shopping trolleys grudgingly, women's participation in paid work and the growth of new family forms have exposed many men's previously accepted domestic roles and contributions to scrutiny, potentially excluding even their 'grudging' participation in family life. Moreover, the more visible presence and social participation of men, and women, from different ethnic backgrounds and with different sexualities has offered men a much greater variety of representations of masculine embodiment, as Chapter 7 describes.

In Chapter 3, we examine these broader trends as manifested within the specific occupations we selected, giving accounts of historical change within hairdressing, estate agency and firefighting, as well as presenting data that show how particular, older men have lived out and through periods of radical change in both their occupational cultures and domestic lives. In Chapter 5 we described how younger men imagined and sought to realise their future life course trajectories and associated milestones. As we showed, many men spoke in chronologised terms, an indicator that a modernist standardized life cycle (Elchardus and Smits, 2006), remained relevant, albeit potentially in conflict with female partners' redefinitions of femininity and parenthood. Chapter 6, however, indicated that the role models and stereotypes men were exposed to within their everyday lives were nonetheless a focus for precisely the ironic detachment or displacement which Rapport (2009) describes. As such, then, men were able to identity in ways that reflected their own particular appraisal of themselves and what it meant for them to be a man.

Men doing gender

Alongside a focus on masculinity, as a concept, albeit one with consequences, the book has considered men and their embodied practices as they move into and out of work, both at the beginnings and ends of their lives and, on a daily basis, as they return home. Hearn (2004) has problematised the notion of hegemonic masculinity, arguing that it is often used in a way which tells us little about what men actually do and how gender power is operationalised. Instead, Hearn advocates work on 'the hegemony of men in the social world'. This, he says, 'concerns ... that which sets the agenda for different ways of being men in relation to women, children and other men, rather than the identification of particular forms of masculinity or hegemonic masculinity' (2004: 60). In our accounts of men working in three different occupations we have shown how those environments carry specific implications for men, particularly in terms of how they understood both the requirements of a particular occupational identity and their capacity to establish themselves in relation to it. To some extent, these data show men finding ways of undoing gender – often by doing it differently and not, therefore, necessarily destablising if not eradicating a gender binary. However, what our data also show is gender undone. That is to say, men finding themselves in contexts where their sense of themselves, as men, is out of kilter with a particular set of changes or requirements: for example, the young men in Chapter 5 whose homosociality is called into question by female partners; the fire fighters who are no longer able to manage emotional distress in ways that 'fit in' with fire service culture (Chapter 13); the hairdresser whose performances of choice around his sexuality then earned him unwanted attention from other men (Chapter 10).

Estate agency, as Brett Hardwick describes in Chapter 3, was an occupation where 'you know, you'd shake hands on a deal and a gentleman's word was his bond and that was it'. The moral status he attributes to this way of working, the particular kind of man who performed it – a gentleman – then gave way to a form of estate agency that offered a lucrative opening for go-getting individuals who needed only a gift for selling, ambition and confidence (Beaverstock et al., 1992: 167). In Chapter 13, however, we find Brad Charrier describing the 'the nature of the business' in very different terms when he says 'we deal with people who are in matrimonial break-ups, who are very you know highly emotional and they need to be erm, you know nurtured and, and carefully dealt with who can be in quite a, a, a frenzied emotional state ... its very difficult to remain totally dispassionate about situations where, where people are very upset'. It is clear from our data that individual men responded to these kinds of changes in different ways. Brett, for example, had moved from away from a conventional estate agency work and set himself up, free lance, as a consultant because he had become 'uptight and frazzled' through moral battles with colleagues. Younger, successful men might adapt to such settings, offering emotional support as appropriate, schooling themselves in reliable, transparent approaches to their job (see Chapter 8). As such, we might consider that they are doing male femininity and, in the particular case in point, a man was not only achieving a very successful reputation but also providing a different, potentially feminised model, of how other men might practice. In some ways, then, estate agency has become a more feminised occupational culture where 'nurturing' people experiencing the emotional demands of clients undergoing traumatic life course transitions had become integral to successful business. To consider this a masculinised practice, in that it is instrumental, reflects an unthinking assumption that women nurture in response to an emotional imperative to 'care', something critiqued in Dalley's (1988) account of the gendering of 'care', where women must 'do' care work to show they are 'caring', whereas 'caring' men can pay others to 'care' for a relative.

Men entering the fire service were similarly encountering an occupation which, in itself, was in transition. The erstwhile preserve of military discipline, training ground of 'the last working class heros' (Baigent, 2001), the fire service now attracts men from a broader range of backgrounds. Our participants had come from a variety of previous occupations and social class locations, some leaving more lucrative jobs for the relative freedoms of a job which was more compatible with parenting and leisure pursuits such as climbing. What was required of men was now less well-defined. Our data show the prevalence of banter and teasing which at times pushed men to their emotional limits and, while responding appropriately was some men's passports to 'fitting in', for others it was at best an occupational hazard that they avoided and at worst a source of humiliation and anger. Moreover, the physicality of risk, as men respond to fire calls, now contributed far less to their working lives, the capacity to engage with the public and with local communities, along with the ability to take on positions of responsibility on the basis of management skills, becoming equally as important. This more ambiguous set of demands disconcerted or even angered men, particularly those with long careers behind them. The bosses, now, in Clive Bell's view had 'never been to a bloody fire ... they don't strike you as physical guys who've ever struggled in their lives to do anything ... they've never pulled anybody out ... they've never been cold'. Yet for those men who had 'pulled someone out', the emotional implications of that experience were being more openly acknowledged as Chapter 14 describes. When asked whether expressing distress to the fire station counsellor might attract stigma, Alec Simpson said 'There's a little bit, there is a little'. Yet he cited the need to do things differently, to undo gender stereotypes of emotionally unmoved macho firefighters. 'The only way you can get rid of that sort of stigma is by using the services, that's what they're there for', he asserted.

With regard to hairdressing, we might expect to find considerable scope for 'undoing' gender in that work within a feminised environment exposes men to potential gender strain. As Chapter 10 describes, historical changes in hair fashion, for example, the bobbing of women's hair in the 1920s, shifted the profile of hairdressing in such a way that men skilled as barbers somehow needed to 'undo' their gendered identities. Even in 1882, such men had been described in the Hairdressers Weekly Journal as 'in a state of perspiration and greasy; he wears a paper collar; his fingers are pudgy and his nails are in mourning, evidently for some near relation' (cited in Cox, 1999: 65). To counteract this image, and enhance business, a new gendered identity developed, one that indeed represented an undoing of gender. To forestall accusations of inappropriate cross-gender proximity in the public space of the salon, the French, effeminate hairdresser constituted a new and aspired form of masculinity for men entering hairdressing. In his autobiography, Raymond Bessone (aka Mr Teasie Weasie) said 'the majority of women thought that unless you were both queer and French you could not possibly be a good hairdresser' (1976, cited in Cox, 1999: 94). As Chapter 11 demonstrates, however, this stereotype was both available to and avoided by the men we interviewed, some of them choosing to adopt it when working among older women, others asserting their heterosexuality when meeting new clients, attractive younger women, or when out with other men who might otherwise view them as sexually available. Among 'out' gay men, effeminacy was eschewed and masculinity's associations with science and technological expertise were drawn upon in attempts to de-feminise hairdressing, in the sense of enhancing its status.

Public men

Whitehead argues that, historically, the public domain has been the site at which 'manhood and manliness' were engaged with and replicated: '[t]he public sphere is a place that males are supposed to inhabit naturally, a place they must colonize, occupy, conquer, overcome, control. It is the site where men come to be (men)' (2002: 114). In D. Jackson's poem about men without work, however, all that remains to them of that public world is 'the betting shop and boozer' which 'greet/them with the old, rough handshake' (2009). In other words, the public world, masculinity, men and work are historically entangled. Our data suggest, however, that within men's everyday lives, and across the life course, the public/private distinction is a complicated concept, an achievement even, that some men and their female partners pursue without consistent success (see Chapter 4).

In terms of the undoing of gender, however, it is often that complexity of how home and work relate to one another that troubles gender identification, and demands or induces men to reinvent or resist hegemonic masculinity. For the 69-year-old novelist, Piers Paul Read, that distinction remains clear cut, manifesting in a fiercely hierarchical gender binary that seems to permit no reflexivity on his part. His career as a writer began after leaving Cambridge University in 1959, a career that has enjoyed sustained success, evidenced in a double spread article in *Saturday Guardian Review* in July 2010. He is quoted as saying that he sees children as 'the victims of the triumph of feminism', going on to argue that 'the nurturing of children is more important than anything else, and I think it is very hard for women to pursue a career and bring up children' (Wroe, 2010: 10). Read himself is the father of four children, a parental role he enjoys alongside his highly successful literary career. The article gives no evidence at all that being a parent caused him to break stride in the pursuit of this career, nor to reflect on parenthood's relationship with success in the public sphere. His wife of 43 years is mentioned only as the other occupant of the Shepherd's Bush home he shares with her. While Read is described as someone 'fuelled by social and religious conservatism', who 'enjoys enraging liberal opinion', his lack of gender reflexivity reflects the pervasive gendering of work and domestic life (Wroe, 2010: 10). Orr (2010) reports shadow welfare secretary Yvette Cooper's decision not to contest the UK Labour Party leadership because 'she has small children, and it is a big job', noting that the same 'small children' are seen by her husband, Ed Balls, as no bar to undertaking this job. The unremarkable nature of this outcome, like Read's unthinking acceptance of his entitlement to parenthood and a career, is indeed enmeshed in thought and language; as Orr (2010) points out, the notion of the 'working father' has yet to enter a prevailing, reflexive consciousness.

The resilience of this perspective, which assumes incompatibilities between the worlds of work and domesticity, unless they are organised according to a gender binary, reflects a robust elision of men, paid work, and a public world. It is a persistent divide, yet one across which many men are in transition. As our data have shown – and as exemplified by key figures within public life, some, it would seem, have further to go than others.

References

Allan, J. (1994) 'Anomaly as exemplar: The meanings of role-modeling for men elementary teachers' (Dubuque, IA: Tri-College Department of Education (Eric Document Reproduction Service No ED 378 190)).

Alvesson, M. (1998) 'Gender Relations and Identity at Work: A Case Study of Masculinities and Femininities in an Advertising Agency', *Human Relations*, 51 (8) 969–1005.

Ashforth, B. E. and Kreiner, G. (1999) 'How can you do it?: Dirty Work and the Challenge of Constructing a Positive Identity', *Academy of Management Review*, 24, 413–34.

Atkinson, P. and Silverman, D. (1997) 'Kundera's *Immortality*: The Interview Society and the Invention of the Self', *Qualitative Inquiry*, 3 (3), 304–25.

Bagilhole, B. and Cross, S. (2006) '"It Never Struck me as Female": Investigating Men's Entry into Female-Dominated Professions', *Journal of Gender Studies*, 15 (1), 35–48.

Baigent, D. (2001) *One More Last Working Class Hero: A Cultural Audit of the UK Fire Service*, published by fitting-in ltd, www.fitting-in.com.

Baigent, D. (2008) *Early Summary for "One Decade On"* (4 April 2008), published by fitting-in ltd, www.fiting-in.com.

Barber, K. (2008) 'The Well-Coiffed Man: Class, Race and Heterosexual Masculinity in the Hair Salon', *Gender and Society*, 22 (4), 445–76.

Barley, N. (1990) *Native Land* (Harmondsworth: Penguin).

Battersby, C. (1998) *The Phenomenal Woman* (Cambridge: Polity Press).

Bauman, Z. (2007) *Liquid Times: Living in an Age of Uncertainty* (Cambridge: Polity).

Beaverstock, J., Leyshon, A., Rutherford, T., Thrift, N. and Williams, P. (1992) 'Moving Houses: The Geographical Reorganization of the Estate Agency Industry in England and Wales in the 1980s', *Transactions of the Institute for British Geography*, NS 17, 166–82.

Beck, U. (1992) *Risk Society: Towards a New Modernity* (London: Sage).

Beck, U. and Beck-Gernsheim, E. (2002) *Individualization: Institutionalized Individualism and its Social and Political Consequences* (Oxford: Sage).

Beynon, J. (2002) *Masculinities and Culture* (Milton Keynes: Open University Press).

Billington, R., Hockey, J. and Strawbridge, S. (1998) *Exploring Self and Society* (Basingstoke: Macmillan).

Black, P. (2004) *The Beauty Industry: Gender, Culture, Pleasure* (New York: Routledge).

Blaikie, A. (1997) 'Age Consciousness and Modernity: The Social Reconstruction of Retirement', *Self, Agency and Society*, 1(1), 9–26.

Bondi, L., Davidson, J. and Smith, M. (2005) 'Introduction: Geography's "Emotional Turn"', in J. Davidson, L. Bondi and M. Smith (eds) *Emotional Geographies* (Aldershot: Ashgate).

Bordo, S. (1989) 'The Body and the Reproduction of Femininity: A Feminist Appropriation of Foucault', in S. Bordo and A. Jaggar (eds) *Gender/Body/ Knowledge: Feminist Reconstructions of Being and Knowing* (London: Rutgers).

Boscagli, M. (1992) '"A Moving Story": Masculine Tears and the Humanity of Televised Emotion', *Discourse*, 15(2): 64–79.

Bourdieu, P. (1977) *Outline of a Theory of Practice* (Cambridge: Cambridge University Press).

Bourdieu, P. (1984) *Distinction: A Social Critique of the Judgement of Taste* (Cambridge, MA: Harvard University Press).

Boyle, M. V. (2002) '"Sailing twixt Scylla and Charybdis": Negotiating Multiple Organisational Masculinities', *Women in Management Review*, 17 (3): 131–41.

Bradley, H. (1993) 'Across the Great Divide: The Entry of Men into "Women's Jobs"', in C. Williams (ed.) *Doing 'Women's Work': Men in Nontraditional Occupations* (London: Sage).

Bradley, H. and Hickman, P. (2004) 'In and Out of Work? The Changing Fortunes of Young People in Contemporary Labour Markets', in J. Roche, S. Tucker, R. Thomson and R. Flynn (eds) *Youth in Society* (London: Sage/The Open University).

Bragg, R. J. (1992) 'Regulation of Estate Agents: A Series of Half-Hearted Measures?' *The Modern Law Review*, 55(3): 368–76.

Brannen, J., Moss, C., Owen, C., and Wale, C. (1997) *Mothers, Fathers and Employment: Parents and the Labour Market in Britain 1984–1994* (London: Department for Education and Employment).

Brannen, J. and Nilsen, A. (2002) 'Young People's Time Perspectives: From Youth to Adulthood', *Sociology*, 36(3), 513–37.

Brittan, A. (1989) *Masculinity and Power* (New York: Blackwell).

Burke, R. and Cooper, C. (2008) *The Long Work Hours Culture: Causes, Consequence and Choices* (Bingley: Emerald Group Publishing Ltd).

Burton, C. (1991) *The Promise and the Price: The Struggle for Equal Opportunity in Women's Employment* (Sydney: Allen and Unwin).

Butler, J. (1990) *Gender Trouble: Feminism and the Subversion of Identity* (London: Routledge).

Butler, J. (2004) *Undoing Gender* (New York: Routledge).

Chaney, D. (1996) *Lifestyles* (London: Routledge).

Clarkson, J. (2005) 'Contesting Masculinity's Makeover: Queer Eye, Consumer Masculinity, and "Straight-Acting" Gays', *Journal of Communication Enquiry*, 29, (3) 235–55.

Cockburn, C. (1983) *Brothers: Male Dominance and Technological Change* (London: Pluto Press).

Collinson, D. and Hearn, J. (1996) *Men as Managers, Managers as Men: Critical Perspectives on Men, Masculinities and Management* (London: Sage).

Collinson, D. and Hearn, J. (2001) 'Naming Men as Men: Implications for Work, Organisations and Management', in S. Whitehead and F. Barrett (eds), *The Masculinities Reader* (Cambridge: Polity Press).

Connell, R. W. (2000) *The Men and The Boys* (London: Polity).

Connell, R. W. (2002) *Gender* (Cambridge: Polity).

Connell, R. W. (2005) *Masculinities* (Berkeley: University of California Press), p. 32.

Cooper, R. (1995) 'The Fireman: Immaculate Manhood', *Journal of Popular Culture*, 28(4), 139–70.

Cox, C. (1999) *Good Hair Days: A History of British Hairstyling* (London: Quartet Books).

Craik, J. (2005) *Uniforms Exposed: From Conformity to Transgression* (Oxford: Berg).

Csordas, T. (2002) *Body/Meaning/Healing* (Basingstoke: Palgrave Macmillan).

Dalley, G. (1988) *Ideologies of Caring: Rethinking Community and Collectivism* (London: Macmillan).

Davidoff, L. and Hall, C. (2002) *Family Fortunes: Men and Women of the English Middle Class 1780–1850* (London: Routledge).

Davidson, K., Daly, T. and Arber, S. (2003) 'Exploring the Social Worlds of Older Men', in S. Arber, K. Davidson and J. Ginn (eds) *Gender and Aging: Changing Roles and Relationships* (Buckingham: The Open University Press).

Davis, K. (2002) 'A Dubious Equality: Men, Women and Cosmetic Surgery', *Body and Society*, 8 (1), 49–65.

De Visser, R. O. (2009) '"I'm Not a Very Manly Man": Qualitative Insights into Young Men's Masculine Subjectivity', *Men and Masculinities*, 11 (1), 367–71.

De Witte, M. and Stijn, B. (2000) 'Automation, Job Content and Underemployment', *Work, Employment and Society*, 14(2), 245–65.

Delphy, C. (1984) *Close to Home: A Materialist Analysis of Women's Oppression* (London: Hutchinson).

Dennis, N., Henriques, F. and Slaughter, C. (1956) *Coal is our Lives* (London: Spottiswoode).

Donaldson, M. (1991) *Time of Our Lives: Labour and Love in the Working Class* (Sydney: Allen and Unwin).

Douglas, M. (1966) *Purity and Danger: An Analysis of Concepts of Pollution and Taboo* (London: Penguin Books).

Duncombe, J. and Marsden, D. (1993), 'Love and Intimacy: The Gender Division of Emotion and 'Emotion Work': A Neglected Aspect of Sociological Discussion of Heterosexual Relationships', *Sociology*, 27: 221–41.

Edwards, T. (2006) *Cultures of Masculinity* (London: Routledge).

Elchardus, M. and Smits, W. (2006) 'The Persistence of the Standardized Life Cycle', *Time and Society*, 15(2/3), 303–26.

EOC (2004) *Plugging Britain's Skills Gap: Challenging Gender Segregation in Training and Work, Report of Phase One of the EOC's Investigation into Gender Segregation and Modern Apprenticeships* (http://www.equalityhumanrights.com/).

Evans, J. (2004) 'Bodies Matter: Men, Masculinity and the Gendered Division of Labour in Nursing', *Journal of Occupational Science*, 11(1), 14–22.

Fagan, C. and Burchell, B. (2002) *Gender, Jobs and Working Conditions in the European Union, Dublin*, European Foundation for the Improvement of Living and Working Conditions.

Faizan Ahmed, S. M. (2009) 'Making Beautiful: Male Workers in Beauty Parlours', *Men and Masculinities*, 9 (2), 168–85.

Featherstone, M. and Hepworth, M. (1989) 'Ageing and Old Age: Reflections on the Postmodern Lifecourse', in B. Bytheway, T. Keil, P. Allat and A. Bryman (eds) *Becoming and Being Old: Sociological Approaches to Later Life* (London: Sage).

Featherstone, M. and Hepworth, M. (1991) 'The Mask of Ageing and the Postmodern Lifecourse', in M. Featherstone, M. Hepworth and B. S. Turner (eds) *The Body, Social Process and Cultural Theory* (London: Sage).

Finch, J. and Groves, D. (1983) *A Labour of Love* (London: Routledge and Kegan Paul).

Firestone, S. (1970) *The Dialectic of Sex: The Case for Feminist Revolution* (USA: William Morrow).

Foucault, M. (1977) *Discipline and Punishment: The Birth of the Prison* (London: Tavistock).

Furlong, A. and Cartmel, F. (1997) *Young People and Social Change: Individualisation and Risk in Late Modernity* (Buckingham: Open University Press).

Furman, F. K. (1997) *Facing the Mirror: Older Women and Beauty Shop Culture* (New York: Routledge).

Garmarnikov, E., Morgan, D. J., Purvis, J., Taylorson, D. (eds) (1983) *Gender, Class and Work* (London: Heinemann).

Geertz, C. (1983) *Local Knowledge: Further Essays on Interpretive Anthropology* (New York: Basic Books Inc Publishers).

Giddens, A. (1991) *Modernity and Self Identity* (Oxford: Polity).

Giddens, A. (1992) *The Transformation of Intimacy: Sexuality, Love and Eroticism in Modern Societies* (Cambridge: Polity).

Giddens, A. (1992) *The Transformation of Intimacy: Sexuality, Love and Eroticism in Modern Societies* (Cambridge: Polity).

Gill, R. (2003) 'Power and the Production of Subjects: A Genealogy of the New Man and the New Lad', in B. Benwell (ed.) *Masculinity and Man's Lifestyle Magazines* (Oxford: Blackwell).

Gillis, J. R. (1996) *A World of their Own Making* (Oxford: Oxford University Press).

Gimlin, D. (1996) 'Pamela's Place: Power and Negotiation in the Hair Salon', *Gender and Society*, 10(5), 505–26.

Giroux, H. A. (1998) 'Stealing Innocence: The Politics of Child Beauty Pageants', in H. Jenkins (ed.) *The Children's Culture Reader* (New York: New York University Press).

Glaser, B. and Strauss, A. ([1971] 2010) *Status Passage* (Piscataway, NJ: Aldine Transaction).

Goffman, E. (1968) *Stigma: Notes on the Management of Spoiled Identity* (Harmondsworth: Pelican).

Goffman, E. (1971) *The Presentation of Self in Everyday Life* (Harmondsworth: Penguin).

Goldthorpe, J. H., Lockwood, D., Bechofer, F. and Platt, J. (1968) *The Affluent Worker: Industrial Attitudes and Behaviour* (Cambridge: Cambridge University Press).

Gregory, M. R. (2009) 'Inside the Locker Room: Male Homosociability in the Advertising Industry', *Gender, Work and Organisation*, 16(3): 323–47.

Grogan, E. (1999) *Body Image: Understanding Body Dissatisfaction in Men, Women and Children* (London: Routledge).

Grosz, E. (1989) *Sexual Subversions: Three French Feminists* (Sydney: Allen and Unwin).

Grosz, E. (1994) *Volatile Bodies: Towards a Corporeal Feminism* (Bloomington: Indiana University Press).

Gutterman, D. (2001) 'Postmodernism and the Interrogation of Masculinity', in S. Whitehead and F. Barrett (eds) *The Masculinities Reader* (Cambridge: Polity).

Halberstam, J. (1998) *Female Masculinity* (Durham: Duke University Press).

Halford, S. and Leonard, P. (2006) *Negotiating Gendered Identities at Work: Place, Space and Time* (Basingstoke: Palgrave Macmillan).

Hall, A., Hockey, J. and Robinson, V. (2007) 'Occupational Cultures and the Embodiment of Masculinity: Hairdressing, Estate Agency and Firefighting', *Gender Work and Organisation*, 14(6), 534–51.

Hall, E. (1993) 'Smiling, Deferring and Flirting: Doing Gender by Giving Good Service', *Work and Occupations*, 20 (4), 452–71.

Haywood, C. and Mac an Ghaill, M. (2003) *Men and Masculinities* (Buckingham: Open University Press).

Hearn, J. (1993) 'Emotive Subjects: Organizational Men, Organizational Masculinities and the (De)construction of "Emotions"', in S. Fineman (ed.) *Emotion in Organizations* (London: Sage).

Hearn, J. (2004) 'From Hegemonic Masculinity to the Hegemony of Men', *Feminist Theory*, 5 (1), 49–72.

Hepworth, M. (1999) 'Privacy, Security and Respectability: The Ideal Victorian Home', in T. Chapman and J. Hockey (eds) *Ideal Homes: Social Change and Domestic Life* (London: Routledge).

Herzog, D. (1996) 'The Trouble with Hairdressers', *Representations*, 53 (Winter), 21–43.

Hochschild, A. (1979) 'Emotion Work, Feeling Rules, and Social Structure', *The American Journal of Sociology*, 85 (3), 551–75.

Hochschild, A. (1983) *The Managed Heart: Commercialisation of Human Feeling* (Berkeley, CA: University of California Press).

Hockey, J. and James, A. (2003) *Social Identities across the Life Course* (Basingstoke: Palgrave Macmillan).

Hockey, J., Meah, A. and Robinson, V. (2007) *Mundane Heterosexualities: From Theory to Practices* (Basingstoke: Palgrave Macmillan).

Hockey, J., Robinson, V. and Hall, A. (2009) 'The Life Course Anticipated: Gender and Chronologisation among Young People', *Journal of Youth Studies*, 12 (2), 227–241.

Holland, J., Ramazanoglu, C., Sharpe, S. and Thomson, R. (1998) *The Male in the Head: Young People, Heterosexuality and Power* (London: Tufnell).

Holmes, M. (2010) 'The Emotionalization of Reflexivity', *Sociology*, 44(1): 139–54.

Horrocks, R. (1994) *Masculinity in Crisis: Myths, Fantasies and Realities* (Basingstoke: Palgrave Macmillan).

Hubbard, P. (2005) 'The Geographies of 'Going Out': Emotion and Embodiment in the Evening Economy', in J. Davidson, L. Bondi and M. Smith (eds) *Emotional Geographies* (Aldershot: Ashgate Publishing Ltd).

Irving, Z. (2008) 'Gender and Work', in D. Richardson and V. Robinson (eds) *Introducing Gender and Women's Studies* (Basingstoke: Palgrave Macmillan).

Jackson, D. (2003) 'Beyond One-Dimensional Models of Masculinity: A Life-Course Perspective on the Processes of Becoming Masculine' *Auto/Biography*, X1, No 1 and 2, 71–87.

Jackson, D. (2009) 'Men Without Work', *Journal of Gender Studies*, 18 (4): 325.

Jackson, S. (1997) 'Women, Marriage and Family Relationships', in V. Robinson and D. Richardson (eds) *Introducing Women's Studies* (Basingstoke: Palgrave Macmillan).

Jackson, S. (1999) *Heterosexuality in Question* (London: Sage).

Jackson, S. (2008) 'Families, Domesticity and Intimacy: Changing Relationships in Changing Times', in D. Richardson and V. Robinson (eds) *Introducing Gender and Women's Studies* (Basingstoke: Palgrave Macmillan).

Jackson, S. and Scott, S. (eds) (2002) *Gender: A Sociological Reader* (London: Routledge).

James, A. and Hockey, J. (2007) *Embodying Health Identities* (Basingstoke: Palgrave Macmillan).

Jamieson, L. (1998) *Intimacy: Personal Relationships in Modern Societies* (Cambridge: Polity).

Jenkins, R. (2004) *Social Identity* (London: Routledge).

Johnson, P. (2005) *Love, Heterosexuality and Society* (London: Routledge).

Johnson, P. and Lawler, S. (2005) 'Coming Home to Love and Class', *Sociological Research Online*, 10, 3.

Karasek, R. A. and Theorell, T. (1990) *Healthy Work: Stress, Productivity, and the Reconstruction of Working Life* (New York, NY: Basic Books, Inc).

Kelan, E. K. (2010) 'Gender Logic and the (Un)doing of Gender at Work', *Gender, Work and Organisation*, 17 (2); 174–94.

Kerfoot, D. (1999) 'The Organization of Intimacy: Managerialism, Masculinity and the Masculine Subject', in S. Whitehead and R. Moodely (eds) *Transforming Managers: Gendering Change in the Public Sector* (London: University College London).

Kerfoot, D. (2001) 'Managing the "Professional" Man', in M. Dent and S. Whitehead (eds) *Managing Professional Identities: Knowledge, Performativity and the 'New' Professional* (London: Routledge).

Labour Force Survey (2004) http://www.statistics.gov.uk/downloads/theme_labour/LFSQS_1004.pdf (accessed July 2010).

Laclau, E. (1990) *New Reflections on the Revolution of Our Time* (London: Verso).

Lawler, S. (2008) *Identity: Sociological Perspectives* (Cambridge: Polity).

Leder, D. (1990) *The Absent Body* (Chicago: University of Chicago Press).

Lewis, S., Smithson, J. and Brannen, J. (1999) 'Young Europeans' Orientations to Families and Work', *Annals of the American Academy of Political and Social Science*, 562, The Evolving World of Work and Family: New Stakeholders, 88–97.

Lindsay, J. (2004) 'Gender and Class in the Lives of Young Hairdressers: From Serious to Spectacular', *Journal of Youth Studies*, 7(3), 259–77.

Lopez, S. (2006) 'Emotional Labor and Organized Emotional Care: Conceptualising Nursing Home Care Work', *Work and Occupations*, 33 (2) 133–60.

Lupton, B. (2000) '"Maintaining Masculinity: Men who do "Women's Work"', *British Journal of Management*, 11, 33–48.

Lupton, D. (1998) *The Emotional Self* (London: Sage).

MacCormack, C. and Strathern, M. (eds) (1980) *Nature, Culture and Gender* (Cambridge: Cambridge University Press).

Mansfield, P. and Collard, J. (1988) *The Beginning of the Rest of Your Life? A Portrait of Newly-Wed Marriage* (London: Macmillan).

Marchbank, J. and Letherby, G. (2007) *Introduction to Gender: Social Science Perspectives* (London: Pearson).

Martin, P. Y. (2001) 'Mobilizing Masculinities: Women's Experiences of Men at Work', *Organization* 8 (4), 587–618.

McArdle, K. A. and Hill, M. S. (2010) 'Understanding Body Dissatisfaction in Gay and Heterosexual Men: The Roles of Self-Esteem, Media and Peer Influence', *Men and Masculinities Online* (first published on October 24, 2007 as doi:10.1177/1097184X07303728).

McMahon, A. (1999) *Taking Care of Men: Sexual Politics and the Public Mind* (Cambridge: Cambridge University Press).

Mead, G. H. (1934) *Mind, Self and Society from the Standpoint of a Social Behaviorist* (ed. C. W. Morris) (Chicago, IL: University of Chicago Press).

Mercier, P. (2008) *Night Train to Lisbon* (London: Atlantic Books).

Merleau Ponty, M. (1962) *The Phenomenology of Perception* (London: Routledge and Kegan Paul).

Messner, M. A. (2001) 'Friendship, Intimacy and Sexuality', in S. M. Whitehead and F. J. Barrett (eds) *The Masculinities Reader* (Cambridge: Polity Press).

Middleton, P. (1992) *The Inward Gaze: Masculinity and Subjectivity in Modern Culture* (London: Routledge).

Miller, D. (1987) *Material Culture and Mass Consumption* (Oxford: Blackwell).

Miles, S. (1998) *Consumerism* (London: Sage).

Miller, S. (1983) *Men and Friendship* (San Leandro, CA: Gateway Books).

Moi, T. (1999) *What is a Woman? And Other Essays* (Oxford: Oxford University Press).

Monaghan, L. (2005) 'Big Handsome Men, Bears and Others: Virtual Constructions of "Fat Male Embodiment"', *Body and Society*, 11 (2), 81–111.

Mörck, M. and Tullberg, M. (2005) 'The Business Suit and the Performance of Masculinity'. Paper given at Interdisciplinary Conference of Fashion and Dress Cultures, Copenhagen, 26–28 October.

Morgan, D. (1992) *Discovering Men* (London: Routledge).

Morgan, D. (1996) *Family Connections* (Cambridge: Polity Press).

Morgan, D. (1999) 'Risk and Family Practices: Accounting for Change and Fluidity' in E. Silva and C. Smart (eds) *The New Family?* (London: Sage).

Morgan, D. (2002) 'You Too can have a Body Like Mine', in S. Jackson and S. Scott (eds) *Gender: A Sociological Reader* (London: Routledge).

Morgan, D. (2009) *Acquaintances: The Space between Intimates and Strangers* (Maidenhead: The Open University Press).

Morgan, D., Brandth, B. and Kvande, E. (eds) (2005) *Gender, Bodies and Work* (Aldershot: Ashgate).

Mort, F. (1996) *Cultures of Consumption: Masculinities and Social Space in Late Twentieth Century Britain* (London: Routledge).

Mythen, G. (2005) 'Employment, Individualisation and Insecurity: Rethinking the Risk Society Perspective', *Sociological Review*, 53 (1), 129–49.

Nettleton, S. (1992) *Power, Pain and Dentistry* (Buckingham: Open University Press).

Nettleton, S. and Watson, J. (eds) (1998) *The Body in Everyday Life* (London: Routledge).

Newton, E. ([1972] 2002) 'Drag and Camp', in S. Jackson and S. Scott (eds) *Gender: A Sociological Reader* (London: Routledge).

Nickson, D. and Korczynski, M. (2009) 'Editorial: Aesthetic Labour Emotional Labour and Masculinity', *Gender, Work and Organization*, 16, (3) 291–9.

Nilsen, A. (1997) 'Forever Young? A Life Course Perspective on Individuation', *Proceedings of the International Seminar on Work, Family and Intergenerational Solidarity* (Lisbon: ISCTE).

Nixon, D. (2009) '"I Can't Put a Smiley Face On": Working-Class Masculinity, Emotional Labour and Service Work in the "New Economy"', *Gender, Work and Organization*, 16, (3), 300–22.

Nordberg, M. (2005) 'It's Important to Make Him Look and Feel Masculine!', paper given at Interdisciplinary Conference of Fashion and Dress Cultures, Danmarks Designeskole, October 26–28.

Olsen, S. (2007) 'Daddy's Come Home: Evangelicalism, Fatherhood and Lessons for Boys in Late Nineteenth Century Britain', *Fathering*, 5(3), 174–96.

Orr, D. (2010) 'Women will Suffer Most from Job Cuts in the Public Sector', *The Guardian G2*, 8.

Pahl, R. (2000) *On Friendship* (Cambridge: Polity).

Popp, A. and French, M. (2010) '"Practically the Uniform of the Tribe": Dress Codes Among Commercial Travellers', *Enterprise and Society*. doi: 10.1093/es/Khq029, First published online: April.

Rapport, N. (1993) *Diverse Worldviews in an English Village* (Edinburgh: Edinburgh University Press).

Rapport, N. (2009) *Of Orderlies and Men: Hospital Porters Achieving Wellness at Work* (Durham, NC: Carolina Academic Press).

Richardson, D. (1996) 'Heterosexuality and Social Theory', in D. Richardson (ed.) *Theorising Heterosexuality* (Buckingham: Open University Press).

Richardson, D. and Robinson, V. (eds) (2008) *Introducing Gender and Women's Studies*, London: Palgrave.

Robinson, V. (1996) 'Heterosexuality and Masculinity: Theorising Male Power or the Male Wounded Psyche?' in D. Richardson (ed.) *Theorising Heterosexuality* (Buckingham: Open University Press).

Robinson, V. (2008) *Everyday Masculinities and Extreme Sport: Male Identity and Rock Climbing* (Oxford: Berg).

Robinson, V., Hockey, J. and Hall, A. (2007) 'Negotiating Sexual and Gender Boundaries' in C. Beckett, O. Heathcote and M. Macey (eds) *Negotiating Boundaries?: Identities, Sexualities, Diversities* (Newcastle: Cambridge Scholars Publishing).

Roche, J., Tucker, S., Thomson, R. and Flynn, R. (2004) (eds) *Youth in Society* (London: Sage/The Open University).

Roethlisberger, F. J. and Dickson, W. J. (1939) *Management and the Worker* (Cambridge, Mass: Harvard University Press).

Rose, D. (1995) 'Official Social Classifications in the UK', *Social Research Update*, 9 http://sru.soc.surrey.ac.uk/SRU9.html.

Rutherford, J. (1992) *Predicaments in Masculinity* (London: Routledge).

Sanders, T., O'Neill, M. and Pitcher, J. (eds) (2009) *Prostitution: Sex Work, Policy and Politics* (London: Sage Publications).

Sargent, P. (2000) 'Real Men or Real Teachers?' *Men and Masculinities*, 2 (4), 410–33.

Scourfield, J. and Drakeford, M. (2002) 'New Labour and the "Problem of Men"', *Critical Social Policy* 22(4), 619–40.

Segal, L. (2007) *Slow Motion: Changing Masculinities, Changing Men* (3rd edn) (London: Virago).

Seidler, V. (1989) *Rediscovering Masculinity: Reason, Language and Sexuality* (London: Routledge).

Seidler, V. (1992) *Men, Sex and Relationships: Writings from Achilles Heel* (London: Routledge).

Seidler, V. (1998) 'Masculinity, Violence and Emotional Life', in G. Bendelow and S. J. Williams (eds) *Emotions in Social Life: Critical Themes and Contemporary Issues* (London: Routledge).

Seidler, V. (2006) *Transforming Masculinities: Men, Cultures, Bodies, Power, Sex and Love* (London: Routledge).

Seidler, V. (2007) 'Masculinities, Bodies and Emotional Life', *Men and Masculinities*, 10 (1), 9–21.

Seremetakis, C. N. (1991) *The Last Word: Women, Death and Divination in Inner Mani* (Chicago: University of Chicago Press).

Sharma, U. and Black, P. (2001) 'Look Good, Feel Better: Beauty Therapy as Emotional Labour', *Sociology*, 35 (4), 913–31.

Shildrick, M. and Price, J. (eds) (1998) *Vital Signs: Feminist Reconfigurations of the Bio/logical Body* (Edinburgh: Edinburgh University Press).

Simpson, R. (2004) 'Masculinity at Work: The Experiences of Men in Female Dominated Occupations', *Work, Employment and Society*, 18 (2): 349–68.

Simpson, R. (2005) 'Men in Non-Traditional Occupations: Career Entry, Career Orientation and Experience of Role Strain', *Gender, Work and Organization*, 12 (4) 363–80.

Simpson, R. (2009) *Men in Caring Occupations: Doing Gender Differently* (Basingstoke: Palgrave Macmillan).

Smeaton, J. (2006) 'Work Return Rates after Childbirth in the UK: Trends, Determinants and Implications: A Comparison of Cohorts Born in 1958 and 1970', *Work, Employment and Society*, 20(1), 5–25.

Smith, R. (2005) 'Hotter than the Average', *The Guardian*, 17 October 2001.

Spector-Mersel, G. (2006) 'Never-Aging Stories: Western Hegemonic Masculinity Scripts', *Journal of Gender Studies*, 15(1), 67–82.

Stevenson, R. L. ([1886]1998) *Dr Jekyll and Mr Hyde* (Oxford: Oxford University Press).

Swain, S. (1991) 'Covert Intimacy: Closeness in Men's Friendships', in B. J. Risman and P. Schwartz (eds) *Gender in Intimate Relationships* (Belmont, CA: Wadsworth).

Tosh, J. (1999) *A Man's Place: Masculinity and the Middle Class Home in Victorian England* (London: Yale University Press).

Tracy, S. J. and Scott, C. (2006) 'Sexuality, Masculinity and Taint Management Among Firefighters and Correctional Officers: Getting Down and Dirty With "America's Heroes" and the "Scum of Law Enforcement"', *Management Communication Quarterly*, 20, (6), 6–38.

Turner, B. S. (1992) *Regulating Bodies: Essays in Medical Sociology* (London: Routledge).

Turner, V. (1969) *The Ritual Process* (Harmondsworth: Penguin Books Ltd.).

Turner, V. (1974) *Dramas, Fields and Metaphors: Symbolic Action in Human Society* (Ithaca: Cornell University Press).

VanEvery, J. (1995) *Heterosexual Women Changing the Family: Refusing to be a 'Wife'!* (London: Taylor and Francis).

VanEvery, J. (1996) 'Heterosexuality and Domestic Life', in D. Richardson (ed.) *Theorising Heterosexuality* (Buckingham: The Open University).

Van Gennep, A. ([1908] 1960) *The Rites of Passage* (Chicago: The University of Chicago Press).

Vincent, J. (1995) *Inequality and Old Age* (London: UCL Press).

Voth, J. (2000) *Time and Work in England 1750–1830* (Oxford: Oxford University Press).

Walby, S. (1986) *Patriarchy at Work* (Cambridge: Polity).

Walker, K. (1994) 'Men, Women and Friendship: What They Say, What They Do', *Gender and Society*, 8(2), 246–65.

Walkowitz, J. (1980) *Prostitution and Victorian Society: Class and the State* (Cambridge: Cambridge University Press).

Walls, S. (2007) '"Are you being Served?": Emotional and Aesthetic Labour of Men in the Retail Sector', Paper given at BSA Conference.

Warhurst, C. and Nickson, D. (2009) '"Who's Got the Look?"': Emotional, Aesthetic and Sexualised Labour in Interactive Services', *Gender, Work and Organization*, 16, (3), 387–404.

Watson, J. (2000) *Male Bodies: Health, Culture and Identity* (Buckingham: Open University Press).

Webster, J. (1995) 'Age Differences in Reminiscence Functions', in B. Haight and J. Webster (eds) *The Art and Science of Reminiscing* (Washington, DC: Taylor and Francis).

Wellington, C. A. and Bryson, J. R. (2001) 'At Face Value? Image Consultancy, Emotional Labour and Professional Work', *Sociology*, 35, (4), 933–46.

West, C. and Zimmerman, D. H. (1987) 'Doing Gender', *Gender and Society* 1(2), 125–51.

Weston, K. (2002) 'Lovers through the Looking Glass', in S. Jackson and S. Scott (eds) *Gender. A Sociological Reader* (London: Routledge).

Wetherell, M. (2005–6) *Society Matters* (8), 14, Newsletter for the Open University.

Whitehead, S. M. (2002) *Men and Masculinities* (Cambridge: Polity).

Whitehead, S. M. and Barrett, F. J. (2001) *The Masculinities Reader* (Cambridge: Polity).

Williams, C. (1995) *Still a Man's World: Men Who Do Women's Work* (California: University of California Press).

Williams, C. (2003) 'Sky Service: The Demands of Emotional Labour in the Airline Industry', *Gender, Work and Organization*, 10 (5), 513–50.

Williams, S. J. (2001) *Emotion and Social Theory: Corporeal Reflections on the (Ir)Rational* (London: Sage).

Williams, S. and Bendelow, G. (1998) *The Lived Body* (London: Routledge).

Winlow, S. (2001) *Badfellas: Crime, Tradition and New Masculinities* (Oxford: Berg).

Witz, A., Warhurst, C. and Nickson, D. (2003) 'The Labour of Aesthetics and the Aesthetics of Organization', *Organization*, 10:1, 33–54.

Wolkowicz, C. (2003) 'The Social Relations of Body Work', *Work, Employment and Society*, 16 (3): 497–510.

Woodward, K. (1997) (ed.) *Identity and Difference* (London: Sage).

Woodward, K. (2007) *Boxing, Masculinity and Identity: The 'I' of the Tiger* (London: Routledge).

Woodward, K. (2008) 'Gendered Bodies: Gendered Lives', in D. Richardson and V. Robinson (eds) *Introducing Gender and Women's Studies* (Basingstoke: Palgrave Macmillan).

Wroe, N. (2010) 'A Life in Books: Piers Paul Read', *Review Saturday Guardian*, July 3rd, 10–11.

Young, I. M. (2005) *On Female Body Experience: 'Throwing Like a Girl' and Other Essays* (Oxford: Oxford University Press).

Index